...et the Martyrology from the Yom Kippur service ... be their epitaph.

y soul grieveth

Kurt

אלה

Ludlin

Buchenwald

Sobibor

אזכרה

Throughout the years

ignorance hath

Dora

Lvov

Claude

devoured our martyrs as in one long

day of blood.

בינדל

Kiev

Natzweiler

Guys

Sachsenhausen

בת גבריאל

Bialystck

Auschwitz

Riga

Paula Jochsberger Schild

pressive, savage in their witless power, filled

Elfriede Schild with a futile thought:

Psalm 42:5

la Haas Meyer

Mauthausen

Stutthof

Amzert

Inge

בריבל בת יהודה

THESE I DO REMEMBER

Fragments from the Holocaust

GERDA
HAAS

THESE
I
DO
REMEMBER

Fragments from the Holocaust

THE CUMBERLAND PRESS, INC.   FREEPORT, MAINE

International Standard Book Number: 0-87027-203-9
Library of Congress Catalog Card Number: 82-71674

The Cumberland Press, Inc., Freeport, Maine 04032
The Bond Wheelwright Company

PERMISSIONS

"MAIN STREET HUNGARY" (pp. 10-14) and "January 23, 1945" (pp. 68-71) from
FRAGMENTS OF ISABELLA: A MEMOIR OF AUSCHWITZ by Isabella Leitner
Copyright 1978 by Isabella Leitner and Irving A. Leitner
Reprinted by permission of Thomas Y. Crowell, Publishers, Inc.

Pages 174-189 from GHETTO DIARY by Janusz Korczak
Copyright 1978 by Holocaust Library
Reprinted by permission of Holocaust Library

From Fania Fenelon, PLAYING FOR TIME, transl. by Judith Landry
Copyright 1977 by Michael Joseph Ltd. and Atheneum Publishers
(First published in France under the title SURSIS POUR L'ORCHESTRE, copyright
1976 by Opera Mundi, Paris)
Reprinted with the permission of Atheneum Publishers

Pages 123-126; pp 216-218; pp 158-162 from THE TULIPS ARE RED by Leesha Rose
Copyright 1978 by Leesha Rose
Reprinted by permission of the author.

Pages 46-50; pp 69-71; pp. 94-96 from THE VAPOR by Bryna Bar Oni
Copyright 1976 by Visual Impact, Inc.
Reprinted by permission of Visual Impact, Inc.

Pages 74-76; pp. 107-113; pp. 160-161 from THE DEATH TRAIN by Luba K. Gurdus
Copyright 1978 by Luba Krugman Gurdus
Reprinted by permission of the author

Pages 53-59; pp. 103-110; pp. 142-145 from SO MUCH TO FORGET:
A CHILD'S VISION OF HELL by Alain Stanke
Copyright 1977 by Gage Publishing
Reprinted by permission of Gage Publishing Limited

RECOUNTED BUT NOT REPRINTED

Young Moshe's Diary: THE SPIRITUAL TORMENT OF A JEWISH BOY IN NAZI EUROPE
By Moshe Flinker, translated from the original Hebrew entitled HANA'AR MOSHE-
YOMANO SHEL MOSHE FLINKER, published by Yad Vashemin in 1958. Yad Vashem
Jerusalem, 1971

In Memory of

My Mother, Paula Jochsberger Schild

ברײנדל בת גבריאל

My Sister, Elfriede Schild

חוה בת ישראל

My Husband's Sister, Paula Haas Meyer

ברײנדל בת יהודה הלוי

Her Daughters, Margot & Inge

&

My Husband's Sister, Erna Haas Weinstock

חוה בת יהודה הלוי

Her Children Kurt, Ruth, Claude and Micheline

Let the martyrology from the Yom Kippur service be their epitaph

אלה אזכרה ונפשי עלי אשפכה

These I do remember. And my soul grieveth.
All through the age hatred hath pursued us.
Throughout the years ignorance hath devoured our martyrs
As in one long day of blood. Rulers have risen through the endless years
Oppressive, savage in their witless power.
Filled with futile thought: To make an end to that which
God hath cherished.

Contents

Foreword

Why another book on the Holocaust?

There are, of course, many reasons which justify the continuing study of one of the greatest tragedies of human history. The growing literature in this field has already increased our historical knowledge of the background and details of the destruction process, awakened us to the moral implications of genocide and portrayed for us the human drama of individuals caught up in the maelstrom. But why *this* book?

These I Do Remember: Fragments From the Holocaust offers its readers a unique diversity of perspectives which encompass all of the above. It is in part the personal memoir of Gerda Haas (nee Schild), a survivor of Theresienstadt concentration camp at age 23. It is also a collection of the narratives of six survivors — including one non-Jew — of Nazi persecution throughout occupied Europe, each account carefully set against the national traditions and circumstances of occupation for each country. Finally, the book breaks new ground in the history of the Holocaust with an extensive treatment of the extraordinary escape of twelve-hundred Jews to Switzerland on the authority of *Reichsfuehrer* SS Heinrich Himmler in February 1945 — an event integral to this work as the author was one of the twelve-hundred.

I met Gerda Haas when she first came to the National Archives to research this incident among the records of the Nuremberg war crimes trials in the custody of the Modern Military Branch. Her work exhibits her diligence and attention to detail, enriched by the hues of personal experience. In all of her attributes as a survivor of the Holocaust, lecturer, librarian, parent and a person involved in education, Mrs. Haas understands the importance of communicating the unbelievable so that it may never recur — a difficult, painful and necessary task, which is accomplished here with skill and dignity.

Through these narratives the statistics of the Holocaust assume flesh-and-blood identities. Most of the individuals who appear in these pages survived yet they remain victims of the Nazi terror in their sufferings and lost years. For the human mind, the figure of eleven million victims is virtually impossible to grasp except as a mathematical abstraction; only with the names, personalities and individual accounts of those who suffered can we begin to comprehend the loss. That is why this is an important book for all.

Timothy P. Mulligan

Preface

Hitler had been dead for a year less three days when I stepped down the ramp of the *S.S. Mulholland* at Boston Harbor. Behind me were twelve years of oppression, six of those twelve spent in wartime and two of the six war years in a concentration camp. Behind me war criminals were being judged in Germany, and bombed cities were being rebuilt all over Europe from Poland to the Netherlands, from Italy to England. Before me was New England, America. The date was April 27, 1946; I was twenty-three years old.

Today the youngest of my four children is the age I was then, back on the pier in Boston. How different my four children's youth has been from mine; how difficult for them to understand my story. They know bombing and killing and fear only vicariously, and when I tell them fragments of my experience in the war and in the Holocaust they do not comprehend them. And yet they must understand, must know how my life has been influenced by the system under which I lived. Perhaps they will then be better able to appreciate the freedom they enjoy and the society they live in.

I first began to realize that my American-born children took for granted the privileges which, for me, were so prodigious on a day in September of 1977. At that point I had already been successful in completing the formal education that was interrupted in my youth: I had graduated from Bates College in 1971, from the University of Maine Graduate School in 1974 and was by then catalog librarian at Bates College; I had already served once on jury duty; I voted conscientiously and proudly at every chance; my family and I freely practiced the Jewish orthodox religion in Lewiston, Maine. Life, liberty and the pursuit of happiness had become a reality, and the oppressed past was history, however real. Then, in late summer of 1977, Governor James B. Longley nominated me for membership on the Maine State Board of Education. My children, by then all in their twenties, and my husband shared my excitement and the sense of honor over the Governor's nomination. But when the official letter arrived notifying me of my confirmation hearing before the Education Committee of the Senate, my heart sank: the date for the hearing was September 14, the second day of Rosh Hashanah, the Jewish New Year, and I knew I could not travel to Augusta on the High Holiday.

With immeasurable regret that this honor and opportunity would now slip through my fingers, and with a deeply imprinted fear of approaching Government, I called the chairman of the Education Committee and explained my dilemma to him, certainly not expecting the Committee to accommodate me. Warmth spread through me when he invited me to come for my hearing the following day. He assured me that the Education Committee would not mind meeting especially for that purpose.

I told my children about the phone call, but they seemed curiously uninfected by my excitement. One of my daughters said: "Why do you think that's so special, Mom?" She seemed to expect that the Committee would routinely reschedule the hearing if I could not attend because of the Jewish holiday. Her reaction was so different from mine that I was startled. The stark contrast in our very different expectations caused me to consider why our views were so different. That very evening I went to the basement and looked for the notes I had taken in 1945 after my liberation from concentration camp. I knew then that it was time to translate those yellowing pages. I knew that it was time to tell my children, and perhaps others brought up in a free society, what it was like to have lived under Hitler's Third Reich.

But even as I was translating my experiences, I began to understand two things: for one, my story was incomprehensible to my children without some sense of the history in which it occurred, and I knew that I should write about Hitler's rise to power and the ensuing war, however briefly. The other thing I realized was that one story — whether it was mine or another's, even when told in historical perspective — could not possibly give a sense of the range and variety of experiences nor the depth of human suffering that was endured during the Holocaust years. I resolved to add Holocaust accounts from other countries in Europe to my story and to tell them also in the context of their history. To add an account of every country that came under Hitler's domination seemed unnecessary for my purpose, and so I looked for only eight other examples besides mine. My intention is to show nine lives changed by history; to show history borne on the shoulders of nine of us: fragments picked from the millions of shattered lives.

I became aware of many such fragments in my library work. Book after book on the Holocaust crossed my desk: memoirs, biographies, diaries, first-hand reports of both Jewish and non-Jewish observers. At the same time I read works on the history of the Third Reich and the Holocaust. Slowly my book took form for me.

I wanted to present human experience in historical context and impress the reader with the geographical range of the Holocaust. All this I wanted to include in my book and convey to my children and, by extension, to children of a generation who may regard the Holocaust as remote and difficult to understand.

As my book took shape, a sense of urgency claimed me. Since nearly the whole of Jewish youth under eighteen was killed, the few of us who have survived, the men and women who are now in our late fifties and older, have a special responsibility to share what we know and have experienced in the Holocaust. This responsibility, this awareness is my justification for telling this story, for writing this book.

January 1982   *Gerda Haas*
Lewiston, Maine

Acknowledgments

I thank the editors of LIBRARY JOURNAL for asking me to review for them in the area of Holocaust and Judaica. They thus helped initiate the idea for this book and, unaware of its genesis, supplied material for it as well.

During the next four years of research, work and worry, my colleages at the Bates College Library buoyed me with their interest and support. I thank Werner Roemer who spent his American holiday doing initial research for me. After he went back to Frankfurt, Nancy Levit did my research with the greatest dedication and devotion; she is now applying the same energy to her law studies. Jane Lindholm took pains with my English. Joe Derbyshire, Librarian at Bates College, read the first draft and I am very grateful for his sensitive comments and suggestions. Drs. Lawrence Langer, Glenn Pate, and Kenneth Shapiro read the manuscript in part or whole: I thank them for their criticism and help.

The archivists at Leo Baeck Institute in New York were very helpful to me, as was the staff of the Cartographic Department of National Archives and Records Service in Washington, D.C. But my special gratitude goes to Timothy P. Mulligan of the Modern Military Branch at the Archives who guided my research and later read the manuscript, catching inaccuracies. Any which remain are my responsibility.

The scholarly works which I consulted and from which I benefited are listed in my bibliography. I express my debt to the scholars of history and Holocaust who wrote them.

I know now how much a writer depends on the cooperation of his or her family and on the comfort that comes from a spouse. I thank my father for letting me open his wounds and allowing me to publish some of my mother's, my sister's and my letters to him. I thank my stepmother for her patience throughout this long ordeal, which naturally brought to the fore her own suffering and loss. My four children each have a part in this whole work: Hedy by asking the question that first moved me to write; David by his queries about what went on in other countries during the years 1933 to 1950, which resulted in my adding "World Highlights;" Leonard in giving me editorial suggestions gleaned from his own writing experience; Polly and her husband, Jean Hammel, in supplying the grandchildren — Benjamin, Jonathan and Sarah Hammel — in whom I find recovery.

The sum of my gratitude is reserved for my husband, Dr. Rudolph Haas, for his forbearance and encouragement during the long months of writing and rewriting. This book is for him too.

Introduction

From the many first-person accounts of survivors and the diaries of victims in Holocaust literature, I have selected for inclusion here eight accounts to be added to my own story: six other survivors' memoirs and two victims' diaries. My first criterion for inclusion was a geographical one: I wanted human stories from different countries of Europe. My second criterion was historical: Though the Jewish persecution took priority, half-Jews, communists, gypsies, homosexuals, mental patients, Blacks, Slavs, Serbs and other non-Aryan races in Europe were equally in danger of their lives. Jehovah's Witnesses, Christian leaders and labor spokesmen, even if they were Aryan, were in similar danger. I have therefore included the story of a half-Jew and the memoirs of a non-Jew, a Lithuanian Catholic boy. My final criterion was diversity: Though Holocaust experiences seem alike in certain respects, they each tell of a very different kind of experience.

My story is the first one. It could be the story of a thousand young Jewish women growing up in Nazi Germany and being taken away to concentration camp. Only I was luckier than most of the others: I was taken to Theresienstadt and worked there until I was liberated and taken to Switzerland while the war was still going on.

Two accounts from Poland are next: the ghetto diary of Janusz Korczak and the biography of Luba Gurdus. Korczak was a famous pediatrician and the beloved director of a Jewish orphanage in Warsaw. When Hitler overran Poland, Korczak had to relocate his orphanage behind the red walls of the newly created Warsaw Ghetto. He kept a diary, jotting down his thoughts in a notebook during sleepless nights or in the early morning hours before facing yet another ghetto day. Finally Korczak was ordered to lead his children to the cattle cars for "relocation" and was offered the chance to stay behind. He did not accept that offer. He made sure that his diary was sent out of the ghetto, and he went into the cars with his children.

In contrast, Luba's biography is testimony to the will to survive. She too lived in Warsaw when German troops marched into the city, and she managed against all odds, with great determination and with the help of sympathetic Polish gentile friends, to slip through the hands of her persecutors.

Denmark, Norway, Holland, Belgium, Luxembourg and France fell quickly to the Nazis, and the Jews in those countries became immediate targets. Leesha Rose of Holland tells how she escaped death by her courageous actions and by joining the Dutch Underground Movement. As an active member of that movement, she helped others — Jews and Dutchmen alike — get through the grim German occupation.

For the Belgian experience I chose Moshe Flinker's moving diary. Moshe's story is a familiar one: the Jewish child in hiding. Unhappily, so many of these brave children went through the nightmare of their submerged lives in vain. Moshe, too, was denounced and sent to the gas chambers, leaving us his diary.

Fania Fenelon speaks for France and also for the many people who barely knew that they were Jewish. Fania, a *Mischling*, was sent to Auschwitz like so many others — Jew and non-Jew alike — from all over Europe. She walked through the portals under the sign that proclaimed: "Work will set you free." It should have said, like the inscription in Dante's *Inferno*: "Abandon hope all ye who enter here." Fania did lose hope, time and again, in that modern-day Inferno and nearly lost her life there too, but by luck and determination she survived the death camp as a member of the camp's bizarre women's orchestra.

Hitler moved against the Balkan countries in 1941, swiftly bringing Rumania, Bulgaria, Albania, Yugoslavia and Greece under his domination. Then he reeled north and took the Ukraine, Lithuania and Latvia away from Russia before attempting to conquer even Russia herself. Let Alain Stanké's memoirs of his childhood first under Russian occupation, then under German domination represent the plight of non-Jews in Eastern Europe. Alain and his family were Catholic and lived in Kaunas, Lithuania. After unbelievable hardship and harassment, they were sent to Germany to do slave labor for the "master race." Alain, a ten-year old laborer, tells a story all too true, one that should not be forgotten.

Let Bryna Bar Oni from the *shtetl* of Byten in the Ukraine speak for the Jews of Eastern Europe. Bryna saw her parents killed in a roundup and ran, crazed with grief and guilt, into the forest nearby. She joined the partisans and fought for her and her country's freedom. Not many Jews survived the relentless persecution in that part of Europe. Bryna was one of the few who did.

Even as German armies were defeated in Russia, Hitler sent troops and SS into northern Italy in 1943 and overwhelmed Hungary in 1944. Isabella Leitner's biography of Auschwitz and her death march through Germany are typical of the condition of Hungarian Jews and of the last months of Hitler's grip on Europe.

In order to make these nine fragments as understandable as possible, I precede each account with a brief overview of the history in which it took place. A picture of the way

Hitler used deceit, speed, brute strength and the element of surprise in his military conquests is essential in understanding that history. I also precede each of the accounts with a short description of how the Jews fared in a given country before Hitler came and how he prepared for mass slaughter as soon as he arrived. The short descriptions of Jewish history in the countries of Europe help explain the reaction of native populations to Hitler's Final Solution, illuminating and supporting individual eyewitness narratives.

For seven of the narratives, I have chosen to give extracts, letting their authors speak for themselves and thus conveying a more immediate sense of the Holocaust than would be possible by the mere retelling of the story. Moshe Flinker's diary is an exception here. So is my own story which, in contrast to the others, has not been published before. In a postscript I report on my own and the post-Holocaust lives of the survivors whose stories I have used.

In a short time survivors of the Holocaust will have joined its victims, and that great catastrophe will be but a footnote in the history books. Let us, while we are still able to do so, pass on to a new generation of readers the memory of this Holocaust as living experience.

THESE I DO REMEMBER

Fragments from the Holocaust

EUROPE
During the Holocaust

Key

City •
Ghetto ✦
Transit Camp ▬
Concentration Camp ▲
Death Camp ☆

Shaded area is Nazi-occupied

World Highlights, 1930–1935

*Spain becomes a republic. Britain goes off the gold
standard. Japanese troops occupy Manchuria. The
discovery of the neutron is announced. Vitamin C and
D are identified and synthesized. Franklin D. Roosevelt
becomes President of the United States and the New
Deal goes into effect. There is a famine in the Soviet
Union. Adolf Hitler assumes absolute power in
Germany and inaugurates a policy for the persecution
of the Jews. Albert Einstein leaves Germany. There is a
growing unrest in Palestine. Prohibition is repealed in
the United States. Salazar establishes a dictatorship in
Portugal. Germany signs a ten-year non-aggression pact
with Poland. Premier Dollfuss of Austria is murdered.
Mustafa Kemal adopts the name of Kemal Atatuerk.
King Alexander of Yugoslavia is assassinated in Marseilles.
Persia changes her name to Iran. Huxley writes*
Brave New World *and Arnold Toynbee,* A Study of
History. *Kazantzakis translates* The Divine Comedy.

PART I
Germany

ONE

The Beginning of Nazi Rule in Germany

The *Nationalsozialistische Deutsche Arbeiterpartei*, the Nazi Party of Germany, was in power from 1933 to 1945, twelve years: a short span in terms of time, a very long time in terms of human suffering. The Party became both the vehicle which carried Adolf Hitler to power and the instrument by which he ruled. In 1926 when he assumed Party leadership, he proclaimed to its few members that he intended to create a Third Reich for the German people in Europe, a Reich greater than either Charlemagne's First Reich of the ninth century or the Second Reich of 1871–1918, a Reich, he promised, which would last a thousand years and would bring a New Order to all of Europe. No German would live under the Soviet Star or the Star of David; all would be brought into the Reich over which would fly the symbol of German labor, the Swastika, and the New Order would make the Aryan race in Europe master over the Slavic peoples. The Jews, he prophesied, would be done away with. The Party granted him unlimited power.

By 1930 his brown-shirted storm troopers, the *Sturmabteilung*, or SA as they were soon called, were marching by the thousands under the Swastika banner, singing: *"Heute gehoert uns Deutschland und morgen die ganze Welt!"* "Today we rule Germany, tomorrow the world!"

On January 30, 1933, President Hindenburg appointed Hitler *Reichskanzler*, Chancellor of Germany, and a short eighteen months later, Hindenburg was dead and Hitler abolished the post of presidency in the Reich. He was master in Germany now, absolute ruler of the nation, the *Fuehrer*. He claimed that his word was the voice of the German *Volk* and that his will was the will of the people; but in truth his word was the law of the land, the only law, and he spoke with the voice of a man with unlimited power.

From the beginning of his dictatorship to the very end, he broadcast two doctrines above all others, two concepts which he then joined into a twisted theme of war and murder: one was the *Lebensraum* doctrine, his claim that Germany needed more space in Europe; the other was the *Judenfrage*, the question of how to get rid of the Jews. And as he overpowered country after country in Europe, first in frightening take-overs, then in bloody war, he both gained *Lebensraum* and eliminated Jews simultaneously with brutality and ruthlessness.

Lebensraum

Hitler based his clamor for more living space and more land for food production on his contention that Germany was a *Volk ohne Raum*, a people without sufficient territory. Seventy million Germans were forced to live at a ratio of 140 persons to a square kilometer, an injustice, he declared, imposed on them by the terms of the Versailles Treaty. This Treaty was the work of the International Jew; it was criminal, therefore invalid. And in defiance of it he militarized the Rhineland, and he annexed to the Reich the border lands which were inhabited by Germans: the Saar, Austria, the Memel Region, Sudentenland and the Free City of Danzig. He claimed that these territories belonged to the Reich by virtue of the right of a people to self-determination. In March 1939 he seized Czechoslovakia, a country which was not inhabited by a Germanic people. Now, he said, he had no further land claims to make in Europe.

Six months later, in September 1939, Hitler conquered Poland in bloody war. He ordered Poles to be driven off their land and the Polish soil to be resettled with people of German stock; he then declared that he had added Poland to the Reich under the self-determination principle. By employing this process again and again, he expected to justify his stampede through the continent of Europe: the rape of Denmark, Norway, Holland, Belgium, Luxembourg and France; the violation of the Balkans; the devastation of Lithuania, the Ukraine and parts of Russia; the corruption of Italy and Hungary. The *Lebensraum* motive had become World War II; the New Order was beginning to be implemented; men and women of Europe were shipped to the Reich for slave labor, and the Jews in Europe were killed.

The Jewish Question

"Die Juden sind unser Unglueck!" "All our misfortune is the fault of the Jews!" anti-Jewish posters screamed in all languages and rekindled old antipathies. Jew-hatred, *Judenhass*, in Europe was as old as Jewish history, unchanged except for the name: In the nineteenth century, in search of a better term, the expression *Antisemitismus* was introduced.

Hitler legalized anti-Semitism by means of the Nuremberg Laws of September 15, 1935. These laws—the Reich Citizenship Law and the Law for the Protection of German Blood and German Honor—decreed that none but Aryans could be citizens of the Reich. They defined as "Aryan" anyone with four German grandparents; anyone else, if not a Jew, was a *Mischling*, a halfbreed. The Nuremberg Laws forbade marriage between Aryans and Jews and made even sexual relations between the two races a criminal offense, the crime of *Rassenschande*. The same laws proclaimed the Swastika the official national symbol and only citizens of the Reich were allowed to display it. The Jews were now a people unprotected by German law. During the next seven years, a number of ordinances were put into effect which isolated the Jews and disinherited them, then concentrated them in ghettos and camps and ultimately allowed their murder.

By late 1938 Jews in small towns and villages had to "sell" their properties to the Germans and move to larger cities. Three years later, in November 1941, a law supplementing the Reich Citizen Law said that "Jews who take up residence abroad" were no longer Reich nationals and that the Reich can confiscate their property and possessions. No one dreamed that "taking up residence abroad" meant to be forcibly displaced, to be deported beyond the borders of the Reich into occupied territory, there to be penned into ghettos or camps.

To confine the Jews in a designated area within a large town or city was not an original idea. Ghettos had historically been quarters of the city where the Jews felt safe from harassment, where they could move freely and prosper. In the great ghettos of the Middle Ages, the Jewish heritage flourished; religious and social unity lent strength and solidarity to the ghetto inhabitants. Inside their ghetto walls, medieval Jews preserved a unique custom of dress to which, it is true, a mark of their separateness was added in the form of a Jewish Star or a peculiar kind of "Jew hat" but in general these markings were not regarded as invitations to murder in the ghettos. With the emancipation of the eighteenth century, ghetto gates opened and walls tumbled, first in France and then in all of Europe. Restrictions were done away with, marks on clothing became silly —until September 19, 1941.

From that day on, all persons defined as Jews by the Nuremberg Laws had to wear the yellow Star of David, the word "Jude" or "Jood" or "Juif" printed in its center with large, black Hebrew-type letters. Thus branded, the Jews of Europe were herded back into Nazi-constructed ghettos in all towns and cities on the occupied Continent. Once there, the Jews were ordered to govern themselves by Nazi-appointed Jewish Councils, called *Judenraete*, which in turn were under the charge of a Jewish Elder, a *Judenaeltester*, so named because Jews could not use the epithet leader or master. These impotent administrators were put in place for one reason only: to facilitate a destruction process yet to be devised.

Handy as the modern ghettos were for the concentration of the Jewish population, they were not the solution to the Jewish problem. For this purpose the Nazis used concentration camps, *Konzentrationslager*. The first such *Lager* was Dachau, established near Munich in 1933. Others sprang up: Buchenwald near Weimar, Sachsenhausen and Oranienburg near Berlin, Mauthausen near Linz. After the conquest of Poland, sinister camp complexes were built up in the East: Auschwitz, Belzec, Maidaneck, Treblinka— their number grew until there were some thirty of them on the map of the Reich and its territories. What was their purpose? What was the Gestapo and the SS gearing up for?

The Gestapo Empire

The Gestapo, the Nazi's secret police, had initially been called into life to act as an instrument of terror within the Party, just as the *Schutzstaffel*, the feared SS, at first was nothing more than Hitler's body guard. But both these bodies quickly swelled to a powerful German policing force whose business was the destruction of the Jews. In June 1934 Heinrich Himmler became chief of the SS and of all German police with the title *Reichsfuehrer SS*. Himmler organized the Gestapo, the SS, the SD (*Sicherheitsdienst*) and the Sipo (*Sicherheitspolizei*) into the *Reichssicherheitshauptamt*, the ominous RSHA, of which first Reinhard Heydrich, then Ernst Kaltenbrunner, was chief. The Gestapo division of the RSHA was called *Amt IV*, the Office for Combatting Opposition and its Division for Jewish Affairs with offices in Berlin. Their heads were Gestapo chiefs Adolf Eichmann and Heinrich Mueller. When Hitler turned over full authority and responsibility in dealing with the Jews in Germany and in occupied territories to Himmler, orders passed through Heydrich, later Kaltenbrunner, to Eichmann and Mueller and from them to the inspector of concentration camps, Moess, and to all camp *Kommandanten*.

In February 1936 the German Supreme Court passed a law which restricted German courts' interference with Gestapo activities, expressly with regard to actions against Jews: henceforth the Gestapo was the law. In January 1942 Gestapo and SS officers and selected officials of the Reich and the occupied Eastern territories met at Heydrich's invitation at Wannsee near Berlin to discuss the "complete solution of the Jewish question." Unrestrained by German law, these men devised the last step, "the final solution," in the *Judenfrage*, the Jews' annihilation in Polish concentration camps. In their official documents they used guarded language such as "evacuation to the East" and "special treatment," but in effect they meant gassing installations for the murder of their victims and crematoria for the disposal of the millions of bodies. To prevent revolt, the Jews were to be told that they were recruited for work and were "resettled" in labor camps. Lest anyone should question what use the old and sick Jews and permanently disabled veterans might be at hard labor, a ghetto was to be set up somewhere in Czechoslovakia for Jews over sixty-five, war veterans with permanent injuries, partners of mixed marriages and *Mischlinge*. Internationally-known Jewish scientists and artists could also be sent to such a "privileged" ghetto in case the free world should inquire about them.

Did the World Know the Awful Truth?

Did world leaders care or help? In July 1938, President Roosevelt called together representatives of thirty-two states at Evian on the French shore of Lake Geneva for the purpose of establishing international bodies for assistance to the Jews of Europe. An international refugee committee was formed with headquarters in London, which claimed the right to speak out for the Jews. It was never heard from. As the situation worsened, each unoccupied country acted — or did not act — on its own; leading figures spoke out — or were silent.

In Europe England's borders were open; Sweden harbored and saved the Jews from Denmark and all others who could reach her shores; Portugal acted as a stepping stone to freedom; the south of France protected thousands of fugitives before her own Nazi occupation. Switzerland granted temporary refuge to hundreds of thousands of fleeing families during the early years of Nazism in Germany,

but in 1936 the Swiss Chief of Police, Dr. Heinrich Roth-
mund, requested that the Germans stamp Jewish passports
with a visible "J" and from then on, Swiss border police
were instructed to turn fugitives back to the German authorities. Fortunately, the border police allowed many Jews
to slip through. Swiss borders again opened wide in 1944
and 1945, when negotiations with Himmler for the release
of Jews in exchange for American money were successful,
and concentration camp survivors found hospitality in
Swiss refugee camps — at *Pensionskost* at a charge of fr.
3.50 a day — until they could arrange emigration to
America or Palestine.

The United States did not alter immigration policies.
The Jews of Europe, yearning for freedom, had to wait their
turn in an antiquated quota system, and then they could
only get visas if they were able to obtain affidavits which
would guarantee their economic independence. Poverty-
stricken Polish Jews were left out. Even Palestine was not
open to them. Palestine, under British mandate, restricted
Jewish immigration to farmers and capitalists, Jews who
were able to pay a required sum of pound sterling. In this
way, the British hoped to appease the Arabs, knowing how
they hated the Jews.

Cuba accepted the fleeing Jews, but only on a temporary
basis while awaiting their quota entry to America. Shanghai took in thousands of Jews, all who could get ships'
passage. Australia, South Africa and South America
granted refuge, but millions could not afford such expen-
sive journeys. With no haven in reach, the Jews were at the
mercy of the Nazi hunters.

By mid-1942 Roosevelt knew about the mass killings in
Germany and Poland. He spoke out publicly and strongly,
but did nothing more than that. The Pope in Rome, Pope
Pius XII, when asked to make a similar statement, declined,

but when the Nazis occupied Italy in 1943 and began rounding up Jews in the streets of Rome, the Pope ordered the Vatican's convents and monasteries to take in and shelter as many Jews as they could hold. At that late date, he saved Jewish lives. Anthony Eden, Foreign Minister of England, received a letter from Chaim Weizmann in July 1944, pleading that the Royal Air Force bomb Auschwitz, Birkenau and the railroad lines leading to those places. The answer, written a month later, was negative: The project could not be pursued due to "technical difficulties." The remnant of Jewry in Europe was doomed to wait behind barbed wire until the liberators arrived. How appropriate that one of them was called Eisenhower, the slayer of iron.

Growing Up in Nazi Germany: Gerda's Story

I slowed my usual run to school to a hesitant walk that sunny May morning in 1933, my first day at the *Maedchen Lyzeum Ansbach* in the Karolinenstrasse. My sister Friedl urged me on: "Hurry a little bit, Gerda, will you! We have to look for your room before the bell rings!" Friedl could be complacent; it was her second year at the Lyzeum, but I was scared. New school, new teachers, classmates, books, and all that talk at home about the new Reich's Chancellor and his raging speeches on the radio. On the way to school, we saw a large sign: *"Die Juden sind unser Unglueck."* We were embarrassed and tried not to look at it, but on a newsstand we saw a copy of Streicher's anti-Semitic paper *Der Stuermer* which came out of Nuremberg, only 35 kilometers away, and which, my parents had said, proclaimed every Jew an enemy of the Reich. I knew that my parents had to bring proof of my father's military service to Germany in World War I and had to show the school director Father's Iron Cross First Class before the Lyzeum even accepted me. I entered its rococo portals with a sickening feeling in my stomach. Was I an enemy of the Reich too? I was only ten years old!

I stood quietly while the professor greeted the new class with a casual "Heil Hitler," and during recess I quickly sought out my sister and the few Jewish students who were standing in a corner of the yard, quite isolated from the happy, noisy crowd. Nobody spoke to us. When the first schoolday was over and the afternoon bell rang, I ran all the way home. There at least I was part of a solid group, our loving family; everybody, Father, Mother, Grandmother Sofie and Aunt Adelheid wanted to hear about the first day at the Lyzeum. I didn't tell them how lonely I had felt.

Nothing that happened at school in the next five years was meant to change that feeling. I was assigned a seat at the far end of the room and was not allowed to answer questions to the class nor to ask any of the teachers. In *"Deutsch,"* I was given poor grades no matter how happy my German compositions turned out. Textbooks in all subjects were brand new, reflected Nazi philosophy, omitted all references to Jewish scientists or artists, denounced France, denounced Bolshevism, accused the Jews. The older, sympathetic teachers were gradually replaced with splendid young Aryan types fresh from their post-training year at labor service camps and comradeship houses: Their morning greeting was delivered in a forceful declaration and with a stiffly outstretched arm, right there under the *Fuehrer's* picture behind their desk. They told the students that the *Fuehrer* considered them the future of Germany, with the exception of me, of course. They told the class that Jesus was an Aryan and that I and my kind had killed him. They sent me home when the class went on outings and field trips and excused me from participation when the class sang or did physical exercises. They reminded my classmates that their promotion to universities depended as much on their record in the *Hitlerjugend* as it did on their academic achievements. They assured us all that everything Adolf Hitler did was right, and every word he said was true and reminded us often to take that message home to our parents. I envied my sister when she graduated in 1938 and wondered how I would get through the year left to my own graduation. I needn't have worried: I was expelled on April 12, 1938.

Friedl went to a Zionist agricultural school, Wolfratshausen, near Munich, but I wasn't accepted there. I was too young, and besides, I hadn't finished school yet. The family sat around the table many an evening, talking about me, about the future, worrying and yet dreaming. Friends and acquaintances were beginning to leave Germany, selling their homes and businesses as best they could and emigrating to places that had, up to then, only been exotic names on my school atlas: Uruguay, Havana, Johannesburg, Buenos Aires, Chicago. But we had no place to go, and anyway, we were so sure that we'd never have to leave our beloved Ansbach. Hitler would only last till spring, or till fall, or till winter. God would help. And Gerda could go to a Jewish school for a couple of years.

Where was there a Jewish school for me? Our rabbi, Dr. Elie Munk, arranged for my admission to the *Adass Yisroel Schule* in Berlin. Berlin? Another place I only knew from the atlas! That was 450 kilometers from Ansbach, wasn't it? How would I get there? Who would I live with? When could I get home to visit Papa and Mama, and where would

I see Friedl? I did not gladly start school in Berlin that spring of 1938. I did not like to leave home.

I was called back in haste on November 12. On November 7, 1938, a young Jew read in a Paris newspaper that terrible atrocities had been committed against thousands of Jews in the Polish Town of Zbonszyn. Suspecting his own family to be among those maltreated, he stormed into the German embassy in Paris and shot one of the diplomats there, the German Ernst vom Rath. The Nazis reacted with fury to that impulsive act. All through the night of November 7, all the next day and into the night of November 8, the SA and SS invaded the streets of every German city and town, smashing Jewish property, burning synagogues, abusing thousands of innocent Jewish men. In Ansbach a hundred Jews had been picked up from their homes and imprisoned in the *Rezat Halle*, a big meeting place near the slaughterhouse on the edge of town. From there the men were taken to prison in Nuremberg. On November 11 women and children were released and were told to pack their personal belongings and to leave Ansbach. Their homes and businesses would be ''bought'' by *Parteigenossen*, party members; Jewish possessions would have to remain intact for the new ''owners,'' and Ansbach would have to be free of Jews by the end of the year—or we would never see our men again.

When I got home on the twelfth, Mother, Friedl, Grandmother and Aunt Adelheid were packing. *Parteigenosse* Groetz, who had bought our house and my father's butchershop for a slip of paper and a song, was already painting the livingroom and telling us to be faster. His eight children were eating from our dishes, and we didn't yet know where to go.

Grandmother's youngest daughter Berta came with her daughter Edith and took her mother with her to Regensburg; Aunt Adelheid, ill with cancer of the stomach, was able to get into the Jewish hospital in Fuerth; what were we to do? Where would we go before the year was out to get Father back?

On a cold and snowy day we walked out of our house. I couldn't bear to look back, to cast one more glance at Turnitzstrasse 5, at the stately old house where our mother and Friedl and I were born, the wrought-iron shield that told of two generations of industrious men, *"Metzgerei Schild frueher Jochsberger"* Butchershop, Schild, formerly Jochsberger, Father having taken over from his father-in-law. I couldn't bear to look at Mother either, knowing the agony in her soul. I just shouldered what I could carry, Friedl took her burden and we walked away, walked the few blocks to the railroad station and bought three tickets to Munich. We had relatives there; we knew they would stand by us in our need.

I don't know how Father found us, but one day he was at the door, together with the Munich uncles and cousins, baldshaven, bearded, pale. "They didn't beat us," was his only comment.

We dreamed no longer. But we still had no place to flee to; no one to arrange an American affidavit for the four of us; no money to buy any other visa. Because we thought then that the Nazis were after our men only, we persuaded Father to join his brother Berthold and a group of men who went to a transit camp in Sandwich, England, that British Jews had fixed up for German refugees. We rationalized that once there, Father could arrange for our emigration, perhaps find English families who would take us in as domestics—anything. It seemed our only chance to get out, even if it meant, for the time being, to separate.

Papa left Munich in July of 1939, and Hitler marched into Poland in September. Great Britain declared war and the borders to England closed. Papa succeeded in immigrating to America in January, 1941, and Germany declared war on the United States in December. We were trapped in Germany.

During those two years the deprivation of the Jews continued in Germany. We had to turn in all weapons, our gold and silver, furs and bicycles, radios and telephones, all appliances. We had to part with our pets of any kind from dog to canary. What we then thought to be chicanery and malice now stands out as early steps toward making us defenseless, unprotected and poor. We were banned from parks and museums and movies and telephone booths. Notices began appearing proclaiming "Jews are not wanted here" and "Jews are forbidden to enter." Regulations reached into the private lives of Jews as well. Newborn babies could only be named from a published list of Jewish and Yiddish names approved by the Reich, and everybody had to add the names Sara and Israel to their passports, identity cards, foodstamps, and to the name plates on residences.

Foodstamps for Jews did not include meat stamps; we received less butter, jam, and bakery goods stamps, no whole milk or cream coupons. Jews did not qualify for clothing cards, shoe repair cards or cigarette stamps. Since all Jewish stores were forcibly closed in 1940, we had to look for German stores which did not display the ominous sign "We do not sell to Jews," and we were allowed in those few stores from four to five o'clock in the afternoon. We had to walk distances of some kilometers in many cases. Did I mention that we were forbidden to ride the streetcars? Were not permitted to hail a taxi? Buy a newspaper?

Jewish buildings were confiscated in 1940. In 1941 Jews had to hand over to the Germans all their woolen sweaters and part of their household linens. Civil and government offices had special hours for Jews; elevators in public buildings were banned to us. So were air-raid shelters. From September 19, 1941, on we were visibly marked with the yellow star which we had to buy for 20 *Pfennig* at the Jewish Community office, one to a Jew, necessitating frequent sewing onto work clothes and outer clothing. Smaller white stars were affixed to house doors and offices. We were tolerated on city streets from six in the morning to eight at night. Branded, concentrated in the larger cities, confined in our apartments from eight o'clock in the evening till six o'clock in the morning, we were kept in a state of uncertainty and fear. By October 1941 the German borders were closed, and the Jews were in the hands of their assailants.

Munich

By late 1939 we knew we had to take charge of our lives, had to make some plans for a most uncertain future, had to do something to be useful to ourselves and our fellow Jews. Friedl was eighteen and I was going to be seventeen before the year was out. There was simply no point in sitting around and worrying all day or waiting for air-raids to blow Munich to pieces at night. Mother suggested that we go into nurses' training, and that seemed a good idea to us all. But it meant leaving her alone in Munich, which she energetically claimed she did not mind. My sister left in November 1939 to become a student nurse at the Gagernstrasse Hospital in Frankfurt, and I rode off to Nieder schoenhausen near Berlin a month later to start my training as a pediatric nurse. I learned only much later the circumstances by which I could become a nurse. All our assets had long been frozen, and Mother was forced to go to the *Devisenstelle*, the local Nazi banking office on Theatinerstrasse the first of every month to pick up her monthly allotment which, of course, did not allow for our training expenses. No appeal was effective in obtaining extra funds for this from our own money. By sacrifice she was able to pay Friedl's tuition, but there was no way by which she could pay mine too. Determined that both her girls should have useful professions, she made a pilgrimage to a distant cousin who lived in Munich, a wealthy bachelor, and begged him for his help. He understood the situation and helped. These many years later, I thank you, Sigmund Jochsberger.

Berlin, 1940 to 1943

I arrived in Niederschoenhausen on New Year's Day 1940 and was soon very happy at the Jewish children's home there. The work with the babies was great, the lessons were challenging and the other student nurses, young women from different cities of Germany, were soon my friends. In spite of outside pressure, we were gay and happy, and in those months at the children's home we formed friendships that lasted. In September of that year, my friend Golly and I were transferred to the hospital of the Jewish Community at Iranische Strasse in Berlin to continue training at the children's ward and at the gynecological station. We were able to shut out the Nazi presence less successfully there. Because the harassment of the Jews intensified in the fall of 1940 and well into 1941, the hospital admitted many a suicide case. We young nurses wondered privately what these poor people were being revived for. Back in the street of the city, they were only renewed subjects for arrest because of an incorrect street crossing or target for a Nazi pistol because they were on the street minutes after eight o'clock curfew, and they'd be back in the hospital or sent to Oranienburg Prison. Nineteen-forty-one was a turbulent year in Berlin. Air-raids became routine. Every evening we nurses made sure that the emergency delivery cubicle in the basement shelter was in order; every night we hoped that we wouldn't have to wheel and herd all those women down in haste, work under the noise of bombs, lose our much needed sleep—was that part of our nurse's training too? It was, and the young woman whom I helped deliver of a wrinkled baby boy while anti-aircraft machine-guns sputtered high above us became a beloved friend. Eva Simmon, dear Eva, little Dan and proud papa Werner. How could I have coped without your warm friendship in the years that followed?

On September 12, 1941, I graduated and was proud when Dr. Lustig, the director of the hospital, handed me the diploma and pin that signified my new status. I was now allowed to call myself "Jewish baby-and-children's nurse, licensed to care for Jewish babies and children." When he asked me to remain at my station as an employee of the *Juedische Kultus Gemeinde*, the Jewish Community, I accepted gladly. Incredibly, the Jewish hospital had as yet not been closed by the Germans and indeed remained functioning and under Lustig's leadership right through the whole war.

Not so the place where my sister trained. In May 1941, the Gagernstrasse Hospital in Frankfurt was beginning to be dissolved. Friedl and a part of the staff were sent to the Siemens Factory in Berlin to do forced labor for the Germans. They lived at a factory collective at Gormann Strasse, and when our free time coincided we hiked long distances and spent our time together, either on the bunk in her room or in the nurses' residence at Iranische Strasse or at Werner and Eva Simmon's house. We were happy to be together, no matter what the circumstances.

We spent a lot of time writing letters to our mother in

Munich, and we included our letters to Father who had by then, together with his brother Berthold, immigrated to America and had found a job in New York. He was doing his utmost to get affidavits for us while Mother in Munich and I for the two of us in Berlin tried to get visas and ship's passage. Reading those anxious letters today, translating them from the original German, the anguish of those years, the depth of our misery, returns to my heart undiminished.

Munich
October 17, 1941

Dear Siegfried:

I am sending this letter off without waiting for the letters of Friedl and Gerda from Berlin. I want to write to you about something that keeps nagging at my mind. I want to tell you that if you have enough money saved up for only two affidavits, please let the children come over, and if you have enough only for one, let one of them come. Please don't wait until you have enough for three—I fear it will be too late by then. If only I had thought of this sooner! Perhaps it's not too late. Is there no answer from Lina? Oh please, move heaven and earth to get at least two affidavits, please try for the children! I have work here and I still have my room; I can wait it out. Please try! I am sure you won't be fired if you have to miss a day at work!

Forgive, dear Siegfried, I am distraught tonight, and very tired. I ran around all day.

Lovingly yours,
Paula

In October 1941, deportations of Jews to undisclosed destinations in the East began. Jews were rounded up in the streets of Berlin, collected by the thousands and stuffed into boxcars ordinarily used for the transport of animals, *Viehwaggons*, freight trains.

26

Berlin
October 28, 1941

Dear Papa:

I am sure you have heard the latest news events from here, but Gerda and I are o.k. I am in her room now, writing letters. Is there any news in our immigration affairs? Did you get an answer from Aunt Lina? It is so urgent that she help us, Papa! Time is running out.

I have a lot of work to do, but it is not unpleasant, and when I compare my life with a lot of other people's, I can only wish that it will stay this way and won't get any worse. That's how modest we've become. If only we could leave now! Will our friends and acquaintances do nothing for us, even though they know the news from here?

I hope so much that you'll be successful in your efforts for us, dear Papa.

Lovingly yours,
Friedl

Munich
October 28, 1941

Dear Siegfried:

I received your telegram yesterday, but there was no point in cabling back because it is too late. The children can no longer leave, and I will not go without them. A few weeks ago there was still hope, but now it's finished.

I am so sorry to have to write you such a sad letter; my heart is so heavy. Forgive the short note today; I will write more soon.

Lovingly yours,
Paula

In November deportations were carried out from all major German cities. The Jews received written notices to appear, with hand luggage, at certain collection centers for "resettlement" in the East.

Berlin
November 1, 1941

Dear Papa:

Mama sent me your letter and your cable yesterday. You will have heard by now that it's too late. You have worked so hard to get all that money together for us, and for nothing.

We are o.k. Things go on whether we like it or not. I would so much like to have a few days off just now, but now they declared a moratorium on vacations till December. It's so long to December. Last year Mama visited me in Frankfurt, and from there she went to Gerdl to Berlin. I have so much time at work to think about the past few years. Let's just hope everything will turn out all right for us. I still have hope.

Lovingly yours,
Friedl

P.S. Dear Papa, if only you could get Mama out, it's urgent!

Berlin
November 3, 1941

Dear Papa:

Your telegram came yesterday and I went to the HAPAG immediately and cabled back, and I hope you got that telegram. Dear Papa, it's too late. If your telegram had come only two weeks ago, we might have made it, but now everything is so hopeless that Mr. Loewenstein advised me to send you the cable so that you can at least save your hard-earned money. We can't get out anymore. Perhaps some day there'll be a way, perhaps for Mama at least.

I am sending this off without Friedl's letter since I won't see her until Sunday, and this is only Tuesday.

Lovingly yours,
Gerdl

Berlin
November 5, 1941

Dear Papa:

Now it's all over with our emigration! And just after I got the news that no one can get out anymore, I got Mama's letter, telling me about your cable. This is a hard blow for us all. But there has to be some way out for us! And soon!

I don't know of anything interesting or worthwhile to write so I'll just stop here.

Lovingly yours,
Friedl

P.S. I try and try to get those few vacation days I have coming to me, but it's useless. They just won't give me the permission to go to Munich.

Sunday
November 9, 1941

My dear Siegfried:

It is difficult for me to write to you today because I have to give you sad news. I have gotten my notification for transport, for the transport that leaves here on Tuesday.

I am so sorry for you and for the children. I know you will be upset. But I beg you, dear Siegfried, don't grieve, and don't be pessimistic. I am calm and I am not excited.

The children feared deportation already for a long time and have been worried about me all this time. Tomorrow I must call them and talk to them. I only hope that they will be spared.

I beg you, dear Siegfried, don't be upset, don't be sad,

and most of all do not blame yourself. If anyone deserves to be blamed it is I, because it was I who urged you to leave without us. We human beings are a thing of naught. I see it clearer now than ever before. All our planning, our hopes and toil come to nothing when God decides differently.

I think now if only I had done this or that, but it's no use, it is all destined by God.

Here I am, making a farewell speech, but as yet I hope that I can write to you where I am going.

I haven't heard anything from Mutter in Regensburg or from Berta and Edith. I hope they will be spared. I will write you a second letter today before I must go.

Lovingly yours,
Paula

Sunday
November 9, 1941

My dear Siegfried:

To continue. I have a letter to send you from the children, although it is a week old. I had hoped so much that Friedl would be able to come for a few days before I would be deported, but really, I didn't believe that I would actually be called up. And now it's a reality as I told you in the first letter. I am in the first evacuation from Munich.

I don't imagine it all as too bleak and I am not upset and of course I'll write to you from there as soon as possible, but don't be concerned if it takes long. And I repeat, dear Siegfried, don't worry about me, and do not reproach yourself; fate is stronger than we are. If it is God's will that we will be reunited, He can arrange it from there, just as it was His will that I could not get to you from here. I have packed already, have taken all my warm clothes along. Frau Kaufmann, the old lady who lives with me, is also in the transport and many of my old friends too. Together our lot will be easier to bear.

Now, my dear Siegfried, I have just talked with the children. Friedl wants to come with me and Gerdl too. I don't know if they can get travel permission, and at any rate, they should stay and keep in contact with you. Farewell, beloved husband,

With sincere love,
Paula

On November 11, 1941, Mother was deported to Riga. She was forty-five years old. My sister and I drew closer together. We talked about our own very likely evacuation, our almost certain separation. We came to the sorry conclusion that if one of us were caught, it would be pointless for the other one to join a transport voluntarily. We thought of Father. We hoped that somehow, someday, the four of us would be united again. We agonized about Mother, hoping that she would pull through an undoubtedly difficult time. How could we have known the true nature of deportation? How could I have known that when Friedl was deported to forced labor in the East that I would never see her or my mother again?

When I think of them today, now that I know the course that these fraudulent "deportations" took, I pray that God in whom they trusted took their noble souls from them in the freight trains, that He spared Mother from standing naked at the abyss in the forests of Latvia the assassin at her back, and Friedl from having to walk into the gas chambers of Auschwitz.

As an employee of the Jewish Community Hospital, I was protected for a little while longer. But one day in September 1942, all employees were ordered to appear in the meeting room at the building Oranienburger Strasse the next morning at six o'clock. When we nurses arrived, there were about five hundred nervous men and women already assembled, standing around in groups, wondering what to expect. The hours dragged on; we were getting hungry, restless, we needed a toilet. We were not permitted to leave the room for any reason. We were terribly worried now. Finally, at noon, three trim young SS men showed up, laughing and smoking: Rolf Guenther and Adolf Eichmann we recognized, but who was the third, jauntily puffing his cigarette? Someone whispered: "Brunner, from Vienna!"

We stood at attention in deathly silence. The three men joked among themselves and ignored us. Someone fainted. Brunner took the cigarette out of his mouth and said lightly that he had come from Vienna "to show the Prussians how to deal with their Jews!" We waited.

After what seemed an endless wait, Brunner ordered the leaders of the Jewish Community, Dr. Kraindl and Mr. Kotzover, to step forward and requested from them the names of their division heads. Then he told the division heads to come before him and ordered them to select half of the employees of their departments for immediate deportation. A gasp went through the hushed room. Were Jews to fashion their own destruction now? Was this what Brunner had come to show his cohorts?

A month later, on October 27 at four-thirty in the afternoon, we were summoned again. Anyone not showing up would have his family deported. This time we arrived at the Oranienburger Strasse meeting room and found Brunner already there, awaiting us. He called Dr. Kraindl before him. Kraindl, deathly pale, stepped forward, stood at attention and then fell to the floor—dead from a heart attack. Brunner looked at the stricken man at his feet and said, "Take him away; he'll be cold on that floor." The room was like a grave.

With Kraindl gone, Brunner called up by name from

the J.K.G. list before him every employee of the *Juedische Kultus Gemeinde*. We stepped forward as our names were called; Brunner either looked up or did not, sometimes asked an irrelevant question but mostly said nothing. In each case, he pointed with outstretched arms either to the right or to the left of his desk until the room was evenly divided into two groups. This procedure had taken about four hours; it was now eight o'clock. Would he let us all go home now?

He called Mr. Kotzover before him and made him repeat to the assembly a speech he dictated to him, word for word, and that was how we were told that the right group was to go back to work at once and the left group was to go home and prepare for transport. On October 30, three days hence, they were to report for transportation to the East. For each person who failed to show up, a leader of the J.K.G. would be shot.

Three days later, on Wednesday the 30th, the assemblage was short twenty persons. On that day twenty high officials of J.K.G., among them Drs. Lang, Blumenthal, Goldstein, the Messrs. Selbiger and Loose, were taken prisoner and driven to Oranienburg Prison outside Berlin. A few days later their families received cardboard urns filled with ashes.

We went back to work in a state of depression. A month later we were called again. This time the brute from Vienna pulled out another thirty percent of the remaining J.K.G. employees and ordered them directly to the collection center. The only concession he made was that he allowed those of us who were ordered back to work to bring the deportees' rucksacks to them. Since every Jew in Berlin had his rucksack packed and ready in the corner of his bedroom, we were able to help our friends out at least that much.

Brunner left Berlin at the end of February 1943, but before he left, he organized the first mass deportation. It was Friday, February 27, 1943. We were sitting in the dining room of the nurses' residence when the telephone rang and Dr. Lustig called for sixteen nurses, I among them. We were to report at Oranienburger Strasse the next morning at six o'clock in uniform. I checked my rucksack. I said my prayers. I hoped that I would be sent to the same place that my loved ones had been deported to.

In the morning sixteen pale young women faced each other in the meeting rooms. No one knew what to expect; no one had even heard any rumors. We were just waiting, not thinking at all. At two o'clock in the afternoon, Brunner showed up. Now he would tell us to go into a transport or to report to a collection center. He did tell us to report to collection centers, but as helpers, as nurses. He gave us armbands and passes so that we wouldn't be picked up by his henchmen and sent us, two by two, to locations we had never heard of.

Klara and I were ordered to the stables of the Rathenower *Kaserne*, a huge brick barrack. There we found hundreds of people who had been picked up at the factories where they worked and where they had considered themselves safe. They were bewildered and very agitated. What about their husbands and wives who worked at different factories? Their children who were at home with old parents? Old dependents who were waiting for their care? There was panic in the stable. The people needed to urinate, but they were not allowed in the main barrack where the toilets were. With us had come ten Jewish orderlies who set to work at once digging a latrine in the yard; then they brought in some straw, and Klara and I helped to settle the people and to calm them somehow. They desperately wanted some hot coffee, but that was beyond asking for. Coffee in 1943 in Berlin? For Jews?

As more wagons and vans brought more Jews, it was becoming clear that this roundup was an operation of unheard-of proportions, that factories in and around Berlin were being combed for Jews. Once when the doors to one of the vans opened, a bloodstained woman tumbled into our arms. A young girl, perhaps my age, was behind her, blood running from her forehead, and with them was a man with a bullet wound in his thigh. "They resisted the arresting SS officer," their captor said to us. They tried to escape their fates. Didn't they know there was no escape for any of us?

We were not permitted to take the wounded to the hospital, and we tried to stop the bleeding as best we could, there in the stables, without any supplies. We were not permitted to bring these people their rucksacks from home either or to accept letters from them, but we ignored that part of the restrictions. We were able to give out hot coffee, at long last, on Monday morning.

Monday? Had Klara and I spent three days in that pandemonium? I don't remember when we were relieved by two colleagues from the hospital; I only remember that we left the stables, our pockets crammed with notes and addresses and that we walked all over town that long day, protected by our armbands from being picked up, and looked for children left suddenly without parents, for aged parents suddenly alone. We took the children to the community home and the elderly into the hospital.

The *Fabrikaktion*, this factory roundup, finally stopped on March 3, 1943. Twelve thousand Jews had been driven to eight collection centers, Jews who had considered themselves protected against deportation by virtue of their forced labor in the German war factories. They were sent East by freight trains in hundreds of boxcars from Putlitzer Station and never heard from again.

Brunner had gone back to Vienna, but the methods he had brought from there remained. From now on Jews were forced to assist their brothers to the death trains under Nazi orders, only to be dispatched a little later themselves. And instead of collecting their prey in street-or-factory roundups, the Gestapo and the SS plucked their victims from homes — at night — when Jews were certain to be in their well-marked apartments.

On the evening of May 17, 1943, Gestapo came to the nurses' home at Iranische Strasse with a long list of nurses, doctors and patients. I felt a sharp sense of relief when my name was read from that list. One Gestapist marched me to my room, gun at the ready, waited exactly ten minutes by his stopwatch and then showed me the way to the waiting truck.

Theresienstadt

Incredibly, the truck stopped at collection center Gerlach Strasse which had lately been used as the center for Theresienstadt transports. Were we going to the "privileged" camp? I looked around the crowded rooms. There were many employees from the J.K.G. there, some familiar from previous contacts; there were hundreds of old people; there was a group, a little separate from the rest and less excited, whom I judged to be *Mischlinge* or perhaps Jewish partners of mixed marriages, I couldn't be sure. I spotted Werner and Eva Simmon and their baby. "Is it possible that we are going to Theresienstadt?" I asked Werner who was himself a functionary of the Jewish Community. "Yes, we are lucky indeed. There was a new directive from SS headquarters recently that J.K.G. personnel go there. Who knows for how long!'' Werner told me. I was so glad that I was with them.

Eva and I helped settle the elderly and then we just waited to be sent on. I wished that I could send word to my father in America about me, but mail to the U.S.A. had been stopped since December 1941 when Germany and Italy had declared war on the United States. Would I ever see my father again? Perhaps I would find my mother and my beloved sister in Theresienstadt? During those few days in limbo between Berlin and deportation I could still hope. On May 20, 1943, we left Berlin from one of the small side stations. They must have run out of cattle cars for we rode out of the German capital in third-class passenger compartments.

The train halted at a small station. The sign read: BAUSCHOWITZ. On the platform, SS were standing around smoking while young Jews, their yellow stars in plain sight, were waiting at attention; a few trucks stood near the station house. At a command the young Jews began unloading old people and helping them into the trucks. I jumped off the train and helped too. A nice blond Jewish boy came up to me and said quietly:

"If you have any contraband, give it to me; I'll return it to you after the *Schleusse*."

And then he was lost again in the shifting mass. Contraband? *Schleusse*? What was he talking about?

The SS whipped us into a convoy, and I could already see the front of it moving out into the *Landstrasse* ahead of us. I found Werner and Eva and Dan again. An old lady took my arm. We walked for a half-hour without saying very much. At one point the nice young boy was beside me again and pointed into the distance:

"You can see the ghetto now!"

I saw the steeple of a church. Was it a proper town, this

ghetto? A little later I noticed high walls and embankments. Soon I could make out what must once have been a moat. Would a drawbridge fall for us, only to be pulled in after the last straggler had caught up?

No drawbridge fell, but as we neared the gate in the wall, a wooden barrier was moved aside for the trucks and the people, then was closed behind us. We were inside Theresienstadt. It looked indeed like a medieval fortress town, and that is just what it was.

Theresienstadt was built around 1790 by the Austrian Emperor Josef II as a training camp for six thousand soldiers and was named after the monarch's mother, Maria Theresia. Around the little church in the center of town were neat, small houses built in straight-line streets, dwellings for the officers and their families; a city hall; a few small stores; a coffee house; all framing an empty park, probably the former parade grounds. Towering over the houses and arranged in a large octagon around them were perhaps ten sprawling three-story brick barracks, each with its own large inner exercise-yard. Enclosing the whole garrison town were the walls with the embankments that I had seen from the road.

We were led to one of these big barracks, the Magdeburg *Kaserne*, and while we were standing around and waiting for quite a few hours, I learned a little more about the place from the Jewish fellows who acted as transport helpers. My blond friend found me, too, and now, out of earshot of the ss, he really talked. His name was Pavel, he was a Czech Jew and he had been in Terezin, as he called this town, since 1941. He told me that we were about sixty kilometers north of Prague on the Leitmeritz-Prague line not far from the confluence of Eger and Elbe—or, as he called these two rivers, the Ohre and the Labe. In November of 1941, chief of RSHA Heydrich had sent a group of one thousand young

Jews from Prague to this little town to prepare it as a ghetto and collection center for Jews from Bohemia and Moravia, the former Czechoslovakia. This first group had a unique job cut out for them: While the town was still occupied by gentiles, the Prague Jews had to prepare the barracks to hold ten times the number of people they were meant to hold. Beds were disposed of and the floors of all barracks were covered with straw. A big communal kitchen was built; the water supply to the town was enlarged; one of the barracks was prepared to become a hospital. Barracks were named after German towns, and streets were simply designated L and Q, *lang* and *queer*; L for those which ran lengthwise through the town and Q for the ones intersecting them crosswise.

In December 1941 a second group of one thousand Czech Jews arrived, and slowly the gentile population was relocated to other towns. By January 1942, coinciding with Heydrich's Wannsee Conference, Theresienstadt was officially declared a Jewish ghetto.

Transports started coming in from Czechoslovakia, Austria, Germany, later from Poland, Holland and Denmark. And transports began to go out, Pavel said. So that was it: We had just arrived in another collection center.

While I tried to picture the early history of the ghetto ˒ and understand its true nature, my new friend started to tell me about its present setup. There seemed to be plenty of time for my ghetto-government lesson; the lines moved hardly at all; the SS seemed to have disappeared; Pavel had nothing to do. All around us in that cheerless barrack-yard, people were sitting on their bundles, standing amid their suitcases and rucksacks, looking as empty and desolate as the very *Kasernenhof* in which a strange fate had deposited them on that cool May day in 1943.

The ghetto was self-governed, the boy continued. With

one of the early Prague transports had come the leader of the Jewish Community from there, the respected Dr. Jakob Edelstein with his family for the stated purpose of being the ghetto's Jewish Elder, the chief of its *Judenrat*. Soon after him arrived Dr. Otto Zucker, his deputy. Together the two men built up the ghetto, but of course they had to take their orders from the SS. Commandant SS Seidl and his deputy, SS *Sturmfuehrer* Ott, were in charge of the whole ghetto and all contact with the world beyond the ghetto walls. A group of SS men and a few German women helped them at their task; a hundred Czech gendarmes acted as a policing force for the SS, but all internal affairs were the responsibility of the *Judenaeltester*, his deputy and the *Judenrat* of nine prominent Jews from Berlin, Vienna and Prague. They supervised the food distribution, the health care of old people and of the ghetto's children; they had to see that deaths were properly recorded, the bodies burned and the ashes stored; they performed marriages and acted in *Bar Mitzvas*; they were responsible for order in the ghetto and cleanliness in the streets. When transports were called for "resettlement" or "work in the East," they had to furnish the stated number of men, women and children. The Jewish leaders were totally dominated by the *Lagerkommandant*, and he in turn was under the command of SS Chief Heydrich — after his death Kaltenbrunner — and of *Hauptsturmfuehrer* Moess, Mueller, Eichmann and, of course, SS *Reichsfuehrer* Himmler.

Pavel was out of breath, and I had heard enough.

"You will soon learn all the bans and restrictions," he said to me. "Try to get a job in the cleaning detail and keep out of transports to the East! Good luck in the *Schleusse*!" And with that he left. I still didn't know what the *Schleusse* was.

The *Schleusse*, I found out as the line was moving slowly

ahead, was the checkpoint for incoming and outgoing transports. There my body and belongings were searched for contraband, and contraband was just about everything: all food items, cigarettes, coffee, lipstick, books, photos, everything, even sanitary napkins.

With the exception of the napkins, I had no contraband, but I lost most of my belongings just the same. I passed on through the lines: delousing — medical examination — registration — food coupons — ghetto number — work assignment — and finally *Ubikation*, the assignment of living quarters. Quarters? Mine turned out to be a straw mattress on the floor of one of the large barrack rooms, top floor, in the Hamburg *Kaserne*.

Hours later when I laid down on the smelly thing, exhausted, with the remnant of my belongings as a pillow, I was near tears. I had lost track of Werner and Eva and their baby and of everybody else I had known. I was in the middle of dozens of indifferent women. I longed for my mother and my sister. To keep from crying, I mumbled my ghetto name and number over and over again. I fell asleep over "Gerda Sara Schild, I/94-12709."

I cleaned the children's home for the next three weeks, from eight in the morning till five o'clock, with time out to stand in line for my noontime soup and bread. I got to know the dedicated people who worked with the ghetto youth. I wanted to become one of them because I, too, wanted to help shape young lives, try to undo the harm the Nazis were doing to these boys and girls, teach them that there was a better world beyond Hitler, tell them about America and Palestine. I talked to Freddi Hirsch, my idol. Freddi was a Zionist, devoted to children, working with them, teaching them Hebrew and Jewish history, inspiring them to be upright and unafraid. When he heard that I was a pediatric nurse, he arranged for my interview with Dr.

Erich Munk, the head of the health services, and I was in luck. On the 18th of June, 1943, I received official notice that I was assigned to work at the home for new mothers and babies as *Pflegerin* and that I was permitted to wear a nurse's uniform. Freddi rejoiced with me. I wasn't going to shape minds as he did after all, but I was happy that I would work in my profession again.

In the babies' home, Q 721, things seemed almost normal. Q 721 was one of the small houses near the center of town and had been equipped to house a hundred infants and their nursing mothers. Twenty-four nurses cared for them in day-and-night-shifts and kept the home clean at the same time. But the sense of normality was sadly superficial.

Transports to the East were leaving Theresienstadt almost weekly in the summer of 1943. Notices went out to a required number of persons to be at the *Schleusse* a day or two hence. Usually families were ruthlessly separated if the transport called for *Arbeiter* or for the aged; destination and fate of either work transports or resettlement transports were the same. The unsuspecting people would enter the *Schleusse* with their belongings at one end and would emerge, already robbed of their modest possessions at the other, and since the rails had been extended right into the ghetto and to the back of the *Schleusse*, they would be herded into the freight cars without further respite. Family members could, of course, join a transport victim, and that is how we lost most of our mothers and babies. Even not knowing that they went to their death, our agony at seeing them go was without measure, our fear for the future, for them and for us without precedent. Q 721, too, was a collection center.

The only good thing about Q 721 was my fellow nurse

Gerda Schild Haas in 1939.

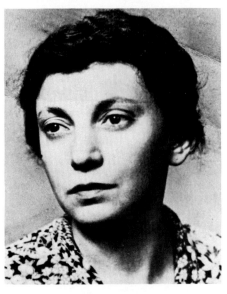

Friedl Schild in 1939.

Paula Schild in 1939.

Opposite page:
Paula and Siegfried Schild,
reunited after Siegfried's release
from prison, Munich, 1939.

Ansbach, Germany.

Luftpost nach Nordamerika

40 25
Deutsches Reich Deutsches Reich

Hr. Siegfried Schild
c/o Bamberger
718 W. 178 Str. Apt. 37
New York City
U. S. A.

MIT LUFTPOST
PAR AVION
BY AIR MAIL

Abs: Paula Sara Schild München 22
Hildegardstr. 1 II
aufgegeben
durch: Leopold Israel Fraenkel
München
Hildegards...

Geöffnet   Geöffnet

Oberkommando der Wehrmacht   Oberkommando der Wehrmacht

Friedl Schild is the last figure on the left. Of the entire group, only four survived. 1936.

Grandmother, Sofie Jochsberger,
her youngest daughter Berta
and Berta's daughter Edith.
Ansbach, 1933.

Opposite page:
Envelope Paula Schild mailed to
Siegfried Schild in New York. Notice that
it's stamped "geoffnet"or opened by the
German High Command and that Paula
had to include her Nazi-assigned name
"Sara" in the return address.

The embankments of Theresienstadt. Grass and trees growing on top act as camouflage.

The nurse's pin worn by
Gerda Schild Haas. It says "Judisches
Sänglingsheim Niederschönhausen"
or Jewish Home for Babies.

Opposite page:
Exit from Theresienstadt, looking out from the
ghetto into the countryside.

Ghetto money in Theresienstadt in *Kronen*, Czech currency.

Gerda Schild Haas' ghetto identification. Every Jew had to carry an ID card at all times and produce it upon request.

JÜDISCHES SIEDLUNGSGEBIET

THERESIENSTADT

PERSONALAUSWEIS

Name des
Inhabers: *SCHILD*

(bei Frauen auch
Mädchenname):

Vorname
des Inhabers: *GERDA*

Geburts-
datum: *23. November 1922*

Geburts-
ort: *Ansbach (Mittel Fr.)*

Familien-
stand: *ledig*

Anschrift: *Berggasse 19*

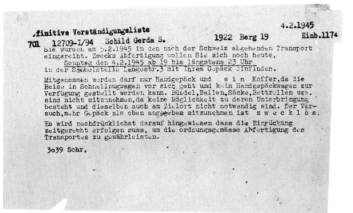

The slip of paper which got Gerda Schild Haas out of Theresienstadt
and into Switzerland. Her transport number — 1174 — is at the upper
right-hand corner.

Gerda Schild Haas holding
Trude Erlanger's son in
Luzern, Switzerland,
summer, 1945.

Gerda Schild Haas *(top, second from left)* on board the ship
Wm. Mulholland approaching the United States, April, 1946.

Eva Hammel in 1981.

Rudolph Haas in 1981.

The Haas family in 1980.
Left to right, bottom: Len Haas; Jean Hammel; Benjamin Hammel.
Second row: Great-grandmother Flora Schild holding Samuel Hammel; Gerda Haas;
Hedy Haas; Polly Hammel holding Jonathan Hammel. *Top:* David Haas;
Great-grandfather Siegfried Schild; Rudolph Haas.

Gerda Haas in 1981.

Eva Atlas from Vienna, whom I met right on the first day of work. She was a little shorter than I, with gray-blue eyes and an abundance of light brown hair. While I looked more Jewish with my dark eyes, jet-black hair, and light complexion, her wonderful exuberance made me seem pale and vulnerable by comparison. She was heavier than I, but we both changed after a few months in the ghetto: My periods stopped and I became positively shapely whereas the cease of menstruation had the opposite effect on her, and she thinned down a bit. Eva was a jolly, fun-loving woman, and I loved her from the start. She, like I, was alone in Theresienstadt. When I was assigned living space in the home's cellar, I made sure that I landed near Eva. We ended up as bunkmates — Eva in the upper, I in the lower bunk — and friends. It was spooky in that cellar. The only source of light was a small window below the cellar's ceiling, level with the sidewalk outside; heat came from a stove if there were wood; there were mice and bedbugs. There was a washroom and a toilet in the basement. But best of all, there was Eva. Eva lit up my life with her cheerful nature, her kindness, her lovely singing voice; she helped me when I was depressed, and she hoped with me that we would find our loved ones again once this ghetto experience was over. It was good to sit with her on the upper bunk and talk and dream and cheer ourselves up with self-invented games. We'd watch shoes and ankles pass by the little window, guessing at the rest of the pedestrians out there; when the passing shoes and trousers were obviously connected to an SS official, we'd give advance alarm for it meant a search of the home for contraband or some other chicanery against us. Or we'd try to forget our hunger by describing to each other our favorite foods, right down to their remembered smells. We'd rub our stomachs while imaginary feasts rose

43

before us and would call our game *Magenonanie*, and we'd laugh at our cleverness: Wasn't it indeed gastronomic masturbation, this futile exercise?

But the day came when we were able to fill our empty stomachs. That came about when one of our young mothers brought her younger brother to the home one visiting day. Jirca Doerfler worked in the ghetto bakery and expressed his feelings in bread. I was soon the recipient of crusty G's and S's and tasty hearts. We looked forward to visiting days and to the ingenious Jirca. The three of us were soon good friends. We went to poetry readings and Zionist lectures, to concerts and discussion groups, all held secretly at first, but later performed with permission of the SS in empty attic rooms or in barrack courtyards. And it wasn't very long before Eva became active in the recreational activities of the ghetto: She joined a choral group and took part in rehearsals for the oratorio "Elijah;" Jirca and I enjoyed sitting through those endless rehearsals. Because Eva had a late pass, we walked home with her after the eight o'clock curfew under starry skies. How wonderful it was to forget reality for a little while.

During my first summer in Theresienstadt I went to meet incoming transports whenever I could, officially to lend a hand, but really to scan the faces of newly arriving women: Perhaps I would see my sister or my mother. Or any one of my dear aunts or cousins, surely long since uprooted from Munich, Regensburg and Frankfurt. I did not look for my grandmother or Aunt Adelheid: Mercifully, God let Grandmother die at her daughter's house in Regensburg before the Germans could deport her; Aunt Adelheid had died at the Jewish hospital in Fuerth soon after her admission there. I only saw Jews and half-Jews from nearly all the countries of the European continent. How much of Europe had fallen into Hitler's hands!

44

In June a trainload of barefoot children in rags arrived, supposedly from the Ukraine. They clung to each other in a state of extreme panic; they shied away from the SS; they looked at us with frightened eyes. On pain of immediate deportation, we were warned not to speak to any of them, but Freddi Hirsch, the kind, courageous Freddi, spoke soothingly to them in Yiddish, trying to put them at ease. He was caught and was sent out with the September transport. We had one card from him, saying that we should do all in our power to remain in Theresienstadt. This short message was our first inkling that other camps were not like Theresienstadt, but we did not know the horrors of those camps until after the war had ended. The children, meanwhile, had been taken to the West Barracks where they were deloused, clothed and fed. It became known that they had witnessed the killing of their parents; it was rumored that they would be sent to Palestine. They were sent away after a little while, together with the physician and the nurses who had cared for them, loaded into boxcars under the personal supervision of *Kommandant* Seidl. Did they arrive in Palestine? There was never any confirmation.

In the early fall of 1943, the first Jews from Holland came to the ghetto and were settled into the Hamburg Barracks in unusual comfort: They got beds with sheets, had towels; a dining room was created for them, meals were served. Billboards, placed where they would notice them, read: "Beethoven-evening in the Rathaus" and "Visit the Theresienstadt Kaffeehaus." That same evening they were asked to write cards and letters back home to Holland. A few days later, they were relocated and forced to live just like the rest of us: The charade was over.

The process was reversed when the Danish Jews came to the ghetto. At first the Danes were treated in the ordinary way, living on straw in barracks for about a month. Then, suddenly, they were moved to two furnished, comfortable houses, one on L-1 street, the other on L-4. They were well-fed and did not have to do any work. They and their leader, Chief Rabbi Friediger, had to report in person to the ghetto commandant once a month to make sure that they lacked nothing. Soon Dr. Friediger was named to Edelstein's *Judenrat*.

In November 1943 Edelstein was arrested and Dr. Paul Eppstein from Berlin was made *Judenaeltester* in his place. The ghetto was alarmed. Amid all the rumors that accompanied Edelstein's arrest, only one was reliable: He was held at SS headquarters in Theresienstadt until the next deportation to the East — the December transport. What had happened? This kind and concerned man had worked tirelessly to create a functioning, self-governing ghetto where before there had been nothing of the sort. He had, if not prevented death for many people, at least prolonged life in many a case. Commandant Seidl, if not very friendly, had at least been correct with him. Why was he now replaced; why was he, his wife, all his associates and their wives and families sent to Auschwitz?

It seemed that twenty Jews who were registered as inmates of Theresienstadt had been arrested in Prague; whether they had escaped from the ghetto or had never even been sent there was not clear. But Edelstein had to pay with his life for a German error in the keeping of German statistics, and Seidl was soon replaced for it too.

Before Seidl left, he embarked on a *Volkszaehlung*, a ghetto headcount. The date was November 11, 1943; the task the counting of fifty thousand human beings. We assembled in the cold and rain at six o'clock in the morning and were marched out of the ghetto, block by block, young and old, some people pulling old parents in makeshift wagons, others carrying their worldly possessions. Who could tell what Seidl would do with us before the day was over?

It was strange to be outside the ghetto walls. We stood there in the Bauschowitz Basin, a huge, open field, waiting, worrying. Many people fainted, some died and we had nothing to help anybody with. We waited and waited till late afternoon when Seidl and his men showed up at last. They ordered rows of tens and blocks of hundreds to be formed; they ordered the counting to begin. There was pandemonium out there that cold, rainy day, and even Seidl could soon see that this was no way to count this mass of people. He was furious. He ordered us to march back to the ghetto and directed his men to shoot us if it became necessary. It was long past midnight before the last inmate was back behind the barriers. Not very long afterwards Seidl was replaced.

The next commandant, Burger, was a sadist who enjoyed the spectacle of transports, never missed one, whether arriving or departing, and struck people with his fist for no reason at all. In the first month of his commandantship, in December 1943, three thousand people were sent to Auschwitz. Did the Jewish leadership know that their people were neither going to work nor to resettlement? If they did have information about the true nature of deportation, about the existence of gas chambers and smoking crematoria, they did not give us any indication that they knew anything. Transports were *"Arbeitstransporte,"* and we did not permit ourselves to think differently.

Some transports really were labor details such as the trainload of young men who left the ghetto in late summer of 1943. They were shipped to Zossen near East Berlin to build underground bunkers at Hitler's Army Headquarters. Their wives and children or parents were promised protection from deportation to the East and were assured that the men would return soon. When I left Theresienstadt in February, 1945, their families were still waiting.

Burger was replaced with Rahm early in 1944. One day after the change, the *Judenrat* received a very strange daily directive: The order was to renovate, beautify and otherwise change the ghetto so that no later than June it would resemble a respectable town. Was *Herr Kommandant* joking with Dr. Eppstein? Not at all. The commandant was acting on the orders of Himmler who had been persuaded by SS Colonel Mildner, chief of SS and SD in Denmark, to permit a visit to Theresienstadt by the Danish Red Cross.

The metamorphosis was astounding. All at once ghetto barriers came down and we were allowed to move about more freely; the curfew was extended; we no longer had to greet the SS servilely on the ghetto streets; the streets were assigned lovely sounding names: We now lived on Bergstrasse 21. All references to "ghetto" disappeared and instead we were inhabitants of the "Jewish Settlement Theresienstadt" now. We were commanded to look happy and to dress neatly. But greater changes took place in the ghetto proper.

Work details, working day and night, painted the houses, paved the streets, seeded the city square with grass and planted roses. They built a pavilion where musicians would play and another where children would romp. They dismantled bunkbeds in rooms that were level with the street and took up the straw in the barracks. Single beds appeared from nowhere, curtains went up on windows visible from streets and the "coffeehouse" was furnished.

But for a "respectable town" the ghetto was grossly overcrowded. The sword of Damocles hung over us: Overcrowding was a situation our jailors knew how to alleviate.

Before Mildner arrived on a pre-visit, ten thousand Jews were sent from the ghetto. I lost my dear friends Eva and Werner Simmon, and I grieved terribly for them. Such lovely people, such good, warm friends. And their little boy, didn't he have a right to live? The ghetto was bleak without them despite the new green lawn and the budding roses. What absurdity! What a farce! Now that they were gone from the ghetto, I longed for them intensely. Would I ever see them again?

While Jews were being shipped out, Jews were being drilled for their part in the upcoming spectacle: Musicians rehearsed on the square; children practiced on swings and slides; bread dispensers got used to handling the bread wearing gloves; Dr. Eppstein began to react to being called *Herr Buergermeister*. Mildner's visit went off well.

In July Adolf Eichmann of RSHA, Rolf Guenther from the Berlin office, Hans Guenther from Prague and a Czech Nazi named Moravec came to Theresienstadt on inspection. The *Stadtkapelle* played the overture to *The Bartered Bride*, and we all had to smile or we'd go into the next selection. Some of us had to sit in the coffee house; others had to play with children in the fine new playground, and still others, I among them, were told to line up behind a hay wagon, shouldering rakes and pitchforks, and march past the inspectors. I don't remember what songs we sang, but I remember well how enraged I felt, how impotent. What if I had not gone along, trotting obediently, smilingly, behind that phoney haywagon? I was already conditioned to obey, especially with the promise of extra food at the end of the act.

And everything worked just fine when the Danish Commission arrived and was driven through the newly renamed streets by "*Buergermeister*" Eppstein, dressed up and out-fitted with a high hat, the car chauffeured by SS Vostrel in civilian clothes, past the concert in the park, past the church whose clock worked and chimed, past a building with a sign on it: *"Schule. Wegen Sommerferien geschlossen."* "School. Closed for summer vacation."

We all had but one thought in our minds: Were the visitors deceived? When they were shown the new "Bread Distribution Center," could they have any inkling that bread was ordinarily sent around in the hearses when those were not otherwise occupied? When they stopped at the homes of Danish Jews and submitted to them the greetings and good wishes of King Christian X, could they guess that the spirited among them were kept under guard at the Magdeburg Barracks?

I had a Danish friend who told me about that later. "At rehearsal when we were told what to say to the Commission and what to answer to questions, I let it be known that I'd tell the truth," she said to me. "And on inspection day, a Jewish ghetto orderly picked me up and kept me in a room with dozens of other people who had also refused to go along with this comedy. Oh, the *Judenrat* apologized, but they explained that Commandant Rahm had threatened mass punishment to the ghetto should anything go wrong, so they wanted us out of the way of the visitors."

How I admired my friend for her courage! The ghetto experience had not cowed this proud Dane; she could still feel the support of her king and country which she had only so recently left. And she could scoff at the extra food too: The Danes received packages from home regularly. Yet as she sat in her little room telling me of her defiance, I was ashamed.

While the roses were in bloom and the paint still new, Theresienstadt was filmed for posterity to see "how well we treated the Jews." It was the hoax of the twentieth century.

Things were different in Theresienstadt after the visit.

Eva and I, who had had to move out of our cellar bunks, were installed in a lovely, narrow, dingy, bedbug-ridden room in Bergstrasse 21, lovely because it was our own and had beds and curtains, but, oh, the bedbugs! We spent many a night in our blankets in the courtyard to get some sleep. Culturally, Theresienstadt was now utopia. Every evening there was a choice of events, operas, oratoria, chamber music and lectures, and we took full advantage of it. We were ''paid'' for our work in the ghetto, paid with specially printed ghetto currency. Eva and I used up our ''salaries'' to get tickets for as many of these events as we could manage to attend. The food was better and more was available.

My friend Jirca had long stopped supplying me with extra bread, but now he was able to offer me a treat of quite a different nature, a real adventure. To him had fallen the responsibility of keeping the church clock wound and running; he was entrusted with the key to the empty church, and he had to climb up into the steeple periodically. When he offered one day to sneak me into the church and take me with him to the loft, I was overjoyed. Today I would call the few minutes high above the ghetto a peak experience, but in late summer of 1944, I had no words for the feeling that gripped me, climbing up, up, inside the dark and narrow tower, reaching the top and sudden sunlight and leaning speechlessly out through its window opening, feeling free and yet confined.

Jirca now pointed to the northern horizon and told me that just out of sight was his beloved Prague. All I could see was rolling, beautiful, unspoiled nature; a blue Eger, or Ohre, as he called this river, winding between tall poplars toward the wide Elbe; and Bauschowitz, Leitmeritz and some farms were laid out below me. The air was brisk and sweet; birds were flying by at eye level. Which was the reality? This dreamy landscape or the nightmare of our condition?

Below us, inside the ghetto walls, puppets moved senselessly. What invisible force directed them? Why were the few fat ones lording it over the many thin? Down there, near the Magdeburg Barracks, why was a column marching through the gate and toward the *Kleine Festung*?

The *Kleine Festung* was a sinister eighteenth-century prison fortress which adjoined Theresienstadt to the East. I had always heard about it but had never seen it; now it squatted bleak and solid just below me. I thought of the student, Gavrilo Princip, who had shot Archduke Franz Ferdinand of Austria in Sarajevo on June 28, 1914: that young boy whose action triggered the first World War. Jirca told me that he had been kept in solitary confinement, chained to the wall in that prison for four years and that he had died just before the war ended; supposedly he was buried somewhere down there near the prison in an unmarked grave. I thought of the many political prisoners who had suffered inside those walls since then and the poor innocent Jews who were mistreated in there now. Perhaps one had smoked a cigarette or another had tried to smuggle out a letter to a loved one? How had the group just entering the prison gates displeased their executioners? I didn't know. I couldn't think clearly; it all seemed so unreal, so absurd, so illogical and bizarre. Just then, strains from the overture to *The Bartered Bride* floated up to us from the square.

A month later, in October of 1944, the honored and beloved Dr. Eppstein was summoned to SS headquarters. We heard later that Commandant Rahm demanded of him his cooperation and active assistance in a major evacuation of the ghetto. Eppstein did not return from that audience. His wife was told to bring food three times daily and clothing once a week to headquarters, but she never received any dishes or clothes back. She made her pilgrimage for three weeks, then the news filtered through that Eppstein had long been sent to *Kleine Festung* because he had refused his cooperation in the mass transportation. The October transports began to move without him.

Dr. Murmelstein became the Jewish Elder. He was not loved then. He seemed to play into the hands of the German masters. But who could judge a man in a position as illogical, as fraught with danger both to the ghetto and to himself as the position of a *Judenrat* in Nazi Germany had to be?

If we hadn't been so preoccupied on the one hand with staying alive and on the other with enjoying every minute of that life as long as it was ours, we might have noticed subtle changes in the activities of our captors in those last months of 1944. In November there came the directive to clear the Sudenten Barracks of its five thousand men and all their belongings in twenty-four hours, a herculean task. Twenty-four hours later, ss trucks with hundreds of thousands of files and documents drove up and the place was taken over by the sd, the *Reichssicherheitsdienst* from Berlin. The two-hundred-man ss personnel that came with the office were installed in great comfort in the *Bodenbach Kaserne* where thousands of Jews had been penned previously. By order of the commandant, high walls were hastily built by the Jews to secure the ss operation; then later we heard that document centers from Lemberg and from Budapest had been relocated behind those walls, too, as the Nazis fled from Poland and then from Hungary.

Simultaneously with the arrival of German archives, the Nazis began destroying their evidence in the ghetto. Documents, papers, medical records and statistics about ghetto mortality were burned. Thirty thousand urns, stored underground beneath the embankments, were loaded into trucks and taken out of the ghetto. The Jewish men who helped with the ghoulish task were sworn to secrecy and later killed. From Jirca I learned what had been done with the urns. In the middle of the night, the Jews had to load them onto an iron barge under the command of Rahm himself. The barge was maneuvered out into the Eger and sunk.

High above the ghetto, I saw silvery formations flying north. I prayed that those planes were Allied planes and that their pilots were successful in their mission and would return safely. We had no newspapers, heard no radio news, didn't even have a calendar. Was the war nearing its end? Would we be allowed to outlive our wardens? We heard the most alarming rumors: The ghetto would be bombed by the Germans and the act would be proclaimed a British attack — we would all be gassed in chambers now being built under the embankments where the urns had been — we would be shipped off and left standing somewhere on rails — and other such enormities. Thirty-five years later, while researching the end of Theresienstadt at the Leo Baeck Institute in New York, I learned that these had been actual plans, not rumors.

Jirca was deported in November 1944. He gave me a piece of ghetto jewelry, a delicately carved phoenix, symbol of rebirth, wrought from metal, strong and durable. I have it still. Eva and I were now quite alone and afraid. Even Eva had stopped laughing.

Incoming transports were more pathetic than ever. Two of them stand engraved in my memory: In November 1944 I saw fifty children and two nurses come to the ghetto, all near death from starvation. They were Dutch, had been on the road for weeks with a long stop in Bergen-Belsen. The children wore tablets around their necks stating their names, in many cases only their first names. They had been

hidden with gentiles and had either been denounced or had been handed over by their foster parents; we never found out what really happened. But here they were and we tried to revive them. Dutch inmates came, looked the children over carefully and took to their hearts those they recognized. In some cases these were their own sons and daughters.

And in December a boxcar full of thin, frozen women came, clutching their babies and infants. Their first question was: "Are our husbands here?" They had been torn from their men, had been hiding in the Slovakian woods around Serreth for months. But the cold and their children's hunger had forced them to give themselves up. Many were shot on the spot; of those who arrived in Theresienstadt, many had typhus and recovered only slowly, if at all. There was a nine-day-old infant in the group, born in a cattle car, which came under our care. This was one baby to whom we permitted ourselves to become attached.

The winter wore on; a new year began; the transports continued. On February 1, the news was that next week a transport would go to Switzerland. Of course! Just like the one that was going to Palestine last year!

No one believed this, least of all Eva and I. And yet, thanks to our youthful optimism, and because we had nothing to lose, and because whatever happened we would endure together, we volunteered for the February 7 transport "to Switzerland."

We had to pass Commandant Rahm's personal inspection. We lined up on February 3, several thousand of us, and waited patiently in long lines in front of SS headquarters. When my turn came and I finally stood before Rahm's desk and faced him in a personal encounter, I began to believe in the Swiss dream. He asked grimly: "Name?

Transport number? Any members of your family here in the Jewish settlement? Any leave from here in transports? Did anybody close to you die here? Have you ever been sick here? Hungry? Maltreated?''

I answered, and answered, and answered. After me, Eva was quizzed. And the next day, Sunday the 4th, I received a brownish slip of paper, my passport to freedom:

> Definite notification Gerda S. Schild, 12709-I/94 Nr. 1174
>
> You are accepted into the transport to Switzerland. You are to present yourself with your baggage today on Sunday, February 4, 1945, between 19 and 23 hours at collection center Langestrasse 3. You may take along *only one* suitcase and your hand luggage since the trip will be taken in an express train and no car will be available for luggage. Do not bring bundles, bedrolls, sacks or such since there is no room for such baggage and you will not need those things at your destination. It will be pointless to try to take more than the permitted things stated above.
>
> It is important that the transport assemble punctually and orderly so that departure can proceed promptly.

I looked for Eva. She, too, had received her notification; we were both overjoyed. We believed now that liberation was in our hands. We looked again at our prized papers, which only twelve-hundred inmates had received. We gasped when the numbers at the top of our slips began to sink in: I was number 1,174 and Eva was 1,175. We had just about made it!

We packed in a daze. We were on time at Langestrasse 3. We sat patiently in the train compartment, amazed when an SS man came through handing out some travel provisions which we didn't even recognize: chocolate, apples, jam, sardines. We waved to the people who saw us off and, when

57

the train finally began to move through the ghetto, we waved to the women who were just coming out of the Glimmer factory — perhaps I saw the one among the many who later became my dear stepmother? It is possible. Certain it is that Eva and I and all the other travelers were happy to leave Theresienstadt.

When we drove through Nuremberg, I looked closely to see if perhaps we might pass Ansbach which was so close by and if perhaps I would see our house from the passing train. I didn't see either, only lots of evidence of bombing. At one point we stopped for a long time, waiting out an air-raid. Near Augsburg the command went through the train for the men to shave and for the women to put on make-up and — did we hear that right? — remove the yellow star! I slipped mine into my pocket without feeling. I have it still. We entered Switzerland at Constance. At Kreutzlingen our escort, one civilian officer from the Foreign Office in Berlin, a group of gendarmes and two SS men left. We were turned over to the Swiss authorities. We were crying and laughing.

We were pampered at Buehler near St. Gallen for a few days and then distributed to various Swiss refugee camps. Eva and I, clinging to each other, went to Les Avants sur Montreux. Never will I forget the symbolic moment when our train emerged from a long tunnel at Puidoux-Chexbres and the azure Lake of Geneva, the snowy mountain ranges of Switzerland and Southern France, glistened in the sunlight before us.

Liberation

What activities had paved the way for the liberation to Switzerland for twelve-hundred Jews from Theresienstadt a full three months before the war was officially ended? To what circumstances, to whose efforts, do these few Austrian,

Czech, Dutch and German Jews, I among them, owe their lives? And why were there no subsequent liberating transports from the concentration camps of Himmler and Hitler? I found the answers to these questions many years later in recorded testimonies and affidavits on file at the National Archives in Washington, D.C. (General Record Division of the Department of State) Decimal File 1945-49, from: 840.48 Faa/1-145 to Refugees/2-2845. Box No. C-523, now declassified.

It appears from the records that by March 1944 Himmler for one began to see that the Thousand Year Reich was about to end and that it might be time to rehabilitate Germany and himself in the eyes of the victorious Allies; certainly that it was time to stop killing the Jews. His view was shared by his subordinates, SS *Standartenfuehrers* Kurt Becher and Walter Schellenberg, but was opposed stiffly by the chief of *Sicherheitsdienst* SS Kaltenbrunner and the SS chief in charge of concentration camps Mueller. In March 1944 Himmler entered into negotiations, through Becher and without the knowledge of his opposing colleagues, with the Hungarian Jewish lawyer Rudolf Kastner for the release of Hungarian Jews imprisoned in the German camps. The neutral contacts for such a release operation were the Swiss representative of the Joint Distribution Committee, Sally Meyer, and the representative of the newly created United States War Refugee Board in Switzerland, Roswell McClelland. Negotiations were successful because forty Hungarian Jews were released to Switzerland in March 1944; twenty-eight hundred more in October of that year and a remnant of seventy-five people in April 1945.

In October of 1944, encouraged perhaps by the liberation of the Hungarians, the prestigious Swiss Jewish family Sternbuch approached former Swiss president, *Bundesrat* Jean-Marie Musy, and asked him to use his influence with

Himmler for the release of their relatives in particular and for the liberation of Jews in German camps in general. Musy's twenty-one page testimony of October 26, 1945, taken in Bern with McClelland as the interpreter, gives insight to the ensuing efforts in this regard. Musy wrote to Himmler and asked for an interview immediately. He received an affirmative answer from Himmler's office and the seventy-five year old Musy set out by car with his son for Germany. At the Swiss-German border at Constance the two Musy's were met by a delegate of *Reichsfuehrer* SS Himmler who escorted them to Berlin to Himmler's deputy, SS Schellenberg, who in time accompanied them to Himmler's private railroad car somewhere near Breslau. In this conference, which took place on a day late in October 1944, the *Reichsfuehrer* said that he was willing to deliver not only Sternbuch's relatives, but a number of Jews from German imprisonment in orderly fashion: One transport every two weeks would be delivered to the Swiss border. In return he asked for "favorable publicity in American newspapers" and a specified number of trucks and tractors for Germany. Musy advised against an exchange of war machinery for Jews and indicated that he would be able to obtain money instead, money from Jewish-American sources, delivered to him through Sternbuch. Himmler then promised to release the Jews regardless of compensation and said that liberating transports "would begin right away, via Constance." The interrogation went as follows:

> Q Were any Jewish people released and delivered to Constance as he said?
>
> A Yes. The first convoy, consisting of 1,200 people from Theresienstadt.
>
> Q When were they delivered?
>
> A Early in February 1945.

Q Were any more people delivered, according to Himmler's statement?

A Young Torel was liberated, and two brothers of Mrs. Sternbuch, since they had not been able to find her father and mother, who had been sent to Auschwitz and were probably dead.

Q Why were no more people delivered than the first convoy and these few extra individuals?

A Although I do not know exactly, this seems to have been due to the intercessions of Sally Meyer.

This last answer of Musy's was quite wrong, as we shall see later in Schellenberg's affidavit. But let us continue with the statements Musy made about his second conference with Himmler, on November 20, 1944, in a hotel somewhere in the Black Forest, when terms for the release of all the Jews were discussed.

MUSY I pointed out to Himmler that the question of compensation in goods was completely impossible. He, therefore, agreed that money would be acceptable and in general was far more accommodating in the whole affair and seemed willing to allow these people to leave. I pointed out to him that he should not give the impression of trafficking in human lives against money but should rather attempt to exploit the political advantages of such a move.

Q Was any sum of money designated at this time?

A No.

Q Was anything said about obtaining publicity for the releasing of these people?

A Yes. That was one of the conditions made, that the press in the United States comment favorably.

61

Q With respect to the question in general of the release of all the Jews, what did Himmler say?

A Himmler agreed, yes, to actively pursue the question of liberating Jews in general.

Q Did he state anything specifically along the lines of what exactly he would do about it?

A He said he would deliver all the Jews . . . via Constance, through Switzerland. . . . Right away.

Q Were any of these Jews delivered as he said they would be?

A No. Outside of the people mentioned, nobody was immediately released.

(Excerpt from: Nuremberg Interrogation, National Archives Record Group 238.)

What happened? Why did release transports stop after the February delivery? Schellenburg's testimony is to the point, and I quote part of it.

The first trainload of Jewish immigrants was delivered early in February. Thereafter Musy submitted a press story of 8 February from the *New York Times* and also submitted proof that he deposited 5,000,000 Swiss francs placed in trust later in February. Thereafter Kaltenbrunner, at the direction of Hitler, prevented further transports of Jews into Switzerland. Hitler threatened the death penalty for anyone attempting to further assist such transfers and ordered that not another Jew nor any American nor British POW's should pass the border with the aid of any German.

Mr. Musy again visited Berlin and expressed great anger and bitter disappointment over the stopping of transfers. Musy and I suggested to Himmler that requests be made to the Western Powers for a four-day armistice to permit sending all Jews and foreign internees through the front lines in an orderly manner. On my own responsibility I informed SS *Obergruppenfuehrer* Berger, Chief of War Prisoners, of the plan. He delayed sending many of Hitler's orders and thereby saved the lives of thousands of people who would otherwise have been evacuated from POW camps or executed where evacuation was impossible. Himmler favored the plan of an armistice but did not have the courage to suggest it to Hitler. I discussed it with Kaltenbrunner who replied to me on 3 April 1945: "Have you too joined the idiots?"

(International Military Trials, Nuremberg, v. VIII, p. 628. Nazi Conspiracy and Aggression, Washington, 1946. Red Series.) This document is not published in the general, now complete *Trial of the Major War Criminals* (Blue Series) and cannot be found anywhere else. A search in the Modern Military Branch of the National Archives in June 1979 could not locate the original document.

In the files of the National Archives, I found documentation referring to the press story of February 8 and also to the deposition of the money used for our release and, at long last, evidence of its sources. Secret Document 840.48 Refugees/2-2245 is a cable, not yet declassified in June of 1979, from the State Department and the War Refugee Board in Washington to McClelland in Switzerland dated March 6, 1945, 9:00 p.m., an authorization "to remit the Swiss franc equivalent of $937,000 to a banking institution in Switzerland for credit to a joint account in the names of Isaac Sternbuch, representative in Switzerland of the Vaad Hahatzala Emergency Committee of the Union of Orthodox Rabbis of the United States and Canada, and Roswell D. McClelland, representative of the War Refugee Board in Switzerland...." And Document 840.48 Refugees/2-945 CS/EG, a telegram from McClelland in Bern to the Secretary of State in Washington dated February 9, 1945, begins thusly:

With regard Musy affair following is translation of article

which appeared number of Swiss morning papers February 8: "Mr. Musy arranges liberation of Jewish internees in Germany first convoy 1,200 civilians coming from concentration camp Theresienstadt arrived Wednesday 11:45 a.m. at Kreuzlingen. It is thanks to efforts former Federal Councillor Musy acting on request of European Executive Council of Union Orthodox Rabbis of United States at Montreux and of world organization of Agudas Israel that these civilians were liberated by Germany. Other transports will follow which will all be sent from Switzerland abroad as soon as transportation possibilities exist. . . .

When these possibilities became reality a year after liberation and I had my visa and my ship's passage on the S.S. Mulholland for April, 1946, I left Switzerland.

World Highlights, 1935-1940

Italy invades Abyssinia. Edward VIII becomes British monarch. Farouk becomes King of Egypt. Margaret Mitchell writes Gone With The Wind. *The XIth Olympiad is held in Berlin. Civil war breaks out in Spain. The Montreux Convention permits Turkey to fortify the Dardanelles. A Rome-Berlin Axis is proclaimed by Mussolini. Edward VIII abdicates the British throne to marry Wally Simpson. The skull of a Pithecanthropos is found in Java. Nylon stockings make their appearance. German troops occupy Austria. In an effort to appease Nazi Germany, Chamberlain and Daladier sign a pact with Hitler and Mussolini at Munich. Kemal Ataturk dies, and Inonu becomes President of Turkey. Sigmund Freud dies in London. Sartre writes* La Nausee. *Italy invades Albania. Czechoslovakia is dismembered. DDT is invented. Hitler and Stalin sign an agreement not to attack each other. The Germans invade Poland. World War II begins. The U.S.S.R. attacks Finland and invades Poland. Germany invades Norway and Denmark. Churchill becomes Prime Minister. British troops, cut off by German advance on Channel ports, are evacuated to England from Dunkirk. Holland and Belgium capitulate. France collapses. The Germans enter Paris. The* Blitz *begins. Italy declares war on Great Britain and France. France and Great Britain guarantee Greek independence.*

PART II
Poland

TWO

Events in Poland

Hitler was in power for six years before he embarked on open war. When he declared in his *Reichstag* speech of January 1939 that the German nation needed ''an extension of living space,'' it was Poland he had in mind. Poland was the largest state in Europe, blessed with a rich soil, great mineral wealth and large coal resources; its thirty million people were made up of many ethnic minorities, of a segment of titled landowners, of a large intelligensia and of Slavic farmers. The majority was Roman Catholic; ten percent of the population was Jewish. Geographically, Poland was the link between Europe and Russia, a vast plain stretching from the Baltic Sea in the north to the Tatry and the Carpathian Mountains in the south.

In 1934 Hitler had signed a ten year treaty of peaceful arbitration with Poland's Marshal Pilsudski so that he could build up his army undisturbed by his eastern neighbor, and Pilsudski had co-signed it, hoping the treaty would pacify the aggressive *Fuehrer.* Five years later Hitler declared that treaty invalid: a treaty was binding to him only as long as it served his purpose. That same year, 1939, he signed another treaty which served him for the next fifteen months, a non-aggression pact with his old enemy, Russia. It allowed him to deal with Poland without fearing Russian interference.

He began his aggression against Poland by demanding the return to the Reich of the city of Danzig. Gdansk, as it is called in Polish, was a predominantly German city separated from the Reich by the Polish Corridor. The Versailles Treaty had declared it an open city in 1919 and had placed it under the authority of the League of Nations, but Hitler wanted it now and wanted the right to build highways across the Polish Corridor into East Prussia at the same time. Poland, backed by France and England, did not permit German access to Danzig nor highways across her territory and got the Allies' assurance that in the event of a war, France and England would come to Poland's aid. It was at this point that Hitler declared the 1934 Germano-Polish agreement terminated because, he said, Poland had subjected him to a policy of encirclement. In the summer of 1939 he stepped up his war of nerves regarding Danzig, but Poland, unlike the countries Hitler had intimidated in the recent past, stood firm.

In August Hitler as the Supreme Commander of the German Army, Navy and Air Force ordered the Army High Command (OKH) to draw up the operation for "Plan White," the invasion of Poland. On September 1, 1939, at 4:45 in the early morning, one million troops crossed the Polish frontiers in Upper Silesia, in East Prussia and near Danzig; a fleet of Stuka bombers and Messerschmidts bombed the airfields and towns of Vilna, Grodno, Brest-Litovsk, Katowice and Krakow and destroyed most of the Polish air power on the ground; Warsaw and Modlin were attacked from the air at 9:00 a.m. Destruction was immense. Polish losses were huge, and the onslaught did not let up for three days. During those three terrible days, the

German Army Group North under General Fedor von Bock mounted two major attacks toward Warsaw and Graudenz while Army Group South under General Gerd von Rundstedt stormed toward Lodz and Krakow. These two gigantic forces, each commanding many strong army divisions of ten thousand and twelve thousand troops to each division, were reinforced by General Heinz Guderian's XIX Panzer Corps and his fifteen-thousand-man fighting force. Armies and generals, making names for themselves in those early days of September in Poland, were to be heard from again and again in all corners of Europe throughout World War II. But as yet Hitler had not declared war.

On the third of September, France and England came to Poland's aid as they had pledged to do and declared war on Germany. The American newspapers immediately called it World War II, and that it was destined to become.

As yet the fighting was restricted to Poland. On the eighth of September the Third Army encircled Warsaw with the help of the XVI Panzer Corps and closed in on Modlin. The Tenth Army in the southeast surrounded Radom; in the southeast the Fourteenth Army seized Lwow on the twelfth and thirteenth, all supported by the *Luftwaffe*. On the sixteenth, with most of Poland already in German hands, the siege of Warsaw began. The city endured incredible hardship, starvation and typhus, with bombs raining down upon the beautiful capital of Poland without mercy. Warsaw capitulated on the twenty-seventh. Modlin surrendered a day later. The Polish operation was over on the sixth of October, and the Germans took hundreds of thousands of Polish troops to Germany as prisoners.

A new kind of war had been introduced in Europe, a war of surprise attack delivered with lightening speed—the *Blitzkrieg*—and Hitler, its creator, considered himself a military genius.

71

Poland was under brutal foreign rule for the next six years. The Polish population was ruthlessly decimated. The Polish government fled to Paris at the start of the German occupation and, after France fell the following year, moved to London and set up a government-in-exile there. From London it organized and supported Polish resistance, directed underground sabotage activities and homefront freedom-fighter movements against the hated occupiers. Russian troops had entered Poland on September 17 and had helped the Germans crush Poland. On September 28, Hitler and Stalin divided Poland between themselves, the eastern part falling to Russia, the whole great rest of it to Germany.

In the German-occupied part, changes were felt immediately. On October 12, 1939, Heinrich Himmler, the powerful *Reichsfuehrer* of the SS, became Commissioner for the Consolidation of German Nationhood of Occupied Poland; Hans Frank became Governor-General; the Austrian Nazi who had helped bring about annexation, Artur Seyss-Inquart, his deputy. Together these men undertook a program of resettlement of ethnic Germans by means of expropriating the Slavic citizens and sending them to forced labor in Germany or to slave labor in Polish concentration camps; those Slavs left in resettlement areas were marked for planned starvation.

As for the Jews, German planning called for total annihilation of the detested *"Ostjuden."* Eastern Jews had traditionally been the most pious, most learned, most revered of all Jews in the eyes of world Jewry. It was from among the Eastern Jews in Poland that the great wonder rabbis arose; it was in Poland that the mystic Chasidic movement emerged, where the most famous Talmudists flourished. But, alas, it was also in Poland where Jew-hatred in Europe was the strongest and where hostilities against Jews had first been

condoned in the fifteenth century and had frequently occurred ever since. Hitler found eager allies in many Poles for
his measures against the almost three-and-a-half-million
Jews he found there in September of 1939.

Measures against them followed the German model and
were carried out with utmost speed: The economical, social
and nutritional deprivation, the physical and mental harassment, the visible ostracism by means of the yellow star or
white armbands with Jewish Stars on them were already
familiar; what was added in the Polish "solution of the
Jewish question" was the ominous establishment of
ghettos.

On October 13, 1940, Hans Frank called the head of the
Jewish Council of Warsaw, Adam Czerniakow, before him
and informed him that a ghetto would be created in the inner city of Warsaw, around the Tomakie Square Synagogue.
The entire Jewish population of Warsaw was to be relocated
within its bounds by the end of October. Czerniakow was
told to form a police force of one thousand Jews to keep
"law and order" among the Jews. A week later, on October
28, the *New Warsaw Courier* published the names of the
streets which had been designated as "Jewish residential
district," an area of roughly one-and-a-half square miles in
the very heart of the elegant city, a district of lovely, three-
and-four story mansions with beautifully carved facades and
wrought-iron balconies. By November 15 the district was
closed off from the surrounding city by a high brick wall,
the "Red Wall," whose ten gates were guarded by SS and
their dogs, terminating all unauthorized movement between city and ghetto. For a while streetcars continued their
normal run through the district, passing through the area at
top speed without stops, SS and Polish police on duty in
each carrige to see that no one got off or on between gates,
but the route was soon changed. The Polish residents

were moved out of that part of the city, and Warsaw Jews were pressed in. Signs in German and Polish proclaimed the area *"Seuchensperrgebiet"*—pestilence area, quarantined — and forbade entrance.

On March 17, 1914, Czerniakow was apointed "mayor" of the ghetto, *Judenaeltester*, and his twenty-four man council, *Judenrat*. By that time the once tree-lined streets and stately houses behind those red brick walls had become prison for the four-hundred-seventy-thousand Jews of Warsaw, with refugees from surrounding towns and villages pouring in daily by the thousands. Nine Stawki Street with its 170 rooms had an occupancy in January of 1941 of eleven-hundred people. Not a single room was heated; there was no running water in the house, and the toilets, of course, did not work. Dysentery and typhus broke out; patients in rags remained in their rooms on narrow cots without blankets; the stench of feces and death was almost unbearable. At 3 Dzika Street there were 153 rooms for sixteen-hundred Jews. At 9 Dzika Street, eight rooms for 136 Jews. Need one spell out the plight, the anguish of the people? Need one describe the despair? Is it describable at all? Imaginable?

In November of that year the Germans changed the size and the shape of the ghetto by tearing down the red wall and building a new one, making the ghetto smaller and dividing it internally; a footbridge led from one part to the other. Food rations were cut down to one-third of those of the Polish population; the death toll reached forty-five hundred a month; people died on the crowded streets, lying there covered by a sheet of paper until a truck collected the many corpses and took them for burial to the other side of the red wall. There was no longer space in the ghetto for the living or the dead.

In July 1942 deportations began. Adam Czerniakow was told to furnish five thousand Jews a day for "resettlement in the East." This daily quota of unfortunates had to appear at the Umschlagplatz, the collection area, where the cattle trains were waiting. The Jews, their spirit at the level of their misfortune, were deported to Treblinka, an extermination camp near Malkinia on the river Bug. On July 23, a few days after the five-thousand-Jews-a-day order had gone into effect, Czerniakow was found dead, slumped over his desk. A note near his cold hand read: "Three p.m. So far, three thousand ready to go. By four p.m., according to orders, there must be nine thousand. I am helpless; sorrow and pity fill my heart. I cannot stand it any longer. My end will show everybody what must be done."

There are always men who know when to die. Janusz Korczak was one of these. He came to the ghetto about the same time Czerniakow did and walked to his death twelve days after Czerniakow's suicide. He kept a record while in the ghetto, a diary, which has been saved. In a house filled to the attic with Jewish orphans, in a room that he shared with seven boys, Korczak wrote at night on his cot by a candle. He escaped the tiny room which smelled of urine, shut out the boys' coughing, his own physical pain and fled to the country of Plato, Marcus Aurelius and Shakespeare. He recalled his own life and thought, his work with the orphans and his love for them and let the realities of the ghetto interrupt only occasionally. He recorded—not the miseries of his predicament, not the grief that filled his heart—the landscape of his mind, the beauty that was in his soul. And when he blew out the candle to sleep before the dawn of another ghetto day, he who had been plagued by nightmares while living a normal life slept dreamlessly while living in a nightmare. He died a martyr and a poet.

The Ghetto Diary of Janusz Korczak

Hersch Goldszmit was born in Warsaw either in 1878 or 1879. His father had been a well-known lawyer, but Hersh remembered him only as a mental patient for when Hersh was still a boy, the elder Goldszmit became insane and had to spend the rest of his years in an institution. The burden of caring for mother and siblings fell on Hersh's shoulders early in life, and the hardship of being a child in a grownup world became an experienced reality. Children were underdogs: They had no privileges, were granted no respect. The boy, Hersh, dreamed of a time when this would be different. He thought of ways to help change the plight of fatherless children.

As a young man Hersh Goldszmit changed his name to Henryk and began a writing career. He used the pen name Janusz Korczak, and became known inside his native Poland and outside as "the Father of Orphans."

Homes for orphans were dreadful places in the late 19th century. Boys and girls unfortunate enough to grow up in one kept themselves alive by cheating and stealing; they were unloved, unkempt and unwanted. Korczak revealed to the world the conditions in those homes in a series of books and at the same time put forth his ideas for change: Let the children have the right to govern themselves, he argued. Allow them their own parliament, court of law, newspaper! Let there be a Children's Republic, a Children's

World Congress, a new slogan: "Children of the world, unite!"

Korczak became a pediatrician. Early in his career he was appointed director of the Jewish Orphanage in Warsaw and had a chance to put his ideas to the test. His orphanage at 93 Krochmalna Street became the first self-governing orphanage in Poland; other institutions adopted the Korczakean principle and slowly the image of orphanages changed. Korczak became a consultant and lecturer on the rights of children.

With the rise of anti-Semitism in Poland, Korczak became more consciously Jewish. He visited Palestine and was impressed with the kibbutz movement. He was even tempted to remain at Kibbutz Ein Harod, but could not in good conscience leave his children, his devoted staff and his dedicated friend Stefania Wilczynska at Krochmalna Street. He returned to Warsaw.

After Hitler took control of Poland and the persecution of the Jews had begun, Korczak was called to Gestapo headquarters at Szuch Avenue and was ordered to resettle the home inside the newly created Warsaw Ghetto. The SS informed him that henceforth he was under the supervision of a German doctor. Korczak worried about the move. How would his children adjust to the closed ghetto quarters? How much interference would he have to expect from the SS doctor? Polish colleagues and friends, hearing of the resettlement, arranged false papers for him and pleaded with him to live among them, but Korczak calmly refused. Two hundred children and a staff of devoted nurses and personnel, led and encouraged by Janusz and Stefa, relocated at Sienna and Sliska Streets inside the ghetto walls.

The children's home became an oasis of order and cleanliness in the chaos of the ghetto. Korczak gave them lessons.

After instructions were over, the children had their assigned
housekeeping chores to do, did exercises, were weighed and
measured and kept clean. Food, though poor, was good by
ghetto standards: In the morning each child had a slice of
bread and coffee substitute with saccharin; at noon a dish of
potatoes or groats seasoned with horseblood; in the evening
there was an occasional piece of horsemeat. The woman who
did the cooking produced rye cookies for special holidays.
Korczak spent much time at the Jewish Community Office
and at the *Hilfsverein* asking for food and money for his
home, and he walked around the ghetto visiting wealthy
Jews, begging for help for his children. If his appeals were
ignored, he threatened to disclose illegal wealth. And even
while he pleaded for his orphanage, he knew that it and all
the children in it were doomed.

The older orphans begged him to allow them to join the
Ghetto Underground, to teach them how to use a gun, but
Korczak refused. Justice, he told them, can only be created
with more justice. Anyway, there were no weapons in the
home. Korczak taught the children songs and plays instead
of killing. They put on the play "Post Office" by Rabin-
dranath Tagore. In the play, Amal, a sick boy confined to
his room, spoke with everyone he could: the passing watchman, the janitor, the delivery boy. The watchman told
him that one day he would be set free by the Royal Physician, Death. The Royal Physician came and sat by his head
and promised him an awakening when the King came.

The supervising ss doctor in the audience was furious at
the idea of this play and informed Korczak that he had better prepare his children for the march to the Umschlagplatz
for deportation. Korczak, thinking fast, told the ss man
that he would indeed prepare his children, that he would
march with them to the Umschlagplatz as if going on an
outing; he would march at their head under the

orphanage's flag — singing. The ss man thought this a wonderful idea — anything to move the Jews in orderly fashion to their death — and offered Korczak his freedom after he had thus delivered his charges. Korczak looked at him in contempt. His Polish friends made a new effort to save him, but he never wavered in his loyalty to staff and children. He promised his friends that he would have his diary smuggled out of the ghetto and brought to one of them. It should, he requested, be used as testimony to the way his staff and children conducted themselves under the sentence of death.

On August 5, 1942, two hundred children marched to the Umschlagplatz. Dressed in the best clothes they could find, carrying their flag, green with the gold four-leaf clover, they marched singing behind Korczak and Stefa. At the Umschlagplatz the box cars were waiting. Korczak, standing by the sloping plank, encouraged the children with kind words and smiles as they climbed up into the awful cars, one hundred children to each car. At the last, Stefa stepped into one, Korczak into the other: two proud, white-haired Jews, two-hundred Jewish orphans. The planks were removed, the cars sealed.

A few days after the closing of the orphanage of Sienna Street, Korczak's friend Igor Newerly received the diary.

Ghetto Diary: The Last Fifteen Days

July 21, 1942

Tomorrow I shall be sixty-three or sixty-four years old. For some years, my father failed to obtain my birth certificate. I suffered a few difficult moments over that. Mother called it gross negligence: being a lawyer, father should not have delayed in the matter of the birth certificate.

I was named after my grandfather, his name was Hersh

79

(Hirsh). Father had every right to call me Henryk: he himself was given the name Jozef. And to the rest of his children grandfather had given Christian names, too: Maria, Magdalena, Ludwik, Jakub, Karol. Yet he hesitated and procrastinated.

I ought to say a good deal about my father: I pursue in life that which he strove for and for which my grandfather tortured himself for many years.

And my mother. Later about that. I am both mother and father. That helps me to know and understand a great deal.

My great-grandfather was a glazier. I am glad: glass gives warmth and light.

It is a difficult thing to be born and to learn to live. Ahead of me is a much easier task: to die. After death, it may be difficult again, but I am not bothering about that. The last year, month or hour.

I should like to die consciously, in possession of my faculties. I don't know what I should say to the children by way of farewell. I should want to make clear to them only this—that the road is theirs to choose, freely.

Ten o'clock. Shots: two, several, two, one, several. Perhaps it is my own badly blacked out window.

But I do not stop writing.

On the contrary: it sharpens (a single shot) the thought.

July 22, 1942

Everything else has its limits, only brazen shamelessness is limitless.

The authorities have ordered the hospital in Stawki Street to be cleared. And the head doctor, a woman, was told to admit all the bad cases to Zelazna Street.

What do we do? Prompt decision, efficient action.

X and Z have 175 convalescent children. They have more than fifteen other institutions, but ours is nearby.

And the fact that over a period of six months the lady in question stooped to every conceivable outrage against the patients for the sake of convenience, through obstinacy or stupidity, that she fought with devilish cunning against my humane and simple plan—that goes for nothing. . . .

While I was out, Mrs. K. agreed to, and Mrs. S. proceeded to put in operation the shameless demand, detrimental in the highest degree, harmful to their children and ours. . . .

To sit on the floor, and clear out. I have long been contemplating it. More—a noose or lead on the feet.

(It has come out incomprehensibly again. But I am too tired to write more.)

Azrylewicz died this morning. Oh, how hard it is to live, how easy to die!

July 27, 1942 Yesterday's rainbow.

Yesterday's rainbow.

A marvelous big moon over the camp of the homeless pilgrims.

Why can't I calm this unfortunate, insane quarter.

Only one brief communique.

The authorities might have allowed it.

Or, at worst, refused it.

Such a lucid plan.

Declare yourself, make your choice. We do not offer a choice of easy roads. No playing bridge for the time being, no sunbathing, no delicious dinners paid for with the blood of the smugglers.

Choose: either get out, or work here on the spot.

If you stay, you must do whatever may be necessary for the resettlers.

The autumn is near. They will need clothes, footwear, underwear, tools.

Anyone trying to wiggle out of it will be caught, anyone wanting to buy himself out — we shall gladly take his jewelry, foreign currency, anything of value. When he has already surrendered all — and fast — then we shall ask him again:

81

"Here or out there? What have you decided?"

So long as there's no sunbathing on the beaches, no bridge and no pleasant nap after reading the newspaper.

You're a social worker? All right. You can even pretend it for a time and we shall pretend to believe you. In general, we believe as long as it is convenient and whatever is convenient. Excuse me: not convenient. Whatever is in the plans.

We are running a gigantic enterprise. Its name is war.

We work in a planned, disciplined manner, methodically. Your petty interests, ambitions, sentiments, whims, claims, resentments, cravings do not concern us.

Of course — a mother, a husband, a child, an old woman, a family heirloom, a favorite dish — they are all very nice, pleasant, touching. But for the present, there are more important things. When there is time to spare, we shall return to such things, too.

Meanwhile, in order not to prolong the matter, things must get a bit rough and painful, and if I may put it that way, without particular precision, elegance or even scrupulousness. Just roughly cut for current expedience.

You yourself are longing to see all this over. So are we. Therefore, don't interfere.

Jews go East. No bargaining. It is no longer the question of a Jewish grandmother but of where you are needed most — your hands, your brain, your time, your life. Grandmother. This was necessary only to hook onto something, a key, a slogan.

You say you cannot go East — you will die there. So choose something else. You are on your own, you must take the risk. For clearly we, to keep up appearances, are obliged to bar the way, to threaten, prosecute and reluctantly to punish.

And you butt in, uninvited, with a fresh wad of bank notes. We have neither time nor desire for that sort of thing. We are not playing at war, we were told to wage it with the greatest possible expedition, efficiently, as honestly as possible.

The job is not clean, or pleasant, or sweet smelling. So for the present we must be indulgent to the workers we need.

One likes vodka, another women, a third likes to boss everyone around while yet another, by contrast, is meek and lacks self-confidence.

We know: they have their vices, shortcomings. But they report in time while you were philosophizing, procrastinating. Sorry, but the train must run on schedule, according to a timetable prepared in advance.

Here are the railroad tracks.

The Italians, the French, the Roumanians, the Czechs, the Hungarians — this way. The Japanese, the Chinese, even the Solomon Islanders, even the cannibals — the other way. Farmers, highlanders, the middle class and the intelligentsia.

We are Germans. It is not a question of the trademark but of the cost, the destination of the products.

We are the steel roller, the plow, the sickle. So long as it bears fruit. And it will, provided you don't interfere, don't whine, get all upset, poison the air. We may feel sorry for you at times, but we must use the whip, the big stick or the pencil, because there must be order.

A poster.

"Whoever does this or that — will be shot."

"Whoever does not do this or that — we will shoot."

Someone seems to be asking for it. A suicide? Too bad. Someone else is not afraid. Hail! A hero?

Let his name shine in letters of gold but — now, out of the way since there is no alternative.

A third is afraid — livid with fear, constantly runs to the toilet, dulls himself with tobacco, liquor, women, and obstinately wants his own way. What would you do with him?

The Jews have their merits. They have talent, and Moses, and Christ, and are hard working, and Heine, are an ancient race, and progress, and Spinoza, and yeast and pioneering and generous. All true. But besides the Jews, there are other people, and there are other issues.

The Jews are important, but later — you will understand some day. Yes, we know and remember. An important issue, but not the only one.

We do not blame. It was the same with the Poles and it is the same even now with Poland and Palestine, and Malta, and Martinique, and with the respectable proletarian, and the fair sex and the orphan, with militarism and capitalism. But not all at once. There must be some order of procedure, some priorities.

It's hard for you, it's not easy for us, either. The more so since there is no buffet handy where formerly one could escape from a wearisome discussion.

You must listen, my friend, to History's program speech about the new chapter.

Why Do I Clear the Table?

I know that many are dissatisfied at my clearing the table after meals. Even the orderlies seem to dislike it. Surely they can manage. There are enough of them. If there were not, one or two always could be added. then why the ostentation, the obstinacy, and even maybe I'm nasty enough to pretend to be diligent and so democratic.

Even worse, if anyone comes to see me on important business, I tell him to wait, saying:

"I am occupied now."

What an occupation: picking up soup bowls, spoons and plates.

But worse still is that I do it clumsily, get in the way while the second helping is being passed. I bump against those sitting tightly packed at the tables. Because of me he cannot lick clean his soup plate or the tureen. Someone may even lose his second helping. Several times something fell from the plates carried clumsily. If anyone else had done it, he would be told off and have a case against him. Because of this eccentricity some seem to feel guilty for letting me do it, others feel guilty because somehow they think they are even taking advantage of me.

How is it that I myself do not understand or see how it is? How can anyone understand why I do it when right now I am writing I know, see and understand that instead of being helpful I make a nuisance of myself?

Odd. I sense that everybody thinks I should not pick up the dishes, but nobody has ever asked why I do it. Nobody has approached me: Why do you do it? Why do you get in the way?

But there is an explanation:

When I collect the dishes myself, I can see the cracked plates, the bent spoons, the scratches on the bowls. I expedite the clearing of the tables and the side table used for the little shop, so that the orderlies can tidy up sooner. I can see how the careless diners throw about, partly in a quasi-aristocratic and partly in a churlish manner, the spoons, knives, the salt shakers and cups, instead of putting them in the right place. Sometimes I watch how the extras are distributed or who sits next to whom. I get some ideas. For if I do something, I never do it thoughtlessly. This waiter's job is of great use to me, it's pleasant and interesting.

But not this is important. It is something quite different. Something that I have spoken and written about many times, that I have been fighting for the past thirty years, since the inception of the Children's Home, fighting without a hope of victory, without visible effect, but I don't want to and cannot abandon that fight.

My aim is that in the Children's Home there should be no soft work or crude work, no clever or stupid work, no clean or dirty work. No work for nice young ladies or for the mob. In the Children's Home, there should be no purely physical and no purely mental workers.

At the institution at Dzielna Street run by the City Council, they look at me with shock and disgust when I shake hands with the charwoman, even when she happens to be scrubbing the stairs and her hands are wet. But frequently I forget to shake hands with Dr. K., and I have not been responding to the bows of Drs. M. and B.

I respect honest workers. To me their hands are clean and I hold their opinions in high esteem.

The washerwoman and the janitor at Krochmalna Street used to be invited to join our meetings, not just to please them but in order to take their advice and benefit from their assistance . . . .

No one is better or wiser because he is working in the storeroom rather than pushing the wheelbarrow. No one is better or wiser just because he wields power. I am not better or wiser for signing the passes or donation receipts. This brainless work could be done more conscientiously and better by a youngster from third or even second grade.

The collector of money, a rude woman, is a nobody to me. Mr. Lejzor is a fine fellow though he digs in the filth of the sewage pipes and canals. Miss Nacia would deserve respect from me if she peeled potatoes instead of being a typist. And it is not my fault that Miss Irka, the nurse, shifts the inferior jobs onto Mira and that Mrs. Roza Sztokman, whom I also respect, once in a while may not scrub the toilet or the kitchen floor just to have a rest.

In farming, this is called crop rotation. In hygiene and medicine—a change of climate. In church—an act of humility. The Pope is called Holy Father, big men kneel down before him and kiss his slipper. And, once a year, the Pope washes the feet of twelve beggars in the church.

The Jews are conceited and that is why they are despised. I believe this will change, perhaps soon. Meanwhile, please don't get cross with me for collecting the dishes or emptying the buckets in the toilet.

Whoever says, "Physical work is dirty work," is lying. Worse still the hypocrite who says, "No one should be ashamed of any work,'' but picks for himself only clean work, avoids what is described as dirty work and thinks that he should keep out of the way of dirty work.

August 1, 1942

Whenever the stems of potato plants grew excessively, a heavy roller would be dragged over them to crush them so that the fruit in the ground could ripen better.

Did Marcus Aurelius read the wisdom of Solomon? How soothing is the effect of his memoirs.

I sometimes hate, or perhaps only try to oppose, certain individuals, such as H., or G., more than the Germans; from their point of view they work, or rather plan, reasonably and efficiently. They are bound to be angry because people get in their way. Get in their way foolishly.

And I get in their way, too. They are even indulgent. They simply catch you and order you to stand in one place, not to walk about the streets, not to get in the way.

They do me a favor, since roaming about I might be hit by a stray bullet. And this way I am safe standing against the wall, and can calmly and carefully observe and think — spin the web of thoughts.

So I spin the web of thoughts.

A blind old Jew remained at the little town of Myszyniec. Leaning on a stick, he walked among the cars, the horses, the Cossacks and the artillery guns. What a cruel thing to leave an old man behind. (ft. Again recollection of World War I.)

"They wanted to take him along" — Nastka says. "But he put his foot down and said that he would not go because somebody must stay behind to look after the synagogue."

I struck up an acquaintance with Nastka while trying to help her find a bucket taken by a soldier who had promised to bring it back but didn't.

I am both the blind Jew and Nastka.

It's so soft and warm in my bed. It'll be very hard to get up. But today is Saturday, and Saturdays I weigh the children in the morning before breakfast. Probably for the first time I am not interested in the results for the week. They ought to have put on a bit of weight. (I don't know why raw carrot was given for supper yesterday.)

In place of old Azrylewicz, I now have young Julek. There's liquid in his side. He has certain difficulties with breathing, but for a different reason.

Here's the very same manner of groaning, gestures, resentment against me, the same selfish and theatrical desire to attract attention, perhaps even to take revenge on me for not thinking about him.

Today Julek had the first quiet night for a week. So did I.

So did I. Now that every day brings so many strange and sinister experiences and sensations I have completely ceased to dream.

The law of equilibrium.

The day torments, the night soothes. A gratifying day, a tormented night.

I could write a monograph on the featherbed.

The peasant and the featherbed.

The proletarian and the featherbed.

It's been a long time since I have blessed the world. I tried to tonight. It didn't work.

I don't even know what went wrong. The purifying respirations worked more or less. But the fingers remained feeble, no energy flowing through them.

Do I believe in the effects? I do believe but not in my India! Holy India!

The look of this district is changing from day to day.

1. A prison
2. A plague-stricken area

3. A mating ground
4. A lunatic asylum
5. A casino. Monaco. The stake — your head.

What matters is that all this did happen.

The destitute beggars suspended between prison and hospital. The slave work: not only the effort of the muscles but the honor and virtue of the girl.

Debased faith, family, motherhood.

The marketing of all spiritual commodities. A stock exchange quoting the weight of conscience. An unsteady market — like onions and life today.

The children are living in constant uncertainty, in fear. "A Jew will take you away." "I'll give you away to a wicked old man." "You'll be put in a bag."

Bereavement.

Old age. Its degradation and moral decrepitude.

(Once upon a time one earned one's old age, it was good to work for it. The same with health. Now the vital forces and the years of life may be purchased. A scoundrel has a good chance of achieving gray hair.)

Miss Esterka.

Miss Esterka is not anxious to live either gaily or easily. She wants to live nicely. She dreams of a beautiful life.

She gave us *The Post Office* as a farewell for the time being.

If she does not come back here now, we shall meet later somewhere else, I'm absolutely sure that she will serve others in the meantime in the same way as she used to distribute goodness and make herself useful here.

August 4, 1942

1

I have watered the flowers, the poor orphanage plants, the

plants of the Jewish orphanage. The parched soil breathed with relief.

A guard watched me as I worked. Does that peaceful work of mine at six o'clock in the morning annoy him or move him?

He stands looking on, his legs wide apart.

2

All the efforts to get Esterka released have come to nothing, I was not quite sure whether in the event of success I should be doing her a favor or harm her.

"Where did she get caught?" somebody asks.

Perhaps it is not she but we who have gotten caught (Having stayed.)

3

I have written to the police to send Adzio away: he's mentally underdeveloped and maliciously undisciplined. We cannot afford to expose the house to the danger of his outbursts. (Collective responsibility.)

4

For Dzielna Street—a ton of coal, for the present to Rozia Abramowicz. Someone asks whether the coal will be safe there.

In reply—a smile.

5

A cloudy morning. Five thirty.

Seemingly an ordinary beginning of a day. I say to Hanna: "Good morning!"

In response, a look of surprise.

I plead: "Smile."

They are ill, pale, lung-sick smiles.

6

You drank, and plenty, gentlemen officers, you relished your drinking — here's to the blood you've shed — and dancing you jingled your medals to cheer the infamy which you were too blind to see, or rather pretended not to see.

7

My share in the Japanese war. Defeat — disaster.

In the European war — defeat — disaster.

In the World War. . . .

I don't know how and what a soldier of a victorious army feels. . . .

8

The publications to which I contributed were usually closed down, suspended, went backrupt.

My publisher ruined, committed suicide.

And all this not because I'm a Jew but because I was born in the East.

It might be a sad consolation that the haughty West also is not well off.

It might be but it is not. I never wish anyone ill. I cannot. I don't know how it's done.

9

Our Father who art in heaven. . . .

This prayer was carved out of hunger and misery.

Our daily bread.

Bread.

Why, what I'm experiencing did happen. It happened.

They sold their belongings—for a liter of lamp oil, a kilogram of groats, a glass of vodka.

When a young Pole kindly asked me at the police station how I managed to run the blockade, I asked him whether he could not possibly do "something" for Esterka.

"You know very well I can't."

I said hastily: "Thanks for the kind word."

This expression of gratitude is the bloodless child of poverty and degradation.

10

I am watering the flowers. My bald head in the window. What a splendid target.

He has a rifle. Why is he standing and looking on calmly? He has no orders to shoot.

And perhaps he was a village teacher in civilian life, or a notary, a street sweeper in Leipzig, a waiter in Cologne?

What would he do if I nodded to him? Waved my hand in a friendly gesture?

Perhaps he doesn't even know that things are as they are? He may have arrived only yesterday, from far away....

The Jews were shipped out of the Warsaw Ghetto in continuous transports until the houses and the streets were empty. There was a short, heroic uprising, a magnificent, doomed moment in Jewish history, but it only brought upon the heroes and their ghetto more German barbarity: In April 1943, after they had brutally crushed the revolt, the Germans set the whole ghetto burning and kept the fires alive until every house within the red brick wall was destroyed and every human being there burned to death. By May 10 the inferno died down, and only perhaps ten Jews remained alive, having saved themselves by crawling through the city's sewer system.

As far as the Germans were concerned, the "Jewish question in Poland" was solved. By having corralled the Jews of the country into five or six major ghettos and into dozens of minor ones, by strangling off the ghetto areas and burning the Jews in them alive or shipping them to be slaughtered in the hinterlands of Poland, they had rid the Poles of their Jewish population.

But there were survivors: Some fifty thousand Jews had managed to avoid the German killing processes. Inherently anti-Semitic as the majority of the Polish populace was, some noblemen, true noble men, supplied their Jewish countrymen with false identification papers, with food and shelter, with work and money, thus saving some of them from their German pursuers. Thirty-five years after these traumatic times, one of the Polish Jewesses thus saved told her story and, in telling it, revealed the tragedy of Poland.

The Death Train: Luba's Story

In Warsaw, on a hot August day in 1938, a boy was born to the painter Luba Gurdus and her husband Kuba. The happy new mother and her scholarly husband named their baby Bobus and dreamed of a bright future. But Bobus was barely a year old when, in September 1939, Warsaw was under German siege. The young Gurdus family was not alone in their near-panic when the Germans made it known that water supply and food deliveries to the city were cut off. Chaos broke out among the civilians as the Germans began shooting and bombing without mercy. Under the threat of total devastation, the city surrendered on September 27. Alarmed, Luba and Kuba watched as the German conquerors goosestepped triumphantly through the Polish capital.

They rounded up young Poles and Jews for forced labor immediately. Many men and families fled to smaller towns; others from nearby hamlets and villages crowded into the capital. Fear and confusion gripped everyone. The people from the countryside told fearsome stories of German terror against the Jews. Could it be true that Jewish men, women and children, even babies, were dragged from their homes and killed? That thousands were lined up before mass graves and machine-gunned into them? Luba and Kuba, Luba's mother and father, and Luba's blonde, teen-aged sister Mira held many an agonizing family council, trying to assess their situation, deal with the present and make arrangements for the immediate future. Should Kuba leave Warsaw to escape forced labor? Should Luba and baby Bobus go into hiding? What about the elderly mother and father? Mira? They knew of no place to which they could run, no haven in which they would be safe. They came to the conclusion that it would be best to stay together in their apartment and to live as unobtrusively as possible among their gentile neighbors.

A month after the occupation, Jews were ordered to wear white armbands with the Star of David on their right arms; they were forbidden to ride in streetcars, walk on sidewalks, enter parks and public buildings. They were commanded to remove their hats when passing a German, and they were fair game to be beaten and shot at by Germans and Poles alike. The Germans did not stop with these measures. A year after they had conquered Poland, they established ghettos in all the cities and towns where Jews were still to be found. In Warsaw they cordoned off a section of the inner city, built a brick wall around it, moved the Poles who had lived there out and forced all the Jews into the closed-off area.

Luba watched in horror as the Jews of Warsaw moved themselves and their few permitted belongings into the crowded ghetto. Now she was ready to flee: Anything must be better than living in the Warsaw Ghetto. Kuba had already fled to the Russian-occupied part of Poland where he succeeded in time in reaching Palestine. And Luba, Bobus and Luba's father and mother accepted the help of a friend of father's, a Polish colonel, who helped them to escape. The colonel, in order to keep the Germans out of it, moved into their apartment.

The colonel had arranged for the family to flee to Szczebrzeszyn, a small village in the district of Lublin where he owned a lumber mill and where Luba's father could work. But because he insisted on wearing his Star of David armband to work, he was soon on the SS blacklist and in danger of being caught in one of the frequent round-ups. They feared nothing more than being caught and sent behind ghetto walls. They resolved to flee again. Despairing, they moved to Zwierzyniec, a small town on the Lublin-Lwow railroad line where they knew their benefactor's, the colonel's, sister-in-law was living. Genia helped them to find shelter, and they were still in Zwierzyniec in the spring of 1942 when the death trains began to roll.

Freight trains, barred and seemingly loaded, moved past Luba's window at night, rumbling south. Where were they going? Who was penned inside those sinister trains? Scraps of paper sometimes fluttered in the wake of the passing trains. What was written on them? Who wrote the hasty messages? Luba laid awake at night, listening to the rails, thinking about the rumors that were beginning to circulate among the Jews: Could it be true that these cattle trains were carrying a human cargo to huge camps built just for Jews. But where were these camps?

As spring became summer, the trains became longer and moved faster. They passed by day and night now. The rumors exploded into facts when a boy who escaped his fate, returned and told of the trains' destination: Belzec, a concentration camp near Lublin. Panic gripped the Jews of Zwierzyniec.

Luba, her father and Mira besieged the *Judenrat* to assign them to forest and farm work, for the Jews who worked for the Forestry and Farm Administration were protected from transports for the time being. They were fortunate: the *Judenrat* gave them work permits. They worked long, hard hours and were always hungry and exhausted. Staying at home and taking care of Bobus, her mother could do little to help her loved ones.

Then on August 8, 1942, an order went out for all Jews to report to the marketplace on the following morning, forest and farm workers included. Luba tried desperately to hide her family with Genia, but she managed only to get Mira hidden; she, her parents and her child had to pack their allotted 10 kilo luggage and join the hundreds of their fellow Jews from Zwierzyniec and the thousands more from neighboring towns at the market square. Their great hope was that their working papers would save them from deportation. They clutched their precious *Ausweiss* as they were shoved into the collection center. They stayed there during one night of utter bedlam, and then they were herded out the next morning, through the village and out onto the dusty road toward the forest and an open field beyond. SS and Polish police lined the road on both sides, armed with guns and clubs while the townspeople gathered to watch the exodus. The convoy moved slowly. Her parents were resigned to their fate now, but Luba's mind was in turmoil. She tried to calm Bobus who sensed her terror. She could not accept the situation; some miracle would surely happen to tear them from the shuffling convoy, save them from the trains, from those rows of box cars standing waiting for them in the field below.

> When we entered the field, I spotted a group of Nazi officials dressed in striking green uniforms. They towered over the crowd, supervising the entire operation. The SS sentry who escorted us reported to his superiors. After a short ex-

change, he pointed at us and returned to take us to the officers. A young captain left the group and met us halfway. He asked father for his documents. Father handed over his working papers and explained he was employed by the Foresty Administration. The officer nodded and turned to me: "And you, what is your relationship to this man?"

"I am his daughter."

"What is your occupation?"

"I work at Wywloczka, a farm in the Zamoyski Principality."

The officer checked my document and said without hesitation: "Go, both of you, you are free."

Before I fully realized the meaning of his words, I saw another officer heading toward us.

"What is the problem?" questioned the approaching major.

"They have working papers," the young captain answered.

"Let me see them."

Father handed over his document. The major examined it carefully and stated: "This man works in the forest."

"That's right, he works in the forest, but for the sawmill," said the captain.

"And where does she work?"

"On a farm."

"Who needs farm workers in the winter?"

The captain, seemingly annoyed, gave up and was ready to leave. In desperation, I decided to appeal to the major.

"During my studies in Berlin," I said, "I met many Germans and made many friends; why are you so inhuman?"

The major, amazed by my audacity, asked sarcastically, "And where in Berlin did you study?"

"At the Reimannschule," I said, recognizing him as a student from the workshop of Professor Hertwig.

"Reimannschule?" he wondered. "Which workshop did you attend?"

"I studied with Professors Hertwig, Gadau, Melzer, Schmidt-Caroll."

The major, obviously amused, turned to the captain and said mockingly, "*Schau mal, schau mal, das waere also meine Kollegin,*" (Look, look, this was supposedly my colleague).

"Hertwig," he said, looking at me closely. "quite possible; you are certainly lucky. Go and take your father along."

When we started out the captain whispered to me: "Go quickly before he changes his mind."

"With our family?" I asked.

"Yes, yes, but without delay."

They were thoroughly shaken as they returned to Zwierzyniec, past the deserted ghetto and through deserted streets. They arrived at their apartment just as a truck was taking away all their possessions. They managed to save only a few pieces, and with those they set about making their place liveable once again. Soon Mira rejoined her family but even while they told her about their experience and escape, they wondered aloud and with great emotion how long they would be able to stay together and remain free. Mira had heard rumors of mass executions in nearby Szczebrzeszyn and Rutobin. The inferno was closing in on them. Was there no end to their anguish?

Then they heard that Jews who worked for the war effort were promised protection, and they rushed to a friend of her father's for jobs in one of his enterprises. They were lucky once more: Prince Jan offered them work in his furniture factory just outside of town. Luba hurried to get working papers for herself, her father and Mira; her mother again took over the care of Bobus.

Four years old now, Bobus was a bright and lovely child with a talent for drawing. He could occupy himself for hours with a piece of paper and some crayons, and sometimes he made drawings of those horrible trains. He saw and heard them all the time and had developed an intense fear of them. Luba promised him that she would never let him go into one of those monsters. Alas, she was able to keep her promise: before the summer was over the boy contracted diphtheria. A Polish physician cared for him at the risk of his own life, but without hospital care and medication, he was helpless. By summer's end, Luba was left only with her son's sensitive drawing of the trains he had feared so much.

In October the inferno closed in. The executioners came to Zwierzyniec. From her window Luba saw SS men rounding up Jews, saw them beating and shooting their helpless prey right in front of her eyes. This was certain death—and she could not face it. She turned from the frightening scene and begged her parents to flee with Mira and her. But her parents, old and tired, were no longer willing to run. They urged their daughters to go—go before the killers entered the apartment, to run and save their lives while they would stay and face their destiny. The girls grabbed their working papers and escaped through the back door—at the very moment the murderers came in through the front. The shots they heard were for their parents.

As Luba and Mira fled through the town, they had to hide in their neighbor's houses, cellars, barns and fields for a few minutes, an hour or a night to avoid the round-ups. But the Germans soon searched Polish houses as well as Jewish apartments, and in panic the girls ran out of the village and into the forest. Neither was the forest a refuge: Haunted people were moving stealthily from tree to tree, and to their horror the forest floor was littered with dead bodies. They left the woods and hid in a tall wheat field. Their plan was to reach Chobrzany where Mira had a gentile friend, Wladek, who, they hoped and prayed, would help them somehow. They could only hope that they would reach Chobrzany, exhausted and famished as they were, with pursuers all around them. They took off their arm-bands and tried to pose as Aryans.

Exhausted, they finally reached Chobrzany and pleaded for Wladek's protection, but it soon became clear to Luba that Wladek would not hide them. The risk to his family, his job and the whole town seemed too much for him to ac-cept, though he said that he would make some arrange-ments for them. In the meantime they were to go to his sister in Sandomierz and to stay there until they heard from him. He bought two tickets for them at the railroad station, and they continued their flight.

In Sandomierz Wladek's sister Marysia was none too eager to take in two strange girls, but she did not refuse them shelter. Grateful beyond words, the girls made them-selves useful by helping with the housework and with caring for Marysia's little boy Stasio. But they lived in a constant state of fear, always trying to think of ways to dispel the neighbor's suspicion; they even went to church with Marysia and Stasio, although they felt very uneasy.

> Our situation became precarious. One hint to the police could get us in trouble, and in the general upheaval two more victims would be of no importance. Marysia came home at noon and told us that the Jews of nearby Klemen-tynow were being moved along the road to a collection center. Stasio, released early from school, said the children had been dismissed and asked by the teacher to stay in their houses. Around one o'clock Marysia's neighbors went to watch the deportation and insisted we join them. Marysia reluctantly agreed, and we went to the hill overlooking the road.
>
> The sight was overwhelming. A gray mass of people—men, women, children—solidly flanked on both sides by

the Polish police and the SS, moved along the wide road. It was very much like the Zwierzyniec deportation, only on a much larger scale. Hundreds marched slowly in broken rows, supporting the old and the sick. Groups of Chasids kept together, wearing their black coats and wide-brimmed hats. Some carried holy Torahs; others apparently caught during their prayers, still had phylacteries on their bare heads and arms. The pitiful sight of horse wagons loaded with old women and small children was painfully familiar.

Mira, shocked by the sight, lowered her head; I did also. We listened to the shuffling of tired feet, mixed with the whisper that accompanied the marchers like a solemn prayer.

An infant's shrill cry pierced the air. The mother, sensing danger, covered the child with her shawl, desperately trying to quiet him. Instantly, an impatient German grabbed the unruly bundle and dumped it in the nearest ditch. Then he forced the sobbing mother into a row of marchers, and when she protested, he struck her with his rifle butt and threw her unconscious body into another ditch.

Excited voices in the crowd were silenced by Germans shouting: *Vorwaerts, vorwaerts, los, los!* (Forward, forward, move, move!)

Minutes later, the laments of an elderly Jew, beaten by a husky SS man, brought the marchers to a second halt. The old man, apparently stricken by a heart attack, was unable to move; but the German continued to strike him. Trying to put an end to the senseless beating, the victim's son sent a powerful blow to the German's red face. Another SS man shot the young Jew in the back. He fell to the ground, covering the body of his dying father.

This time the stunned marchers refused to move. Women wept, children cried, and men seemed ready to revolt. The air was charged with emotion, but the Germans skillfully terrorized the marchers by sending a volley of shots above their heads; then they aimed their guns at the crowd. Once again their method of persuasion worked; the march resumed.

It started to drizzle. The marchers covered themselves and their children with shawls and blankets; the bizarre procession moved on and on, leaving corpses along the road. The sun disappeared behind the hills, and the sky turned purple. Many peasants dispersed. Others followed the marchers, waiting for the loot, which accumulated with each bundle discarded by each Jew thrown into the ditch.

Marysia finally decided to leave after speculating on what life in the district would be like after the elimination of Jews. Tired and wet, we entered the cottage, trying to contain our grief. Fortunately, Marysia, depressed by the tragedy, did not wish to discuss the deportation.

We were about to go to bed when Adamowa, dressed in a tight jacket and a blood-stained scarf, walked in bubbling with excitement. Undisturbed by Marysia's astonishment, she explained that the scarf and jacket belonged to a woman who was shot. Her son removed it—together with jewelry, which would go toward the purchase of a new horse.

Not discouraged by our silence, Adamowa told us that her son had followed the Jews to the tracks and saw thousands of them collected from the entire district, waiting for trains supposedly taking them to labor camps. According to her son, the Jews paid exorbitant prices for bread and water supplied by the local peasants under the cover of darkness. "Some people have luck," concluded Adamowa. "We could also use the money."

"Stop this nonsense," Marysia said finally. "I could never take advantage of poor, persecuted people." Adamowa, considering it an insult, got up and left in anger. Before retiring for the night, Marysia said her usual prayers and added one for the souls of the deceased Jews.

An unusual noise woke us at dawn. I looked through the window and saw Adamowa's son harnessing his horse. He shouted to a neighbor, who was also preparing for the early escapade. With others, they went to Klementynow and returned in the afternoon, loaded with furniture, bedding and various household utensils, removed from the houses of deported Jews. Apparently the police had not interfered with the plundering.

That night the hamlet celebrated. The peasants, elated by their sudden wealth, tried to outsmart each other in the barter of looted goods. Some of them gambled with the stolen money and stayed up all night drinking and fighting. Those who did not participate in the brawl were scornful of their neighbors but did not interfere. Afterwards, guilty consciences and shame intensified the hamlet's hatred for the Jews, whose money was blamed for the corruption.

The atmosphere was tense. Marysia was nervous, and her neighbors were acutely aware of the presence of strangers. The hostility was growing and we decided to leave before something drastic happened. Marysia informed Wladek, asking him to come.

He came as soon as he could and brought two false *Kennkarten* (identifications) which he obtained for us from the underground. Marysia and Stasio were overjoyed by his arrival and proudly introduced him to their friends and neighbors. Wladek's presence added weight to Marysia's story about us, but there were people who suspected the truth. After the initial excitement wore off, Marysia, unable to hide her anxiety, asked Wladek to leave and take us along.

Wladek was disappointed. He had hoped that his sister would keep us a few more weeks and give him a chance to find another place. However, Marysia's fear was so intense that it left him no choice. We stayed a few more days, then left for Lublin.

In Lublin Wladek found a room for the two girls and left them to their own devices. Much as he wanted to help his friend Mira and her sister, he had to think of himself and his family. Helping Jews was punishable with death.

But what he had done for Luba and Mira was quite beyond measure. Clutching their false identification papers firmly in their hands, the girls set out to look for work. It was not easy; in fact, it seemed to the desperate girls an impossible task and they decided to try to return to Warsaw to their parents' apartment. They knew that their benefactor, the colonel, was still living there and they planned to approach him for his help once more. He did not disappoint them. He gave them money so that they might find a new hideout. And they found one almost immediately: The parents of one of Mira's friends in the suburb of Saska-Keba offered cover and blonde Mira felt at home there at once. But Luba, darkhaired and darkeyed, was uneasy and decided to go back to Lublin.

At Lublin station, an SS round-up was in full progress, and anyone without identification, anyone even suspected of being Jewish, was taken prisoner. An SS man examined Luba's papers and took her to Gestapo headquarters. She was terrified. Did they suspect her of being Jewish? If so, she would surely be deported, and this time she would find no escape.

She spent the night in prison, and in the morning a German guard pushed her onto a truck full of Polish women prisoners. What luck! That meant she would not be killed on the spot! The truck moved and went directly to Maydaneck, a gigantic barrack compound on the outskirts of town. Electric fences enclosed the huge open field in which low barracks stood in long rows; watch towers from which searchlights blazed and guards stared down gave the camp a terrifying atmosphere. Thin men in striped rags pulled and pushed carts heaped with corpses; more thin men sat on the ground sorting clothes. Dense fog came from high chimneys smoking in the distance and hung over the area. A bad smell hovered over the incredible scene. Luba's heart sank.

She spent a grim winter in Maydeneck in the Polish women's compound. She was ordered to hard labor and was cold and hungry every day and night. But the worst aspect of Maydeneck for Luba was her fear of being recognized as a Jewess and sent to Compound Three from which there was no return. With a courage born of desperation she pleaded with an SS man to free her and the miracle occurred: at the next selection for release she was sent along, out of the camp and away from danger, past the doomed, through the gate to freedom. On foot she reached Lublin, and from there it was only a matter of another miracle to reach Warsaw and to find Mira.

April 1943. The sky over Warsaw was red from the fires at the Ghetto where Jews had attempted a revolt. Their uprising was crushed with the most inhuman Nazi cruelty, by burning the inmates of the Ghetto alive. Luba stood at the window, hypnotized by the flames that reddened the sky, grieving for the suffering Jews, repelled by the thought that no one had come to the help of the heroic ghetto inmates. She knew that at this moment the Germans were combing Warsaw for the few Jews who had escaped the ghetto, and she knew that she would have to flee again and hide until the Germans were driven off Polish soil and this war would be over.

The inhumanities of the war and the killing of Jews continued for another year. It was spring of 1944 before Luba noticed signs of retreat: Beaten SS troops dragged themselves through the streets of Warsaw on their way back from the Russian front. But with the German defeat in Russia came a last monstrous effort to crush Poland. In August and September 1944, the Polish Underground rose up and tried

106

to win back their land. They were bombed and slaughtered brutally.

One morning, particularly heavy detonations rushed us out of bed. We left our room half-dressed and almost fell down the stairs when a huge explosion shook the entire building. The crash of broken glass suggested a direct hit. The pressure opened the door to the ground floor apartment where some of the tenants had been injured by glass. One of them in danger of losing an eye needed immediate help. I rushed to the nearest phone and called an ambulance. When the injured were picked up, we returned to our rooms and found that our bed was strewn with debris and broken glass.

In September the Russians further intensified their attack on the capital and forced the Germans to evacuate the eastern part of the city. Several streets were emptied in Saska Kepa, and the population was moved to the western part of the borough.

During the action I met a few relatives and friends who had remained in hiding—including my sister-in-law Anne and her mother, whom I had last seen in 1939. Our emotional encounter was watched by a policeman who supervised the move. We had a chance to exchange addresses but were separated again when the street was showered by an artillery barrage. My group reached a nearby bomb shelter where we spent the night.

Day after day we were moved from one street to another, from one shelter to the next. Totally exhausted, we made a final effort to return at night to the evacuated part of Saska Kepa, which was out of bounds to civilians. The flat on Kryniczna Street was empty. We closed all the windows and stayed in the darkness in order not to attract the attention of the police who were watching the streets. Not far from us the German anti-aircraft continued firing. It was difficult staying in the apartment and we moved to the cellar.

Then came September 10. The earth shook under heavy

artillery fire, and a fierce air battle was underway. German reflectors combed the sky in fruitless pursuit of the Russian formations, flying at high altitudes. The barrage was so intense that it lit up the darkness and started a number of fires, which turned houses into piles of rubble. In addition, soundless missiles came in waves, forcing us to stay in the shelter.

In the middle of the night, all calmed down for a while. Then the bombing resumed at a considerable distance. Totally exhausted, we dragged ourselves upstairs and fell asleep. At dawn, animated voices came from the outside. I couldn't understand what would bring people to this part of the borough in defiance of the German order. I opened the window and learned that during the night Saska Kepa had been taken by the Russians.

Mira and I looked at each other in disbelief. We tried to seal in our hearts and minds the moment of a return to life. If we only could share this precious moment with our dearest ones, our parents and Bobus—and with the nameless and countless brethren who suffered, prayed and hoped to survive—but didn't live to see.

In December 1945 Luba's husband Kuba Gurdus, an officer in the Palestine Jewish unit of the Eighth British Army, came to Warsaw to take his wife and Mira out of Poland.

World Highlights, 1940-1945

*Air battles rage over Britain. Roosevelt is re-elected
President of the United States for a third term. Leon
Trotsky is assassinated in Mexico. Lend-lease begins.
Italy attacks Greece from Albania. Greeks win the first
Allied victories in Europe. Great Britain and Greece are
the only countries left to oppose the Axis. Britain sends
troops to help Greece. Germany attacks Yugoslavia
and Greece. Crete is taken by German parachutists.
Germany invades Russia. Penicillin is mass-produced in
the West. Rudolf Hess lands in Scotland. Japanese
troops land in Indo-China. The Japanese attack Pearl
Harbor, and the U.S. is drawn into the War. Singapore
falls to the Japanese. Following the Battle of
El-Alamein, Rommel retreats across North Africa.
Intensive research on a new weapon begins in the
United States. German V-1 and V-2 rockets are
launched against England. George Orwell writes*
Animal Farm, Camus, *L'Etranger and Eliot "Four
Quartets." The Russians defeat the Germans at
Stalingrad, and the tide of war changes. Germany
surrenders in North Africa. The Allies land in Sicily,
then Italy. The Allies land in Normandy and D-Day,
the greatest military invasion in history, begins.
Mussolini falls. The Germans are driven from Russia.
The Allied leaders meet at Yalta. Roosevelt dies. Harry*

109

S. Truman becomes President of the United States. Mussolini is executed. Hitler commits suicide. Germany surrenders. Churchill is defeated in British elections, and Attlee forms a Labor government. The Allies assume control throughout Germany. The Americans drop their new weapon, two atom bombs, on Hiroshima and Nagasaki.

PART III
Northern Europe

THREE

The Occupation of Denmark and Norway

While Hitler was overrunning his neighbor to the east in September of 1939, six countries to his north and west declared to him and the world their absolute neutrality, which he promised publicly he would honor. But privately he said that such neutrality was meaningless and must be ignored. Of the six neutral countries, only Sweden escaped his invasion, perhaps because it did not lie directly in his warpath; Denmark and Norway were to him but northern stepping stones to England as was Holland to his west; Belgium and Luxembourg were his route to France. He conquered these five countries in two swift operations only a month apart: Denmark and Norway were invaded on April 9, 1940, and Holland, Belgium and Luxembourg on May 10.

Adjoining Germany at her northernmost tip and jutting out into the North Sea, Denmark was a monarchy with a population of four million people of Nordic stock, predominantly Lutheran Protestants. The lush, flat country yielded an abundance of dairy products and had a wealth of iron ore both of which Hitler needed. Furthermore, he planned to use Danish airfields as bases to Norway.

113

Lying across the Skagerrak Straits from Denmark, out in
the Norwegian Sea, Norway was much larger but had fewer
inhabitants. Its three million people had settled away from
the mountainous interior, toward the fjords and the sea
and were an industrious fishing and seafaring nation
with a history of greatness in shipbuilding. Like Denmark,
Norway was a monarchy; the two kings were in fact brothers. In 1933 a socialist party had sprung up in Norway, the
National Union Party of Vidkun Quisling. Quisling approached Hitler for his support of the movement and
received it. When Hitler was pressed into action against
Norway in order to keep the British out of Scandinavia, he
made use of Quisling and his party.

An operation called *"Weseruebung"* was drafted, which
was no harmless "exercise on the Weser," the river that
empties into the North Sea at Bremerhaven; it was a plan to
conquer both Norway and Denmark in the quickest way
possible. Denmark was to act as a base to Norway; Norway
was to provide naval bases for attacks on Britain. The exe-
cution of the plan was given to General Nikolaus von Falkenhorst.

In the early days of April 1940, seven German cruisers,
fourteen destroyers and several torpedo boats set out from
Bremerhaven, steaming toward Norway. On April 9, very
early in the morning, while darkness was still covering their
activities, these ships spewed forth ten thousand combat
troops at five points along the Norwegian coast. The troops
made their way quickly into Kristiansand, Stavanger,
Trondheim, Bergen and Narvick while, at the same time on
that cold Tuesday morning, three thousand fighters
dropped from German airplanes into Oslo and twenty-five
hundred into Sola. The sun rose abruptly, and when it was
fully daylight, only minutes after the troops had landed,
the major cities of Norway were full of Germans.

Denmark was attacked and overrun simultaneously. Both kings were handed German ultimatums at 8:30 in the morning, hours after the surprise invasion had taken place. The ultimatums stated that the invaded lands had broken neutrality in favor of England and that a British takeover, invited by Denmark and Norway, was imminent; the German soldiers came not as enemies, but rather as protectors against the takeover and as guardians of neutrality. The ultimatums requested the cooperation of each king and country and promised "no interference in governmental affairs, either now or in the future." But should this request be ignored and resistance encountered, there would be bloodshed and all loss of lives and damages would be the sole responsibilities of King Christian X of Denmark and King Haakon VII of Norway.

The aging King Christian X capitulated at once on that fateful Tuesday, and perhaps because of the prompt surrender or because Hitler liked the tall, blond, blue-eyed Vikings or for both these reasons, he made Denmark a *Musterprotektorat*, a model domain under German protection. King and cabinet remained in place and were not interfered with, at least not until 1942 when Hitler sent SS chief of Security Police Administration, Werner Best, to Copenhagen as *Reichskommissar* for Denmark with SS *Standartenfuehrer* Rudolf Mildner in charge of Jewish affairs. The Danes resented the ever-tightening grip of these two Germans on their country and organized one of the most effective resistance movements in all of occupied Europe. Germans found themselves hindered in every way and their orders ignored. When Best issued a decree which was to impose the wearing of the yellow star upon the Jews of Denmark, Christian X announced that, if this were enforced, he and his family would be the first Danish citizens to wear this star as a badge of honor. "We have no Jews," he said; "We have only Danes." The decree was not enforced.

Eight thousand Danish citizens were of the Jewish faith, all very much assimilated and respected. When the Germans stole a list of these citizens' residences from official files, and the Danish prime minister received secret word that the Jews were to be taken from their homes and sent to German and Polish concentration centers, he threatened his and his cabinet's resignation should the Jews be harmed. At the same time he personally alerted Jewish leaders, and the Danish resistance made preparations for their evacuation to safety. During the summer months of 1943, thousands of Jews were secretly shipped across the Kattegat to Sweden, among them the scientist Niels Bohr; hundreds were hidden with Danes whom they had in many cases never seen before. In October, when the Gestapists came with their stolen lists, they found very few Jews at home. Eventually some four hundred were rounded up and sent to Theresienstadt; their chief rabbi, Dr. Friediger, went with them. In Theresienstadt the Danish Jews remained under the protection of their king and were exempt from transports to death camps. In 1945 when German occupation came to an end, all Jewish Danes, including Niels Bohr, returned home, their travel expenses paid for by the monarchy.

Things were very different in nearby Norway. Upon reading the German ultimatum on that April morning in 1940, King Haakon VII told his ministers that he would fully understand a decision to accept the German yoke in order to avoid the spilling of Norwegian blood. In such an event, however, he would see himself forced to abdicate. The cabinet decided to resist, and Haakon was able to turn down Hitler's demands. Norway immediately organized a strong fighting force and asked for British naval aid.

General Falkenhorst, as Hitler had threatened, met the resistance with a crushing assault. By April 16 he had built up the German strength to eighty thousand troops by utilizing the forces that had overrun Denmark and through continuous supplies of parachutists; his ruthless ground fighting was supported by heavy air attacks aimed both against Norwegian cities and the British Navy in the Norwegian Sea. The British fleet was forced back, and the king and his cabinet fled to London where they set up a government-in-exile and directed effective underground resistance throughout the long five years of German tyranny in Norway. For in spite of fierce Norwegian defense, the Germans gained the upper hand all through southern and central Norway, and the country surrendered on June 10, 1940.

For the Jews Norway had been one of the few islands of peace in Europe, but with the invasion, peace for Norwegian Jews ended abruptly. In May, only a month after their landing, German soldiers smashed the synagogue of Trondheim to pieces, placed their swastika where the Star of David had been, demolished holy objects and used the religious lamps for target practice. Injustices inflicted on the Jews continued and increased. Radios were confiscated, travel was restricted and trips abroad were forbidden. The Germans demanded membership lists from all Jewish communities, the first step toward deportation. At first only Jewish refugees from mainland Europe were arrested and taken to the Norwegian concentration camp at Grini. The Jewish community was agitated but not alarmed. But in June 1941, at the time of the German invasion of Russia, with SS *Kommissar* Terboven and Quisling and his party firmly in place, all Jews living in northern Norway were arrested and sentenced to forced labor in arctic camps. Jewish property and real estate were confiscated. Jews still living in central Norway were declared "illegal aliens." In Trondheim Jews were executed without trial for repeating news items they had heard on BBC radio: Listening to BBC was a crime in Norway, but only Jews were put to death for it. Many now fled to Sweden, but many others remained, considering the conditions bad but not dangerous. But things were fast approaching a state of alarm for the Jews in Norway.

In September 1941 a Norwegian policeman was shot by a group of young Jews trying to escape to Sweden. Now Quisling ordered the roundups to begin. "Europe is overrun by Jews like grasshoppers," he said, and it was time that Norway dealt with the Jews that had settled there.

Mass deportation followed. Jews were loaded into the troopship *Donau* conveniently anchored at the harbor and were shipped to German ports. From there they were transported by train to their death at Auschwitz. With the exception of one letter of protest from a group of Norwegian bishops and professors, the Christians did not object.

In contrast, the Christian population of neighboring Denmark spontaneously organized into a body of resistance when the Germans tried to deport their fellow countrymen. When the German freighter *Wartheland* anchored at the Danish coast but failed to unload a cargo, rumors that the ship had come to take away the Jews were soon confirmed by German officials. Yes, the roundups would begin October 1, 1941; the Danes would be rid of their Jews by October 2, a simple matter of two operations for the Gestapo.

The news spread by word-of-mouth through the Jewish community. Danes warned their Jewish friends; friends warned acquaintances; officials, both Jewish and Christian, made sure that all Jews were notified of the planned action. At first people would hear the message but not understand it; once they understood, they would not believe it; but when they took in the meaning of it, their reaction was: "I must warn others!"

Jews were startled when strangers on the street approached them, offered their homes for refuge, handed them keys to cottages to hide there for a few days, gave them money or just walked up to them with tears in their eyes and a warm word on their lips.

The roundups took place, but the Jews were not in their homes. The magnificent Danes had saved their fellowmen. After the acute danger was over, they embarked on a nationwide and successful effort to ship the Jewish Danes to Sweden for the duration of the German occupation.

FOUR

The Invasion of Holland, Belgium and Luxembourg

While Hitler's soldiers were falling out of the skies over Norway in April 1940, he was giving orders to implement his "Plan Yellow," the corruption of Holland, Belgium and Luxembourg. His ruthless *Blitzkrieg* method with the added element, used for the first time in modern warfare, of parachuting troops and equipment into the theater of fighting, had proved to be successful for him. He had extended his nation's living space toward the north and had assured food supplies and war materials by bringing two more countries under his heel. Now he resolved to occupy the Netherlands to the west of the Reich for the same reasons he had occupied the two Scandinavian countries to his north. He resolved to get into Belgium because he planned to invade France, not via the Maginot Line that divided France and Germany as the French expected him to do, but over the Franco-Belgian borders. The small Duchy of Luxembourg was to be overrun simply because it lay between Germany, Belgium and France. "Plan Yellow" meant to attack Luxembourg, Belgium and Holland all on the same day.

The monarchy of the Netherlands had considered itself invasion-proof, protected by an elaborate system of Dutch dikes, canals and man-made waterways that crisscrossed the flat land. The green, colorful countryside had almost no natural obstacles besides those waterways to protect its dairy farms and tulip fields, its industrial plants and its lovely cities. That civil little country which had given the world Rembrandt, Vermeer, Van Gogh and Van Eyck had in 1940 a population of thirteen million people of stolid Saxon descent, half of whom were Roman Catholic and half of whom were Protestant. Most of them wanted nothing more than to be left in peace. But this was not to be their fate: Holland was overrun in five days and suffered the most hardship and famine of all the occupied countries in Europe during its five years of subsequent bondage for Hitler had planned his heaviest strikes against lovely Holland.

He ordered three army groups into the campaign of the West: Army Group A under General Gerd von Rundstedt; Army Group B under Fedor von Bock; Army Group C under Wilhelm von Leeb. Rundstedt was to drive through the Ardennes Forest with forty-five divisions into Belgium; von Bock with thirty divisions was to march into Holland across the Ruhr region and through the Dutch Peel Marches; von Leeb was ordered to take the southern route through Luxembourg into Belgium with nineteen divisions; airborne troops were to be provided primarily to Bock's Army Group B and all groups were to be supported by over two thousand tanks and three thousand aircraft. A truly Hun-like onslaught scheduled to strike the unsuspecting West at precisely 4:10 a.m. on May 10, 1940. Later that morning the familiar ultimatums were to be delivered to Grand Duchess Charlotte of Luxembourg, King Leopold III of Belgium and Queen Wilhelmina of Holland. This time, Hitler declared, the stricken countries had to be pro-

121

tected not only from an English invasion but from an imminent French conquest as well.

Everything went according to Hitler's plan. On May 10, the Grand Duchess quickly accepted the German ultimatum and fled to London. Her tiny country was taken over by the SS *Kommissar* Gustav Simon who sent most of its three hundred thousand inhabitants to German labor camps and wiped out its ancient Jewish community of five thousand before many Jews had a chance to flee across the French border.

In the Netherlands, while Queen Wilhelmina was reading the German declaration on that fateful May morning, German *Stukas* divebombed The Hague, Rotterdam and Moerdyk, devastating those cities. Dutch General Winkelmann's forces, with Allied aid, tried to defend the country but were not able to halt the bombing nor stem the invasion. The days from the 10th to the 15th were tragic days for Holland. On the 11th, the German Eighteenth Army penetrated Holland as far as Utrecht. On the 12th, they captured Langstraat and Moerdyk. A day later, on the 13th, Queen Wilhelmina, the Royal Family and the Dutch cabinet fled to London to set up a government-in-exile; on the 14th, Rotterdam fell and the Grebbe Line, Holland's major defense, had to be surrendered. Loss of life and damage to the cities were so great that Winkelmann asked for an armistice on the 15th, and Holland capitulated. An underground movement, supported by the government-in-exile, went immediately into action, harassing the captors and, in time, saving the lives of many Jews.

Holland had a Jewish population of about one-hundred-forty thousand in 1940, one of the oldest Jewish communities in Europe. Jews had enjoyed citizenship in the Netherlands since the Middle Ages and had taken an active part in the affairs of government there since 1797. They had settled almost exclusively in the three major cities: Amsterdam, Rotterdam and The Hague; when anti-Jewish measures began taking effect in 1941 and 1942, this natural concentration aided their persecutors in collecting them and sending them to their deaths. Few were able to escape since the country offered no rural hiding places, no thick forests or remote mountains and no neutral nearby borders. Safety could be found only in attics of sympathetic Dutch gentiles and in hidden backrooms. At the start of the occupation, the Austrian SS man Artur Seyss-Inquart was recalled from his post in occupied Poland and appointed *Reichskommissar* for occupied Holland, and another feared Austrian, Hans Albin Rauter, was made his deputy; Willi Zopf and Ferdinand Aus der Fuenten were picked to deal with the Jews. When the war was over and these tyrants had been driven out, the Netherlands had been decimated: One-hundred-twenty thousand Jews had been deported and only fifteen thousand survived; hundreds of thousands of Dutchmen had been deported to do slave labor in Germany; thousands had been mercilessly killed by the invaders. No one could have foreseen such suffering that day in May of 1940 when the German onslaught occurred. No one could have predicted that Holland would be caught in a pocket of German resistance so strong that it took a year before the Allies were able to break it, a year to take the short distance between the Normandy beaches and the suffering Netherlands.

German Tyranny in Holland: Leesha's Account

May 10, 1940, was a Friday. In the Bornstein house in The Hague, the day normally would have been one of joyous preparation for the Shabbat. Preparations did take place, but mother, always gentle and calm, seemed agitated and preoccupied as she saw to the cooking while father, the deeply religious head of the Bornstein household, was unusually quiet. Hava, age 15, and her brother Paul, who was two years younger, tried to dispel a sense of doom. Only four year old Jackie played unconcerned.

The concern of the Bornstein family was justified: During the early morning hours German fighter planes had landed on Dutch airfields and five days later, on May 15, the Germans, the hated *Moffen*, marched into a somber Holland. Immediately the Dutch Nazi Party, the black-shirted N.S.B., helped set up a German administration: Seyss-Inquart became *Reichskommissar*; Rauter his assistant; SS captain Aus der Fuenten was made commissioner in charge of the "Jewish question."

The Dutch tried to resist their conquerors and protect the Jews, but the Germans crushed all protests and strikes and put the Nuremberg Laws into effect: Jewish professors were fired from their posts; doctors and lawyers were forbidden professional exchange with non-Jews; bankers and brokers were forced to withdraw from their firms. Jewish children were expelled from their schools. Jews turned in their bicycles, their gold and silver, their stocks and bonds.

124

Radios, too, were to be handed over, but the Bornsteins kept theirs and hid it in a closet and listened secretly to the nightly BBC broadcasts from London.

SS Captain Aus der Fuenten ordered the Jews to form a *Joodse Raad*, a council of Jewish Elders. Through them he ordered the Jews of Holland to be marked with the yellow star. Once that was accomplished, he had the Jews sent to the collection center at Westerbork. He proclaimed that the Jews were deported to work in the east, an operation that he called *Arbeits Einsatz Osten*. He announced that Jews would be rounded up in the streets and taken from their houses for this purpose. As yet the Jews believed him, though each single one of them tried to avoid the deportation.

Hava begged her parents to let her join a group of young Jews who were planning to emigrate to Palestine, but her parents, underestimating all signs of doom, forbade their daughter to leave home. Hava was terribly disappointed. Going against her dear parents' will was out of the question, and so she began to think of what she could do with her young life in this climate of uncertainty and fear. She decided to become a nurse.

To her joy she was admitted as a student nurse at the Joodse Invalide Hospital for the chronically ill at Sarfatistraat and Nieuwe Achtergracht in Amsterdam. It meant leaving her beloved family, but it also meant helping people who really needed her. She drove herself hard to overcome her homesickness for The Hague and tried not to think of her own or her family's future.

Hoping to be able to stay together, the family paid out a great deal of money to get onto a waiting list for Palestine, tried to find a contact to smuggle them across the border into Switzerland, even tried to have their identity papers removed from official files, all to no avail. Still they deluded themselves into thinking that Nazi rule in Holland would soon end. Didn't Dutch gentiles continue to stage courageous protests and organize in secret resistance movements to rid themselves of the invaders and to save the Jews? To avoid being sent to Westerbork, the collection center, Hava's father had himself admitted to a mental hospital; her mother underwent plastic surgery; Paul went into hiding in another town; little Jackie stayed with friends.

Hava heard of many Jews who committed suicide, of many others who went into hiding with sympathetic gentiles and became *onderduikers*. Then one black day she heard that her father had been sent to Westerbork right out of the mental hospital. She wished desperately that she could contact the Underground Resistance movement which, she knew, was helping Jews, but she did not know how to get in touch with it, and no one at the Joodse Invalide Hospital seemed to have that information. In spite of her valiant efforts, she was homesick, lonely and afraid.

On February 28, 1943, the Joodse Invalide Hospital was notified that it was to be liquidated the very next day. Many nurses and staff members escaped that night and Hava, too, was tempted to run away, home to mother and Jackie, home to The Hague. She knew well enough that travel on the Dutch railroad system, even on the local transit system, was forbidden to Jews, but she would remove her star and take the risk. Surely God would help her to get home safely. She spent a sleepless night praying for guidance.

In the morning when she saw the despair of her unhappy patients, she knew that she had to stay with them. All that long day she helped the old, the blind and the senile into SS vans. She knew in her heart that these poor people were being driven to their death—and that she would go with them. By late afternoon all her patients were in the van. She was about to step into the gloomy truck after them when her eyes fell onto the seemingly normal street, onto the calm, blue, distant horizon, and she was suddenly buoyed by a strong will to live; she could not give up life voluntarily. She hid her white uniform under her coat, tore off the yellow star and walked calmly past the van, past the SS guards, the motorcycle brigade, the police, the blackshirted N.S.B.. She walked out into the traffic of Sarfatistraat, away from the Nazis. Once out of their sight, panic engulfed her and she began to run. She ran for hours until at last she was able to control herself.

She took the risk and traveled illegally to The Hague. To lie in mother's arms again, to be with Jackie was worth anything! And she made it. Mother was overjoyed to see her. Jackie, sweet child, wouldn't let go of her. Now at last she could relax for a while. But her illegal presence endangered mother's and Jackie's lives. The Joodse Invalide Hospital was dissolved—what should she do now? Her mother advised her to continue her nurse's training at the other Jewish hospital in Amsterdam, the Netherland Israelite Hospital, the N.I.Z. Hospital at Nieuwe Keizergracht.

She was happy when the director at N.I.Z. accepted her and assigned her to duty on the male ward. This was a new phase of her training, and she made every effort to overcome her inexperience with acutely ill men and gave herself fully to her work.

One day she was told to bring medication to a "special patient," a man under police guard. When she stepped into the room, she found a young man, obviously very ill, gazing at her intently, and she understood in a flash of insight that this man was dying and needed to tell her something. She bent over him pretending to give him medication, and she listened carefully to his low voice. Instinctively she knew what he was going to say would have to be memorized. He whispered an address and said: "The

password is 'The tulips are red'!'' This had to be a contact
with the secret Underground Resistance movement! Why
was he pleading with his eyes that she go there? Who was
he? What should she do?

Again Hava spent a sleepless night, asking God for guidance. Should she go to the address the dying man had given
her? Was she ready to risk her life in working with the
Resistance? What if it were a trap? Oh God, what should
she do? What would her mother advise her now?

That night an urgent call came through for her: It was
Paul, who was still in hiding, telling her breathlessly that
mother and Jackie had been caught in a roundup and had
been sent to Westerbork! Now Hava had no trouble making
up her mind: She would join the Resistance and would take
up the work her dying patient had to leave unfinished. She
hoped it would be work by which she could help save innocent lives. On her next day off, Hava searched for the address she had memorized and gave the password for admission.

She found herself in an ordinary house, in a room full of
Dutch citizens, some young, others middle-aged, and she
sensed that they were members of the Underground Movement. They introduced themselves to her with what she
realized were their assumed names; they all seemed to know
her. Her courageous escape from the Joodse Invalide
Hospital had made news in the Underground Movement.
The members told her that they were secretly fighting the
German occupation and that they were hiding Jews with
Dutch gentiles as part of their mission. They then informed
her that her dying patient had been assigned to provide
false papers and food stamps for the hidden Jews, the
onderduikers, and had been caught by the Germans. They
wanted her to continue his activities. As a first step she was
to be the link between the Underground and the hospital.

They expected her to keep her eyes and ears open for patients who seemed to want to go into hiding and for young mothers who wanted to save their babies. The Underground would then find sympathetic people who would take them into their homes. She also learned that day that the Underground was supported and financed by the Dutch government-in-exile. She left her new friends elated: at last she could help keep Jews out of Westerbork! When she got back to the hospital, she found a pretext to enter her "special patient's" room and, with her eyes, she told him that she was involved. She could see his relief.

In June of 1943 SS orders came to the N.I.Z. Hospital to get ready for immediate evacuation. Again Hava helped unfortunate Jews climb into those terrible vans. This time she stepped into the last one, rucksack in hand, ready to share her patients' fate. The vans drove directly to the railroad station and unloaded their freight into waiting boxcars. The patients lay or sat on the floor of those cars and were frantic. With a composure she did not feel, Hava walked among them with reassuring gestures and words. Outside on the platform, the SS waited for SS Captain Aus der Fuenten to give the signal for the train to start. She heard an SS man calling up and down the long freight train: "Brother de Leeuw! Lilly Bromet!"

Hava was electrified: Were these two people to be pulled out of the transport? And yet they could not be found anywhere. Without thinking clearly, she grabbed her rucksack and jumped to the platform. She stepped firmly before Aus der Fuenten and said: "I am Lilly Bromet," praying that he would not ask to see her papers. He looked at her icily— then told her to go back to work at the hospital. As she struggled to keep her knees from giving way under her, the boxcars behind her began to move.

Amid ongoing roundups and deportations, Hava worked

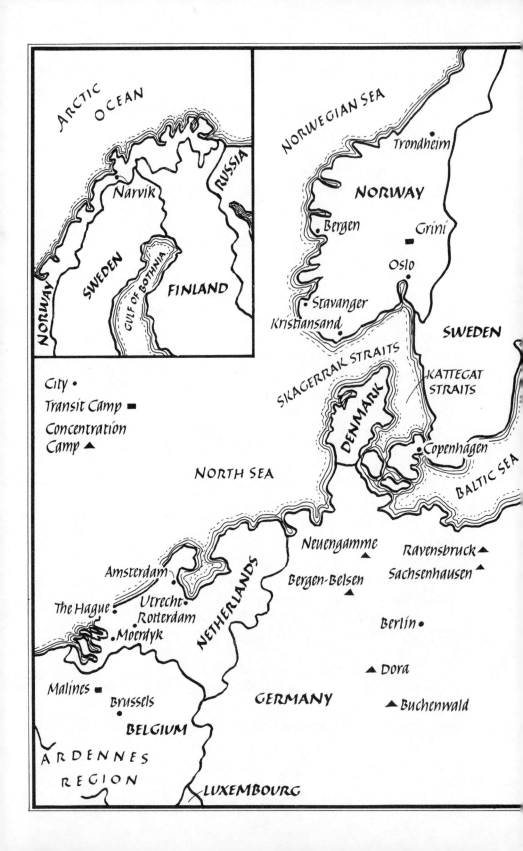

at the hospital as hard as she could. In her free time, she immersed herself in her work with the Underground Movement, and she was happiest when her efforts resulted in saving a few souls from the transports. She thought much about her dear parents, praying to God to protect them in the labor camps where she imagined them to be. She expected that one day she would join them there.

In July, just a month after the first evacuation, the hospital again received notice of evacuation. This time all remaining patients were to be taken and the place to be closed down and handed over to the Germans. Again the monster vans appeared; again Hava helped her charges to their doom and entered the last van.

This time the vans stopped at the Hollandse Schouwburg, a collection center in the city of Amsterdam where the Jews had to wait until freight trains were available. Hava's patients were close to hysteria. There was no food, no water, no medicine for them; they lay on the floor, one next to the other, so close that Hava had trouble stepping between them. She did all she could to quiet them, but as the waiting grew into days, she reached the end of her endurance too. On the fifth day of their stay at the center, a young man approached her casually and looked around quickly to make sure no one was close enough to overhear him. Then he said to her quietly:

> "You have been selected to be rescued, after which you'll be placed in hiding. Keep this strictly to yourself. Go through the motions of preparing for transport. Listen carefully! Be in the attic of the Hollandse Schouwburg tomorrow morning at 6:00 a.m. After the rescue you are to go to Alan Hartog and Jules Godefroi in the Joodse Invalide. Ring the bell at the side entrance on the Nieuwe Achtergracht." We shook hands and he left.

I was terribly excited at this new development. There was hope for life again! I wondered how the Underground Resistance could arrange such a dangerous act of escape. How could it be accomplished if every exit was controlled by armed guards?

That night the drunken Aus der Fuenten came again to the Hollandse Schouwburg, proudly inspecting "his fruitful efforts."

I had not slept well that whole week, but that night I did not permit myself to even doze off for fear of oversleeping.

It was still dark when I noiselessly made my way to the attic. I could not see, but I felt that I was not alone and I kept absolutely still. A few minutes later I heard someone else come in and I was afraid that I had made a mistake.

Maybe it was a trap?

Finally a flashlight pierced the dark, revealing the same young man from last night and, with him, I saw five of my friends. I was so happy that they also had a chance to escape, since I felt guilty that I was the only one chosen. The young man introduced himself as Ron and he gave us our instructions.

"Don't utter a word and follow me closely. You may have to take some extreme risks but this is your last chance. You can still back out if you want to. O.K. Let's go!"

He led us up a small ladder to the roof, opened the door, and one by one we climbed out. The air, the sun, and the wind hit me all at once and took my breath away. I had to get used to the light. We were on top of the three-story building of the Hollandse Schouwburg, which was detached on all sides.

It was impossible to jump to the next rooftop because the distance was too great. Armed soldiers were stationed around the building on the sidewalk halfway down the block, occupying positions in between the houses and the Hollandse Schouwburg. Ron motioned us to go toward the back.

Looking down we saw an iron fire escape between the buildings. A partially protruding wall formed a niche hiding the fire escape from the street.

In the building opposite there was a side door situated not far from the sidewalk where an armed German walked on patrol. Ron explained to us:

"Climb down the fire escape and wait in the niche. When you see the German move away from the space between the buildings run to the door. It's open, go in and wait. This will take agility and nerves. Good luck!"

He left first. We laid down on the roof and watched. It took him almost a half hour until the German guard moved away and gave him the opportunity to cross to the door of the opposite building into which he disappeared.

The next was a girl. She tied her skirt up so that it would not get caught while climbing down the fire escape. She had to wait more than an hour till she could cross to the door. She kept looking up desperately from the niche. Finally the German moved and she ran quickly to the door. The boy who was next in line was luckier. After a few minutes he disappeared into the next building.

When it came to my turn I almost became dizzy because I have a fear of high places. I grasped the sides of the fire escape and my body shook as I climbed down. I kept on saying, *Shma Yisrael*, "Hear, O Israel." I crossed, after what seemed to me an eternity, and entered the side door.

It took more than three hours until everybody managed to cross. We followed our guide, Ron, up the backstairs of the house, which seemed to be empty. When we reached the attic, he opened the small front window and he pointed to a narrow gutter ledge leading from the front to the side of the building. From there we would have to jump to the next rooftop and hide behind the chimney. The dangerous part was to make sure not to be seen by anyone.

I climbed out of the window and walked in the gutter along the front side of the roof. I steeled myself because I realized that it was either now or never. One by one we managed to land behind the chimney of the next building. The suspense of waiting for each other kept us tense, since we depended on each other's successful movements. If one person were to make a mistake, we would all be caught and the consequences would be fatal. By now the sun was beginning to warm us.

We climbed up to the next roof, which was covered with red tiles. There was hardly room for our feet to walk along the edge and we had to move sideways on our tiptoes with our backs against the roof.

We all managed to get to the next rooftop, which, Ron said, would be our last lap. He instructed us to enter through the roof window, go down into the building, and come out on the other side into a garden. From there we would be on our own.

He went to the window and tried to open it but. . . it did not move. The other men tried but still it would not budge. It would be risky to break the glass and take the chance that someone might hear it. There was no other entry from the roof into the building.

What should we do?

Ron contemplated the space between the two buildings. There was a fire escape on our side that extended halfway down. On the building opposite there was a small window level with the end of the fire escape. We all watched as he climbed down the fire escape. From the last rung he quickly swung himself over and grasped the ledge of the small window, which was one-story from the ground. He bounced off the wall with his feet and landed safely with catlike agility. He waved to us and beckoned us to follow him.

I shall never understand how I managed to get to the ground safely. I felt as if Satan were chasing me and that I had to escape his clutches. I landed on all fours and only scraped my hands, whereas one of the girls twisted her ankle.

We had to move cautiously one by one through a garden and a passage between two houses toward the street after which we were on our own.

I grasped the hand of our guide, Ron, my eyes expressing my deep gratitude to him—and I left.

How sweet and thrilling this moment was! I stood on the Plantage Muidergracht, FREE!

'You are to go to Alan Hartog and Jules Godefroi in the Joodse Invalide.' Through the waves of joy and gratitude, Hava remembered Ron's instruction. Alan and Jules had both been at the hospital during her student days there, and she had always liked them well. After the Jewish patients had been evacuated, the place had been turned over to the Germans and was now in use as a German supply building. Alan and Jules had stayed on as caretakers. What would they say now when Hava would suddenly show up asking for asylum?

She needn't have worried: Both men were overjoyed to see her and hid her quickly in a narrow room on the fifth floor. A long period of waiting began. Hava, not used to leisure and inactivity, became impatient as the weeks grew into months. Had the Resistance forgotten about her? Jules' and Alan's assurances that the movement was preparing false identity papers for her and that this was a process which required time and patience didn't help much. At last one hot day in August, Jules came to her door triumphantly: The Resistance had obtained a blank card, stolen from the city registry and here it was! He proceeded immediately to fill it out, attached a photograph of Hava, skillfully applied her fingerprint and pasted an official stamp on the card. All she needed to do now was to choose a new name and sign it on her card. Jules gave her the name Elisabeth Bos, Leesha for short, and impressed upon her the necessity to forget her real identity and to start thinking of herself as Leesha, a Dutch gentile. Soon a Resistance contact man came and took Leesha out of hiding.

The man took her to his home in Utrecht where she found a house full of "guests"—guests who disappeared up into the attic and pulled the ropeladder up behind them whenever there was a knock at the door. She didn't have to do that. She was a registered Dutch citizen. All she had to do was to learn to act like one: never show surprise or fear; join her hosts in going to church; feel comfortable with her new personality. She had to live with several different members of the movement before she was able to adjust to her new identity and fully understand the dangers involved in working with the Resistance. The day came when her friends considered her ready for active Underground work. Eddy, a new contact man, took her to a place where she would work as a nurse and could receive her assignments from the movement under cover of her duties.

Situated in Heemstede, a lovely suburb of Haarlem, Het Marishuis was a large, sprawling thatched-roofed two-story house that served as a residential convalescent home for eight well-to-do elderly people.

When I first saw it, on my journey there with Eddy, I was enchanted with its setting in an area of tree-shaded winding streets, colorful and unique houses and gardens, relaxing parks, the canal opposite the house, and a windmill outlined against the horizon.

Heemstede was a fairy-tale village, untouched by time or war. Its well-kept houses were surrounded by shrubs and trees set back into the gardens. I immediately took note of this reassuring fact. It meant that one could not readily be noticed by prying eyes upon entering or leaving the house.

"Good morning, are you the new nurse we are

expecting?'' I heard a voice sing out to me from the entrance. I was so taken by the scene and so enjoyed its every detail that I was hardly aware of having opened the gate leading toward the house.

A pleasant-looking young woman in a nurse's uniform came down the path to meet me. My ''Yes'' was immediately countered with:

''Then you must be Leesha Bos. You have no idea how much I was looking forward to greeting you!''

She helped me with my suitcase, her words just pouring over me.

''I am Inneke and I am temporarily replacing Zuster Marie, who is recuperating from pleuritis. I struggle as best as I can. Can you cook?'' she asked, leading the way.

The large kitchen was a sight to behold. Pots and pans, vegetables, and groceries, covered all available space on the counters and on the center table. There was a smell of burnt milk that had boiled over on the gas stove. Inneke ran to turn the knob.

''You see what's happening? Be an angel and help me. It's eleven o'clock now and by twelve-thirty we have to serve lunch.''

When Inneke stopped talking to take a deep breath, I ventured to answer her:

''I have never cooked for so many people before, but I can try.''

She showed me to a charming attic room under the eaves; the house had a slanted roof sloping toward the back of the house. I opened the small window set in the thatched roof and I could almost touch the lush, green trees that were interspersed between red and black roof tops. I could hardly tear myself away from the picture of sylvan beauty, but Inneke urged me to hurry since I had an important task to fulfill.

Within a few days I had become skilled in caring for the patients. I cooked their meals and attended to the various other tasks that I had undertaken. I performed them efficiently, quietly, and quickly.

No one in the house knew about my second level of activity—contact and cooperation with the Underground Resistance movement. During the train ride from Leiden to Heemstede, Eddy had informed me that I would be in charge of delivering and dispatching important items.

A "mailman" would bring me a package addressed to me. My name would be spelled "Elisabeth Boss," with two S's in red ink. I was to take off the outer wrapping, destroy it, and then repack the package. At times there was an extra message for me to meet someone at an appointed place. Then I was to deliver the package to an address that appeared as the sender on the original wrapping, after deducting ten numbers from the number of the house. All these precautions were of the utmost importance in case someone should intercept the "mailman." It was my mission to dispatch the package quickly and unobtrusively, since finding it in my possession was equally dangerous.

This setup was arranged with the active Underground participation of a registered nurse, Zuster Johanna, who owned Het Marishuis and another convalescent home located fifteen minutes away from ours. This spirited and fearless elderly lady was the only one who knew my Jewish identity. After my placement at the home I heard through the Underground grapevine to what great extent Zuster Johanna was actively involved in helping to hide people in need of refuge.

Some weeks later, our head nurse, Zuster Marie, returned to her post after recuperating from sickness. She was pleased to note that the patients were well taken care of, that the household was running smoothly, and the meals were being served on time. Zuster Inneke ascribed it all to me and praised my efficiency. Since we had set up a certain routine, Zuster Marie had no reason to notice my occasional slipping out of the house in the afternoons or evenings. I utilized my days off for arranging matters in places some distance from Heemstede.

Growing tension could be felt throughout the country. Many people believed that the Allied invasion would take place at any moment. Each night the Allied bombers were heard flying overhead on their way to Germany.

The Dutch submarine base in Ijmuiden was bombed by the Allies in full daylight with thousands of people watching. The coast shook under the impact of the heavy explosions.

There were rumors that large armies were waiting in England and that eight thousand ships were ready to move for a landing on the European coast. In Belgium and France, the railways and the station emplacements were under constant heavy Allied bombardments.

The food situation in Holland was grim and getting worse by the week. It was hardly possible to live exclusively on the rationed allotments. People had to supplement their meager supplies with food bought on the black market, at ever-increasing prices. We were all losing weight gradually and constantly feeling the hunger pangs gnawing at our insides.

How unhappy and restless the people were! Everyone was waiting impatiently to see the end of the miserable, long, and bloody war!

I was deeply worried at the fate that must have befallen my family and friends. Their absence left a cold emptiness in my heart. I feared particularly for the whereabouts and welfare of Jules Godefroi, with whom I had not communicated since the winter of 1943.

In order to sleep at night I drove myself physically to the utmost so that my body would be tired. In spite of this, I was plagued by frightening dreams and nightmares.

One night I woke up, my body shaking with sobs, tears streaming down my face. The utter loneliness I felt and my yearning for my parents filled me with despair. I felt compelled to put my feelings down on paper. I lit the stump of a candle near my bed and poured out the words, which at times were blotted out by my tears.

My darling sweet Mother:

How I long for your caring eyes, your words so sweet and tender. How can a person be so lonely? Do you know what it means to be all alone, when my heart almost bursts with loneliness, and impatient waiting threatens to destroy me?

O my darling little Mother, I yearn so for you, to put my heavy tired head in your lap. Yes, sweet Mommy, I am crying now. I cry so bitterly as only a lonely, longing, yearning soul can do; I can't stand it any longer. I don't know where to look for consolation.

I am looking at your picture, which I keep behind a plank in the closet. Darling Mother, will you ever be able to answer me?

And you, dear Father, my friend? Your penetrating, honest, yet tender glance is so true and confident. I miss your strong protective arms. I know, everyone of us was so self-reliant. But if we uttered just one word or gave a sign that we needed you, your always open hands were there. Will you ever be able to give me an answer? Ever?...I hurt so unspeakably much. You were both such good parents, so honestly good and intensely involved in all that we did, so self-effacing. Will this be the end? So bitterly and unexpectedly? I need you always, your love, your care, it is the most beautiful and dearest feeling in the world, one cannot get another father and mother. We were so close!

Surely the strong love we have for each other will bring us together again?....

Leesha's solace in those lonely months and years was her work with the Underground, and to it she gave all her intensity. Her link with the movement was a tall, kind man of thirty-five, Fritz van Dongen. This noble Christian was an important leader in the *Landelijke Knokploegen*, L.K.P., one of the branches of the Resistance. His main task was hiding and caring for hundreds of Jews. Fritz soon became Leesha's close and trusted friend. Together they bore hardship, and together they rejoiced at good news: the Allied invasion on June 6, 1944; the liberation of Paris on August 25. They hoped and dreamed of the liberation of Holland, grieved over the disappointment of "Mad Tuesday," that crazy day when Dutchmen lined the streets waiting for their liberators in vain.

A dreadful winter was yet to be endured. The Nazis robbed Holland of all her supplies and resources, shipping everything, everything to the Reich. They still hunted for men, sending them to forced labor or to prison. Food and coal became alarmingly scarce. How shall Het Marishuis manage to get through this severe winter without food and heat? A dangerous and exhausting excursion into the country yielded nothing for the patients. Het Marishuis, depleted of everything, was forced to close its doors.

Leesha packed her belongings with a sad heart. She didn't know where to go or what to do. Her suffering and the misfortune of her country seemed without end. A knock at her window startled her out of her worries. Who could be out there? Did Fritz come, even though this was not one of his scheduled days? She lifted the curtain carefully: The man in the snow was a stranger. But he identified himself quickly, and Leesha let him in. He brought bad news, this new contact man: Fritz, her dear friend, had been captured.

Leesha followed the new man to Leiden as if in a nightmare. Fritz's loss, after all she had endured already, was nearly more than she could cope with. She looked at her leader: He, too, seemed stricken by Fritz' arrest. Dare they hope that their friend was still alive, that they would ever see him again?

The man took Leesha to a hastily called meeting at a house in Leiden. They found five somber people sitting around a table, one of them, Victor, acting as the leader of the group. Without ceremony Victor told Leesha that she had to take over Fritz' responsibility in the organization, the care of the hidden Jews. She had to see to it that the *onderduikers* were provided with foodstamps, money, false papers, news and encouragement. How many such *onderduikers* were there? One hundred eighty. Was there a list of their names, of the names of the gentiles in whose houses they were hiding? Leesha had worked with the Underground long enough to know that no such list could exist, that Fritz had carried all information in his head. Where was she to start, then, to find these one hundred eighty people who were now dependent on her alone? Vic had six names and addresses for her; the others she would have to reconstruct with the help of these first six. Vic arranged for a bicycle for her, gave her an address where she would find a room and then she was on her own.

During the next three weeks Leesha ferreted out the whereabouts of her charges, memorizing, as Fritz had done, the long list of names and places. And how glad these people were to see her when she came on her regular visits; how desperately they needed her! Hunger and the fear of being discovered had left most of them pale, many sick; the lack of fuel or wood could kill them. Leesha brought extra food rations, some sticks of firewood and mostly encouragement: hold out just a little longer, my people, she wanted to cry to them; this horrible war has to end one day! Holland will be free again! Soon, soon!

Yet the war dragged on. Jews and gentiles alike suffered terribly during that long, cold winter of 1944. The people ate tulip bulbs to stay alive, cut down their beautiful parks to keep from freezing. Jews and non-Jews had to go into hiding now to avoid being sent to the Reich for forced labor. Rumors circulated that the Germans would shoot the whole population of Holland in one last saturnalia.

The Underground doubled its efforts and its vigilance: to get caught at this late date would be tragic indeed. They needed weapons now, and they embarked on a daring scheme to get guns as well as motorcycles and gasoline from the Germans: They would contact German soldiers, promise them protection after Germany's defeat in return for those items but would kill the hated enemies as soon as they had handed over their possessions. Leesha discovered that she could not kill the German boy who gave her his pistols. Humiliated, she asked Victor to assign her to something else.

Victor had yet another plan against the German occupiers, an action that would at the same time help his countrymen in their hour of need. The Germans had confiscated all Dutch goods, all produce, every farm animal, anything they could possibly move and planned to send their loot by rail to Germany. The Dutch railroad workers were enraged by this plunder, and, encouraged by their government-in-exile, they went on a nationwide strike. This infuriated the Germans, and they threatened terrible revenge on the striking men and their families. The Underground helped hide these patriots, but they needed more money than their government could secretly send from England. Untiring and ever-resourceful, Vic planned a daytime raid on the Rotterdamse Bank in Rapenburg. He gave Leesha a new chance to be useful: She and another young girl from their membership were to stand guard during the daring raid.

It was a cold but clear day and I pedaled against the wind until I got to the Rapenburg, right across from the Rotterdamse

Bank. Julie arrived and we positioned ourselves facing each other, making believe we were talking and holding on to our bikes while we scrutinized the street. Soon we saw our men going in, one by one, with Hans remaining outside the entrance.

Julie and I were nervously talking to each other. "No, nobody. I see no one. I see no *Moffen*. I see no sign of police. I hope everything will go all right. Vic is O.K. He researched everything meticulously. Oh God, let no Nazi come now! I hope the boys make out all right, so that no one will get hurt!"

After what seemed like ages, but in reality, was only minutes, the boys came out two and three at a time, some of them with briefcases. Everything had gone O.K.!

Julie and I jumped on our bicycles and raced away in opposite directions. As I came to the Oude Singel, I saw two big green German vans standing on either side of the canal. The soldiers had cordoned off the street and everyone passing on foot or on bicycle was asked to show identity papers and was frisked for weapons or black market food.

Oh, I was in trouble! I had a small gun in my belt, about fifty ration cards rolled up in my bra, and two blank identity cards. Such evidence of illegality would incriminate me without question.

I spotted the danger but I saw no way out, not even an alleyway I could turn into. I quickly made a complete U-turn and started to race against the traffic. One of the German soldiers saw me and started yelling: "Halt!" "Halt!" He grabbed a bicycle and raced after me.

I was desperate. If he caught up with me it would be the end of me. Who could help me now? Like a flash I got an idea and began to whistle the first four notes of Beethoven's *Fifth Symphony in C minor*. This was a whistle we used in the Underground; if there was a friend nearby he would answer me with the second part of the phrase: "bum bum bum bum."

As if from heaven I heard a whistle answering me and then a crash of bicycles, shouting angry voices and cursing in German:

"*Verfluchte Leute*! Damned people!"

The oncoming cyclists kept to the right of the road leaving me a path. I raced against the traffic and as I turned the corner I looked behind and saw a pile-up with the pursuing German caught in the middle.

I ducked in and out of side streets till I reached the home of the Kruizingas. When I finally caught my breath again, I related my adventure of the day to Ada. I could not get over my miraculous escape. Ada was so happy.

"You see, Leesha, there are some wonderful people in the world. You have to keep on believing."

That night, Vic was the hero of the hour, as he told the story of the raid on the branch of the Rotterdamse Bank on the Rapenburg and how he had planned the whole procedure:

"When our twelve L.K.P. men entered the bank, one by one, I went over to a little man guarding the vault and I said to him: 'In the name of the Prince of Orange raise your hands,' and I stuck a gun in his ribs. The frightened little man put up his hands and started singing: "*Oranje boven*"—"The House of Orange I hold high."

"When the cashier saw two of us approaching his window, he threw everything down and fled. Then we confronted the bank director with two guns under his nose and he had to hand over the money. We pushed all the people in the bank, including the employees, into the vault, while we quickly packed away fl. 95,000 into our briefcases. After we finished, we let the director and the rest of the people out of the vault. We assembled them against the wall and I said to them:

"Gentlemen, this is not a theft or a burglary. This is a raid executed by the Underground Resistance movement. This money, instead of going to the Nazis, will be given to peo-

ple in hiding, whose lives we are saving and to the railway
people who are now unemployed. Long live the Queen.''

Leesha listened with gratitude and satisfaction as Vic relived
for them all that show of heroism. She had been part of this
episode in the history of the Dutch Resistance, and she had
done her part well. She yearned to do more, to help her
country and her people get through this miserable time.
She thought of her hidden charges, the many Jews who had
not been able to go out for a walk in months or even in years.
Might it not be possible to register them under assumed
names so they could move about with a little freedom?

As soon as the thought had crystalized in her mind, she
went to see a fellow Underground worker, Cor van Wijk, an
employee at the Leiden City Registry and asked him if such
a thing were feasible. To her surprise, he answered that it
would not only be possible but actually very simple to register her people in the *Bevolkings Register* of the City Hall.
He handed her blank identification cards and told her step-
by-step how to get the *onderduikers* to fill them out, how to
fingerprint them and then affix legal stamps. Of course they
would have to use fictitious names and birthplaces, even
supply false names for parents and grandparents, but once
that was all in place, he could file the cards at the Register
and their owners were ''legal.''

Leesha was elated. She had helped her people, and she
had made a new friend. Through Cor, she became a
member in yet another arm of the Dutch movement against
the Germans, the *Strijent Nederland*. Disregarding her
own constant hunger, she now served her country to the very
limits of her strength.

Holland was in a desperate situation. Although the Allies
were victorious and had liberated country after country
from the German occupation, Holland was caught in a

146

pocket of German resistance and was subjected to intense Allied bombing. Now the Germans openly and deliberately embarked on a program to starve the population. Leesha lay awake at night wondering if it were humanly possible to live until liberation. She listened to the roar of fighter planes overhead and the growling of her own stomach. If help would not come soon, it would come too late for many brave Dutch men and women.

On April 29, 1945, Leesha heard the sound of help. Four hundred fifty British bombers flew low over Amsterdam and dropped thousands of tons of food. The next day American bombers did the same over all of Holland. The hunger was over. The war would soon be ended too.

On May 5, 1945, five years almost to the day of the invasion, Germany at last surrendered; Dutch flags again flew everywhere. Leesha said farewell to the people for whom she had cared and began to search for her own family. She heard that Jews in concentration camps had been gassed and their bodies burned, but the message did not reach her brain. Her beloved parents and her two brothers must be alive somewhere and able to come back to her one day. God can't mean for her to be left alone in the world forever.

Leesha was alone. But not forever. In 1947 she married one of her liberators, the Canadian Captain Isaac B. Rose, and with him she started a new life and a new family.

PART IV
Belgium and France

FIVE

The Germans in Belgium

Holland's neighbor to the south, the kingdom of
Belgium, was an equally lovely, cultured and industrious
land with green, rolling lowlands and picturesque cities.
Belgium had a population of ten million people of
Teutonic and Celtic descent, most of them Roman Catholics. This land of Rubens and Breughel, of diamond cut-
ters and ship builders resisted the German terror for eighteen days before it, too, was savagely bombed and beaten
into surrender. When Rundstedt's men and tanks came
crashing through the Ardennes Forest and German
bombers unleashed airborne death over cities and airfields,
King Leopold III was ready to submit to the Germans at
once. But his cabinet insisted on resistance, and with
Allied help the Belgians fought heroically against insur-
mountable odds. General Bock directed his major attack
against their Maastricht-Liege Line while at the same time
General Rundstedt's panzer divisions, the XIXth Armored
Corps under Guderian and the Armored Corps of Ewald
von Kleist, mowed their way through the country and
toward the Straits of Dover in the English Channel. Air-

borne reinforcement and heavy air attacks helped them from the first day on.

On the second day of the invasion, May 11, 1940, the Germans took the Belgian fortress Eben Emael by landing on its flat roof under cover of night and working their way down into the stronghold, taking its twelve-hundred-man protective force prisoner. More parachute troops captured strategic bridges over the Albert Canal the same day. On the sixteenth, with German strength forcing the Belgians back toward Antwerp, the ministers advised King Leopold III to flee to London. But the young king stubbornly insisted on staying, even at the risk of falling into enemy hands. His government fled without him and set up an exile government, which influenced Belgian resistance from London. Antwerp fell to the Germans on May 18. Ten days and much bloodshed later, on May 28, Leopold surrendered to the invaders and was eventually taken to Germany as a prisoner. His country came under the military rule of General Alexander von Falkenhausen.

The Belgian community of sixty-five thousand Jews fared better under General Falkenhausen, the military commander, than its neighbors did under the customary SS commissaries. German generals did not see the destruction of the Jews in their territory as their foremost duty while the SS chiefs looked upon the "solution of the Jewish question" in the occupied countries as their primary task. A country considered itself fortunate to get a *Militaerbefehlshaber* as the highest occupational officer instead of an SS *Kommissar*, but such luck was rare.

In Belgium General Falkenhausen permitted, even helped, thousands of Jews to cross the frontiers into France before he embarked on the prescribed anti-Semitic procedures. He postponed the roundups as long as he could, and when at last he did allow mass transportations to take place in October 1941, he declared Belgian Jews exempt from deportation and restricted arrests to the many thousands of Jews from the countries of Europe who had come to Belgium in search of refuge. But even among those unhappy people, many found protection and hiding places with the anti-German Belgians — in many cases, however, only for large sums of money.

In September 1944 the Germans were driven out of Belgium and the king's cabinet returned. Twenty-five thousand Jews were still in the country; many thousands had been killed. Thousands of Belgians had perished during the bloody war and the grim occupation. King Leopold III, who had been liberated from German imprisonment and found refuge in Switzerland, was invited back home in 1950. Five years later he gave up his throne in favor of his son Baudouin.

A few survivors returned to Belgium, among them Eliezer Flinker, survivor of Auschwitz. Alone, old and broken from his ordeal, he searched out the house on the outskirts of Brussels where he, his wife and their seven children had been in hiding for two years. Nothing was there for him but sad memories — and a diary. His son Moshe, dead at sixteen, gave testimony.

Dialogue with God: Moshe Flinker's Diary

Moshe Flinker was born in Holland in 1926 and grew up there, part of a large, deeply religious family. His father, a wealthy businessman, conducted some of his business in

Brussels and so, for many years, Eliezer Noah Flinker would cross the border to Belgium regularly every week. In November 1942, with the persecution of the Jews in Holland in full force, Moshe could hear his parents discussing the future: Should they flee to Switzerland as many of their friends had done? But some of them had been caught and sent back for deportation. With his solid connections in Brussels, the elder Flinker convinced his wife that Belgium should be their destination. He explained to his wife and also to Moshe that the Jews were somewhat safer under German military governance in Belgium than they were under Nazi rule in Holland. Moshe couldn't see much difference in the two arms of German occupation, but when his father arranged for the large family to cross illegally into Belgium, he felt secure. At least the endless discussions about the future stopped for the time being.

By means of large bribes Mr. Flinker registered his family as Dutch citizens living in Brussels, and with the help of his business contacts he found a house for them all. They were safe for the moment, safe if they kept themselves out of sight of the neighbors who might become suspicious of a new family with seven children. They might denounce them to the Germans. Moshe's initial feeling of safety soon gave way to new emotions: He was bored, he was worried, he doubted his God. Because he had no one to talk to, he started a diary. He made the first entry on November 24, 1942, the Jewish date of Kislev 15, 5703, and the last entry on April 7, 1944, Pesach 5704.

These two years of hiding in Brussels were years of boredom for the boy Moshe. Going to school was out of the question, and so he had to remain indoors during school hours. Even after school hours, he did not dare to be seen on the streets or in the parks. He had no friends. He tried for a while to teach his sister French and himself Arabic, but he did not get very far with either of these two projects. His thoughts were taken up with worries.

He knew that his father had to cash in large portions of his stocks to obtain the residents' permit, paying huge sums of money for ration coupons and blackmarket clothes for his many children. Bribing and begging, from month to month. Is that the way You want us to live, God? Do You want us to be shut in, Moshe asked, fearing every knock at the door? Having nothing at all to do but think and pray, God? Is this Your will?

In December 1942, the Festival of Lights, Chanukah, was celebrated in hiding. Moshe begged the Lord for a miracle to occur during Chanukah. Send me a sign, oh God, something, so that I will know You do not mean to destroy Your people! Oh Lord, perhaps You will send the Messiah while I am lighting these Chanukah candles? Moshe sang the *Maoz Tzur* with fervor: Rock of Ages, come to our aid! Hear our prayer! Answer the prayers of saintly men, if mine is not worthy!

But the month brought bad tidings: Moshe heard that one of his friends was killed while trying to cross the border from Holland into Belgium just as he himself had done only a month earlier. Was the friend betrayed? He heard of other friends who were turned back at the Swiss border. Do the nations know that we are being deported by the thousands every day? Will no country help us? Father told the most shocking news of all: He heard that the Jews deported to the East are not used for labor, that they are killed instead. Pain engulfed the boy. He heard his father say that all nations probably know of the massacres yet do nothing to stop them. Moshe wished he could die rather than hear such horrible news. His people, Jews like himself, being killed? Not even the Bible offered solace nor the Prophets peace to his tormented mind. He took up the Book of Lamentations and said the dirges: Return us, Oh Lord, unto Thee and we shall return; renew our days as of old.

In January 1943 Moshe learned that the offensive in Russia had begun and that the German armies were retreating. He took this as a sign from God. You have heard our prayers, Ruler of the Universe! You will not forsake us! You will beat the Germans in Russia!

But all around him in Brussels, Jews were picked up, either on the streets or in their houses, and they were sent to their doom. Moshe panicked every time the doorbell rang. And yet his life seemed normal to him if he compared it with his brethren who were being sent away. He prayed for them from the depths of his heart, morning, noon and evening.

In February 1943 the snow was deep in the city, and the Flinkers were cold. Emptiness was in Moshe's heart. Why does the Lord not hear him? If only he had a friend to whom he could pour his heart out. Why, Lord of the Universe, he wrote in his diary, do You let Your people experience such anguish? Such suffering will not bring the Jews back to You! On the contrary, they will think there is no God at all in the Universe. Do not let Your chosen people endure any more!

Moshe dreamed of a homeland for the Jews; he wished he could go to Palestine. He tried again to study Arabic; perhaps it would be useful one day. He dreamed on. Perhaps he would become a diplomat in his Jewish homeland and help make peace between the Jews and the Arabs. He thought of the many times in history that his people had endured persecution. Was there a difference in persecution through the ages? Earlier actions against the Jews, he reasoned, were localized, the persecutors giving religion as their reason for hunting down their victims. But this time the hunt is official and widespread and the reason for it is

simply that the victims were born Jews. And again he wrote
onto the cold pages: Why do You allow this, Oh Lord? He
delved into the Zohar, the mythical book of Jewish learning
and he thought he found an answer: We were expelled from
our land because of our sins, he wrote. Now we must first re-
pent completely; we must be cleansed by suffering before
the Lord will let us return. As he stood before his God in
daily prayer, he asked fervently that God let His people live
and reach their homeland, Palestine.

The winter crept on. To relieve boredom Moshe sneaked
into the public library to read magazines. Once he even
dared to go into a movie. He saw the German film *Jud Suess*
and was appalled, shocked at the Jew-hatred that this picture conveyed. Was this really what the Christians thought
of the Jews? And if so, how could he help change their mis-
conception? His depression deepened.

March — April — May — one month flowed into the
next. Moshe kept writing into his diary the terrible Why?
He kept saying his daily prayers and yet wondering if they
were heard. But he never lost his faith in God and in God's
mercy.

August 10, 1943, Tisho b'Av, 5703, was the day com-
memorating the destruction of the First Temple in Jerusalem 2,529 years earlier. Moshe fasted and wept, both for
the Temple and for the suffering of his brothers in Europe.
In all of continental Europe, he realized with a start, only
three countries were free of Hitler's domination. The Jews
in only three countries in Europe did not have to fear for
their very lives: Sweden, Switzerland and Portugal — and
he prayed for the Messiah to come to lead all the Jews out of
slavery to safety.

As the summer of 1943 turned into fall, as 1943 became
1944, Moshe wrote less in his diary. What was there to write
about? God had apparently not heard him, was not answer-

ing his call. No sign had come to him. God was silent. Moshe no longer dreamed of safety or of becoming a diplomat. He had stopped studying, stopped trying to find solace in the Bible and the Zohar, stopped being glad that he was part of God's Chosen People. Chosen to suffer?

In April 1944, Pesach 5704, the Flinker family made preparations to celebrate the holy day of liberation in a climate of doom. Father was able to get some matzot, the bread of affliction, and even a chicken, a rare treat. As the chicken on the sideboard was being salted and "koshered," as Moshe helped mother set the Seder table for the evening celebration, Gestapists stormed into the apartment. It was futile to try to deny Jewishness. They were all taken away. Moshe died in Auschwitz soon after his arrival.

Four years after Moshe Flinker's death, God answered the boy's prayers. In May 1948, only three years after Germany's defeat and Hitler's death, the State of Israel was created in Palestine. Cleansed by suffering, Moshe's people at last went home.

SIX

France Falls

The country which was to Hitler Germany's irreconcilable and mortal enemy, the country which, along with England, he most wanted to conquer and humiliate was France. It was in France, at the Palace of Versailles in 1919, that the conditions of Germany's surrender had been drawn up. It was in France, in the woods of Compiègne, that a defeated Germany was made to accept them. The Treaty, in a seemingly endless series of parts, sections, articles and clauses, had imposed political, military and economic submission on Germany; had granted autonomy to formerly German areas; had demilitarized the Rhineland and had ended the German Empire.

Hitler used the Versailles Treaty as a vehicle of propaganda. He said it was World Jewry who had drawn up this document of defeat which restricted his nation, and he declared it invalid. By the time his armed and armored divisions stood before the borders of France, the Treaty lay broken behind him: Germany was fully armed; all the autonomous regions and countries were again part of the Reich: The Saar region, Austria, the Czecho-Slovak state, Memel on the Baltic Sea and the Free City of Danzig were his. The Rhineland was militarized and now, twenty-one years after Versailles, Hitler was ready to take his revenge, to take France.

Beautiful France, country of snowpeaked mountains and windswept shores, land of wines and perfumes, country where equality and the dignity of man was so well understood that a citizen's race was not recorded on his birth certificate, was now within Hitler's grasp. He coveted her iron and wheat, her Cezannes and Manets and Renoirs. But the forty million French felt secure and protected from German attack behind their Maginot Line, a chain of fortress-like military installations which stretched from Luxembourg to Switzerland along her border. On May 19, 1940, General Maxime Weygand took command of the French Army, not dreaming that only a month and a few days later he would be signing the French surrender in the fateful forest of Compiègne while the German band played *"Deutschland, Deutschland ueber alles, ueber alles in der Welt."* For the moment Germany was indeed at the zenith of her might, on top of the world, and Hitler, somewhere in his war headquarters, had reserved for himself the triumph of dictating the battle plan which was to fell France.

While General Bock was still waiting for Belgium to surrender to him, the armies of Kuechler, Kleist, Kluge and Guderian of Army Group A were pressing toward the West, toward the British and French troops who had come to Belgium's aid. But just as Guderian and Kleist's panzer corps were advancing on Calais and Dunkirk and nearly reaching the Dover Straits and the English Channel, a "Halt" order came from Hitler on May 24. This illogical command enabled the British, French and some Belgian troops to evacuate the threatened area and to reassemble on the French border. When the order was lifted on

May 26 and the Germans took Dunkirk, most of the Allied forces were safely out of their reach. On May 28, 1940, Belgium surrendered, and by May 30 the Allies were preparing the defense of France along the river Somme.

German forces were ordered south in a gigantic, wheeling reorganization: A total of one hundred twenty divisions and a backup of twenty-three more thundered toward Weygand's sixty-five French divisions, which were trying heroically to stem the German host.

On June 5, with the *Luftwaffe* ranging almost unopposed in the sky over France, Army Group A launched an attack on Paris, advancing with fifty divisions from the west; on June 9 Army Group B came in from the north with forty-five divisions, spearheaded by Guderian's and Kleist's panzered armies; Army Group C was to make an attack on June 14 with twenty-four divisions against the Maginot Line in the east. Morale on the side of the aggressors was high from their victories of the previous months. The morale on the French side was low, and not even Churchill's radio messages to his French allies could infuse *ésprit*. Nor could his public and private support of French premier Paul Reynaud stave off the demands in Reynaud's cabinet for surrender.

Reynaud had formed a new French cabinet only three months before, on March 20 after Daladier's resignation. In May he had appointed the aging Marshal Henri Philippe Petain vice premier. Petain had favored surrender from the very beginning, believing that with a French surrender the fighting in Europe would stop and France would receive favorable cease-fire terms in reward for her submission. Reynaud, on the other hand, proposed to move the French government to North Africa and continue fighting together with England until Hitler was defeated. Heavy bombing and advancing German armies did force the government to move on June 11, but they fled first to Tours and then to

Bordeaux where Reynaud resigned under pressure from Petain's followers.

On June 17 Petain took over the government and formed a new cabinet with Pierre Laval. Laval supported Petain's defeatist philosophy; indeed he had been an admirer of Hitler's ever since 1933 and looked forward to welcoming Hitler personally in Paris. Together they resolved to surrender at once.

Petain and Laval's request for armistice reached Hitler at his war headquarters in Sedan at the French border on June 17, but he made the French wait until he had conferred with his friend and ally the Italian *Duce* Mussolini. Mussolini had entered the war on Hitler's side only a few weeks before the truce request, and he hoped to get a part of France for his efforts or at least some French colonies in North Africa. But Hitler had other plans. Instead of carving France up, he schemed to divide the proud country against itself: he would occupy the northern part; Petain and Laval would govern the south of France from Vichy. In this way he hoped to weaken France and prevent an uprising.

On June 22, 1940, Hitler presented Weygand with the conditions of surrender — in the woods of Compiègne. This was the very spot of Germany's humiliation in 1919. With Field Marshal Hermann Goering at his side and the German High Command behind him, Hitler marched onto the historic spot, his face ablaze with triumph. The very railroad car where once France had dictated to Germany had been dragged from a museum and erected once again on now rusty rails. And this time Germany did the dictating to a stunned France: the division of the country, the release of all German prisoners-of-war, French payment of the entire cost of occupation. Hitler kept the one million French prisoners-of-war that he had taken in the month of fighting and used them for forced labor. In time he shipped another

million able Frenchmen to the Reich's labor camps. He depleted France of raw materials and food stuff and stripped
the museums. With the band playing German victory
marches, Weygand signed the harsh document. The railroad car was immediately dismantled for shipment to Berlin
and the little memorial park in the woods of Compiègne
demolished.

While the Swastika was being raised over Paris and
Frenchmen openly wept, Hitler with columns of polished SS
strode through Paris: Napoleon's Tomb, the Arch of Triumph, the Tuileries, the Eiffel Tower — it was all his!

A German government was set up in Paris. Two German
generals, General Otto von Stuelpnagel and General Karl
Heinrich von Stuelpnagel took over the military administration of northern France; SS Chief Adolf Eichmann took onto
himself the "solution of the Jewish question."

The Jewish population of France could trace its origin
back to the sixth century, to the movement of the Jews out
of the Roman Empire. By the tenth century French Jewry
was already well established and had produced eminent,
medieval rabbis and scholars, the most famous of them
Rashi of Troyes. In 1791 French Jews were granted individual rights, and the great Emancipation was born in
Europe. It spread to neighboring countries and, by the
beginning of the 19th century, to all of Europe. Ghetto
walls came down and assimilation took place. Jews settled in
all of France as respected citizens. When Hitler stood at the
borders, France had a Jewish population that was estimated
to be three hundred thousand — estimated because France
had never made a distinction between Jewish and non-
Jewish Frenchmen in her statistics.

Immediately upon the conquest of Paris, the Nazis began
the persecution of French Jews and of all Jews who had
sought refuge there from already-occupied countries. Nor

was persecution limited to Jews. Half-Jews, *Mischlinge*, were prey as well, and so was anyone who opposed the German occupation, either openly or by aiding the French Resistance. French prison complexes in and near Paris became collection centers, and the proud French were sent to their fate from there.

Fania Fénelon's Survival in Auschwitz

Fania Fénelon was the stage name of a beautiful and spirited young French singer. Because she was only part Jewish, she had not been deported at once; because she disguised her anti-German feelings cleverly, she managed to continue her singing career, even singing for the Germans when they came to her cabaret. Secretly she was active in the French Resistance and let her friends use her apartment on the nights she was singing. She did not know that the Germans had been watching her place for some time, and one morning as she was coming home from an engagement, she was arrested. She was taken to Drancy.

> At Drancy prison in Paris, the crossed-off days on my calendar formed a little ladder ending at January 20, 1944; I'd been there nine months. Now I was to be taken to Germany in a convoy of deportees.
>
> Six o'clock. From the third story, our group began its descent of the exit stairway. At each landing hands stretched out offering chocolate, a pot of jam, a pair of woolen gloves. On the last landing there was a sudden scuffle and a jeering

voice called, "Don't push, there's no hurry. No danger of getting left behind!"

It was Leon's voice. What was he doing here? Suddenly I felt a firm grip on my elbow, and heard the same voice, wheedling now, close to my ear: "I wouldn't have liked to let you go alone."

It was indeed Leon, brash as ever: a handsome little fellow, whose exact line of business was unclear to me — brown-haired, perky, with a roving eye at present fixed on me.

"You see, I said to myself, 'That little girl is going to need a man to carry her things and put a little romance in her evenings when she's down.' I'm rather taken with you and I don't want someone else stealing my place. So I came back, pronto."

"But hadn't you escaped? You surely didn't come back of your own free will?"

He laughed like a child who has played a good joke. "Something along those lines. The toughest bit was to get myself put in the same group as you. It was hard to get them to swallow that one, because it's not the kind of trip people normally clamour for. But as you see, I've done it."

His words amused me and touched me, yet annoyed me. I preferred to choose the men in my life rather than the reverse. Still, it was certainly a declaration. Poor Leon: we were immediately separated. A security man thrust him into one of the first trucks.

I was surrounded by people I didn't know. My neighbors were a young woman of about thirty, very beautiful, with her two smartly dressed little daughters, and a girl of about twenty with a ravishing head set upon an enormous deformed body. There was an immediate rapport between us; her name was Clara.

Early morning Paris was a sinister place. It was very cold, and stalactites hung from the cracked and frozen gutters. The blue winking of the civil defense lights made the gloom seem colder still. Our truck was covered with tarpaulin and open at the back. The few chilly early-morning passers-by hardly bothered to cast a glance in our direction. And yet our convoy must have been rather unusual, with women wearing fur coats, men of all ages, old people, and children.

Awaiting us at the marshalling yard was a very old train which had seen action in World War I and a wheezing engine which certainly didn't deserve its insolently large, immaculate white V, Churchill's victory sign that had been expropriated by the Germans after Stalingrad.

We staggered beneath the weight of our luggage. Everyone had brought everything he'd managed to get together: clothing, food, drink, cigarettes, jewelry, money. There were a hundred of us, from all walks of life, all ages and races, crowded into the pitch black interior of a carriage meant for cattle. There was clean straw on the floor. The quick thinkers — and the strongest — did what they could to stake claims to their own corners; they dug in, flapping, shuffling their bottoms into the straw like chickens, acting as though they were going to be there for an eternity.

The enchanting young mother was quietly advocating various subtle points of etiquette to her children: "Don't make too much noise, there are other people here." Already there were quarrels of the "I was here before you" type. Laughable. People started telling jokes, groaning, complaining, making conclusive but unfounded statements:

"We're going to a work camp in Bavaria, with little German bungalows, quite clean and decent, and comfortable, with little gardens for those with children."

"He's crazy!"

"I'll say. That camp is the worst of all, I know that for a fact."

Me, I . . . I, me . . . One opinion followed another.

The smell of the improvised lavatory soon became unbearable. At every jolt, there was a worrying, ploshing noise. The straw around it was already filthy. A child sitting on the floor in the middle of the carriage kept repeating in a piercing little voice, "I can see things moving everywhere."

A woman called out, "Make that filthy brat shut up."

"It's obvious you've got no children," shrieked the mother.

"You're wrong — I've got six."

"Where are they then?"

"I'm not saying."

"Are you afraid I'll expose you?"

It was outrageous, but no one laughed. Quite the contrary — the two women leaped at one another. The tension was exhausting.

The time came to eat: it seemed like a picnic without the bonhomie. The whole crowd chewed; it wasn't an elevating moment, but it was restful.

Clara looked worried. "Have you brought something to eat?"

"Of course."

I offered her some of my treasures: sardines, real ones in oil, sausage, pate de foie gras and champagne.

"It's astonishing, it's like Christmas; and your Santa Claus seems to shop on the black market!"

That broke the ice, and she laughed; in the darkness her small, regular teeth gleamed like the pearls in a necklace. Devouring our luxury fare, quenching our thirst with Roederer brut, we swore never to leave one another, to share everything.

In the stinking atmosphere, heavy now with the smell of food, people belched and dozed. Clara confided in me that she had once been very thin. She'd begun to get fat in prison. At Drancy it had been terrible: she had swollen up as though someone had blown air into her with a bellows.

"Only my legs stayed slim. Look, I'm positively deformed. My boyfriend won't want anything to do with me."

Weeping now, she told me about her parents. Hers had

been the life of a little rich girl, an illustration from a children's book, a protected, untroubled youth into which the reality of war had only just intruded. "You see, Jean-Pierre, my boyfriend, belonged to a network. I carried letters and arranged meetings, took telephone messages without understanding their importance. But I think they arrested me because I'm half-Jewish."

Here the young mother joined in. "My children are too. Since they couldn't arrest my husband, who's in the Resistance, they took us. They meant us to act as hostages, as a lure. Luckily it didn't work, my husband wasn't taken in. So, they're deporting us. The main thing for me is that their father has escaped the Germans; he would have been in danger of his life, but for us it will just be a rather grim interlude."

"And what about you?" Clara asked me.

"Rather like you, really. I'm also half-Jewish, and I too did a favour for a friend in the Resistance, taking letters, arranging rendezvous; giving people beds for the nights when they needed them."

"But that was dangerous."

"Of course. Someone informed on me and I was arrested. That night, a friend had slept at my place. I'd slept at a neighbour's. I was going back up to my room in my dressing gown, carrying my clothes. Imagine how I felt — there were three of them waiting at my door. They took me to the Quai de Gesvres. At first I wasn't too worried, my papers were fine, my ration cards absolutely authentic, made out by a police commissioner in the name Fania Fénelon, the name I use as a singer. I even had a night pass issued by the Commandant."

"Did you used to sing?"

"Yes, in nightclubs."

"I couldn't have heard you sing," said Clara rather primly. "We'd stopped going out at night. We didn't mix with the Germans, and no one went to nightclubs except Germans and collaborators.''

I fell silent, slightly ashamed; it had been very good business. How would Clara have judged the proprietress of Melody's, who looked like a madam — indeed, perhaps she was — but who protected us? How she would have despised those tarts who hung from the necks of German officers and gave us papers, photographs, and information.

''Did they find out your real name?''

''No. In the end I gave it to them. I was tired of being beaten — it's oddly monotonous. And they insisted that I was a Communist; it would have been difficult to prove, but they might have managed it. Then I could have been shot. If I was going to die, I preferred to die under my father's name, Goldstein. As soon as they knew I was Jewish, that settled everything. I was sent to Drancy, which seemed to me an acceptable way of staying alive.''

Intrigued, Clara asked, ''How did they beat you?''

''With an iron bar, on my back.''

She clasped her chubby little hands. ''Good Lord!'' And you didn't talk?''

''I hadn't much to say.''

''I don't know what I'd have done in your position.''

Despite her huge body, Clara seemed to me so weak, so vulnerable, that I was overcome by a wave of pity; she was like a child, to be taken under one's wing. She asked me a few more questions, which I evaded. I didn't want to relive the period that led up to the present. The little girls began to hum *Malbrough s'en-va-t-en guerre* and we joined in the chorus. Clara had a pretty voice, a light airy soprano. Other people joined in, euphoria reigned. But my rendering of ''Lying in the Hay'' spoiled everything; my sense of humour wasn't theirs.

''That'll do,'' they burst out.

''We're trying to sleep.''

169

"You wouldn't sing if you knew what you were in for," one woman commented prophetically. . . .

We'd been travelling for over fifty hours. The smell was frightful, the door hadn't been opened once. At first, under the supervision of the SS, the men in each carriage had taken out the buckets to empty them. Since then, our bucket had emptied itself by overturning.

We were desperately thirsty; all the bottles — water, coffee, wine, spirits — were empty. The stinking air was unbreatheable, the ventilation nil; we were beginning to suffocate.

My watch was at twelve when the train stopped — midnight. Our door was opened. "Quick, fresh air," and everyone rushed for the door.

"Get out. Leave all the luggage in the train." The orders were in French.

The younger ones jumped out, others managed as best they could. Searchlights lit the platforms, their blinding glare making the night seem darker still. There was a dizzying succession of images. Clara was beside me; there were cries and shrieks, and orders barked in guttural German:

"Raus! Los! Schneller!" Out! Out! Fast!

Shouts in the Dark: "Mama, where are you?"

"Françoise, Jeanette, where are you?"

"Here," called a child's voice, "Mama, we're here."

"Where's here?"

SS soldiers climbed into the carriages and threw the ill, the stiff, and the exhausted out onto the platform with kicks and rifle blows; last of all went a corpse.

Living skeletons in striped uniforms, their skulls shaven, moved among us like silent shadows, climbing onto the train; these strange "porters" took out our luggage, piled it onto trolleys, and took it away. The snow was thick and dirty, but Clara and I tried to melt some in our hands to drink.

There was a rumble of vehicles, military trucks, but with enormous red crosses set in white circles.

"The Red Cross is here," exclaimed Clara. "We're not in any danger."

The SS thrust the crowd towards the vehicles. Old people and children moving too slowly for the SS stumbled and picked themselves up, clung to one another and were hustled brutally.

Caught up in an eddy, I was about to climb up in my turn. A sergeant stopped me. "How old are you?"

I told him and he pushed me back. "You can walk."

The mother and little girls called to me from the back of the truck. I too could have climbed up there and joined them, under cover of darkness, but Clara stopped me.

"Don't get in there, we've been cooped up for days in the terrible atmosphere; it'll do us good to walk, even in the snow."

Two columns had formed, fifty men and fifty women; everyone else from the train had got into the trucks with the red crosses. The convoy moved off, skidding over the snow, sending up violent flurries of slush. From the back of the last truck the little girls waved goodbye to me; the older one fluttered her handkerchief. I smiled at them until they were out of sight.

At a barked command our column moved off, flanked by soldiers and guard dogs. We walked at a brisk rate, Clara and I arm in arm, almost cheerful. It was very cold and snowing heavily, but I had my fur coat and was comfortably shod in furlined boots.

"I wouldn't actually come here for a Christmas holiday, of course," I said jokingly. "The staff haven't quite been licked into shape yet; they're not what you'd call considerate."

Clara wasn't willing to follow in this vein; she was worried. "Those men at the station!"

"They must have been prisoners."

"Convicts, more like. Dead ones, at that."

"Don't worry, it's nothing to do with us," I said reassuringly. "You saw the red crosses on the trucks."

THESE I DO REMEMBER

"It's odd, you can't see the sky; it's as if there's a sort of great screen of smoke between us and it. Look at the horizon. It's red — you can see the flames."

"There must be factories; that's where we'll be working."

A soldier was walking next to Clara. He had a totally unremarkable face, something between animal and mineral. Suddenly he addressed her in French, in a voice as devoid of expression as he was himself: "I'll get you some coffee if you'll let me make love to you."

Coffee? Either a woman wasn't worth much around here or else coffee was priceless. She said nothing and he let it drop.

"Are we going to a work camp?"

He observed me at length with his small pale eyes. "Don't worry, you'll be all right."

I was hardly convinced.

After half an hour's walk, we arrived at Birkenau, the extermination camp of the Auschwitz prison complex. A sort of porch led into a brick building, briefly lit by the searchlights on the watchtowers which burst through the darkness sporadically to scour the roadways of the camp. They caught on the barbed wire, scanning the night in a dreadful, disquieting dance. Above the main entrance was a sign: "Work Camp." It was almost reassuring.

On a cold January 23, 1944, the two young women walked arm in arm into the "work camp." They were herded into what seemed to be a big amphitheater in the gloomy night and were stripped there of all their belongings: The fur coats went first, then the boots, the handbags, the jewelry, then all the clothing until they stood naked. Their hair was shaven off. Fania's thick, shiny plaits suddenly laid there at her feet. The crowding women pushed her along, made her step over the mass of coiling hair that had so suddenly ac-

172

cumulated on the floor. They were tattooed next: 74862 was pressed indelibly onto Fania's forearm. Someone handed her a pair of men's boots and a striped prison garment with the yellow Star of David sewn onto it, and she was ordered into line and, right alongside Clara, was marched to bunker twenty-five. The mean-looking woman who was giving orders and rushing them on was called *kapo* which stood, as Fania soon learned, for Jewish camp police. As Fania struggled to keep pace in her large men's boots, she dared to ask the *kapo* what had become of the other people from her transport, the ones who rode into camp on those red cross trucks? The *kapo* pointed to tall chimneys fifty yards away: "They are going up in smoke over there," she said laconically. Fania did not understand. And she did not understand either when someone in the marching column whispered to her that bunker twenty-five was the quarantine block. Soon enough she understood that prisoners went from quarantine to the gas chambers and from there their bodies were taken to the crematoria with the tall chimneys.

It was dark inside the hut into which the *kapo* pushed Fania and Clara, dark and incredibly smelly in bunker twenty-five. Fania barely made out three-tiered bunks all along the bare walls. After her eyes had adjusted, she saw hundreds of pathetic women lying on straw on those bunks. Lifeless eyes stared at her. She was horrified. The stench nearly made her faint. Someone came toward her and Clara and assigned them adjoining bunks. The *kapo* had disappeared, and now this new woman seemed to take over. She was called *blokowa* and was the Jewish inmate in charge of bunker twenty-five.

Fania was panic stricken. How could she lie on those filthy straw things? How long would it be before she, too, would stare with unseeing eyes, waiting for death? She resolved in her heart to do anything to get out of this place alive.

Suddenly the door opened and a husky woman bellowed into the darkness: "Madame Butterfly! Madame Butterfly!" Fania's mind reeled. Was someone looking for an opera singer in this place? Clara grabbed her arm and whispered: "It's a hoax!" but Fania, without thinking, jumped from her bunk and placed herself before the large woman. The big woman stopped shouting and, looking down on Fania, motioned her to follow.

The woman led Fania to another section of the camp called Camp B and stopped before a bunker which looked very much like the one Fania had just left. But when her guide opened the door and shoved her inside, Fania gasped: This bunker was bright and clean, smelling of warmth and of normal people. Single beds lined the walls along with a music stand, a piano and instruments. Warmth came from a stove, and young women sat arount it on chairs, looking alive, talking, laughing, and they were dressed in clothes, not in prison garb. Was she dreaming?

A regal looking woman came toward her and asked her to sing an aria from *Madame Butterfly*. In a daze Fania walked over to the piano and began to accompany herself to "Un bel di." She sang with all her soul and wished the aria would never end. When she did come to the last note, an elegant SS woman who had entered while Fania was singing ordered her to begin again. At last Fania stopped and the SS woman, obviously pleased, said in a loud voice that Fania was "in." Fania's heart leaped. Whatever "in" meant, it must be better than going back to bunker twenty-five! Then she remembered Clara and quickly told the SS woman that she could only stay if Clara could audition as well, hoping in her heart that Clara's voice would be good. To her amazement, the SS woman gave the order to fetch Clara and accepted her on the strength of a lovely soprano. Then she demanded that they "get dressed" and marched out of the room.

Now the other inmates crowded around the two new-comers, asking questions and giving information all at once. Fania extracted from their chatter that she was now in the music block of Auschwitz-Birkenau and that she and Clara had just become members of the women's camp orchestra. The women's orchestra had been the idea of Auschwitz commandant Rudolf Hoess. The first conductor had been a Polish prisoner, Tchaikowska, who claimed descendence from the great composer. The first orchestra had consisted of a few random players whose function it was to play marching music every morning and evening, accompanying the *Arbeitskommandos*, the endless columns of thin women, out of the camp to forced labor and back at day's end to their sorry quarters. The orchestra had been located in Camp A in Auschwitz then, but the idea had so intrigued the leader of Camp B, SS *Kommandant* Josef Kramer, that he took the orchestra under his wing and moved it to the adjacent camp complex, Birkenau. Kramer's two women lieutenants, SS Maria Mandel and SS Irma Grese, then moved the group to its present location, demoted Tchaikowska to *blockowa* and made Alma Rosé, a niece of Gustav Mahler, the new conductor. Under Kramer and Mandel, two music lovers, the group had been expanded to its present size of forty-seven women, all taken from transports from the four corners of Europe. Musicians hailed from France, Greece, Holland, Belgium, Poland, Russia and Germany. Some were Jewish, many were not. The Jewish members had their hair shaved and wore the Star of David while the others were allowed to keep their hair and wore their respective identifying patches.

One of the group had seen Fania on arrival and had recognized her from a singing engagement in Paris; Alma Rosé had auditioned her and SS woman Mandel had accepted her and Clara into the women's orchestra.

Fania listened attentively. She asked what the orchestra's function was now, and she learned that it was expected to play at any time in addition to the morning and evening routine: for the inmates in the camp square or in any location the SS directed; for the SS at any time and place at their command. And the SS demanded not just marches, but real concerts. A poor performance, a false note, could send one player or the whole group to its death.

And what, Fania asked, was the composition of the orchestra? A combination of ten violins, a flute, reed pipes, two accordions, three guitars, five mandolins, a drum and some cymbals. How did they get musical scores for such a strange combination? That, her new comrades told her, was the big problem. Alma improvised as best she could. Fania said then that she could orchestrate and everyone, even the regal Alma, jubilated. Alma handed her the score of Suppé's *Lustspiel*, paper and pencils, and asked her to adapt it to the orchestra. Suppé was the Germans' favorite composer, and a concert of his music might win the group their jailors' pleasure.

Throughout the long winter of 1944, Fania sat in the music camp working at her peculiar task. Every day Alma rehearsed the group with Fania's adapted scores, and day and night the women played for their skeletal, apathetic fellow inmates. On Sundays when the SS demanded music, the orchestra played in the Sauna, a huge, cold, concrete sorting center at the far end of Camp B, near the open pits where the corpses burned. In this most hellish of all places on earth, before a grotesque audience of well-groomed SS and half dead prisoners, this absurd camp orchestra played Fania's versions of Strauss and Léhar waltzes, Schubert

176

Lieder and Beethoven symphonies. Evenings, after "selection" and gassing was completed for the day, the SS would charge into the music block to be entertained: Schumann's "Reverie" for Kramer, "The Charge of the Light Brigade" for Dr. Mengele and for Frau Mandel an aria from *Madame Butterfly*. Fania loathed her absurd existence.

From her work table in the music block, Fania could see the incoming transport, for the rails had been extended right into camp. The newly arriving victims no longer had to walk the half-hour from the Auschwitz station, nor were they transported any longer in those deceptive red cross trucks. As they disembarked from their cattle cars some fifty yards from Fania's window, they could hear the orchestra practicing. Fania saw some of them lift their heads to listen, saw surprise and hope in some eyes. Unhappy people! In another minute they would go through their first "selection," passing before camp physician Dr. Mengele who, with a wave of his riding crop, will decide who shall live and who shall die. Fania yearned to run out to them and to scream the truth of Birkenau into their faces. But who would dare to be on the camp roads during *Blocksperre*.

There were two kinds of *Blocksperre* in Auschwitz-Birkenau, both having the same objective: During incoming transports no one was allowed outside her bunker so that the victims could be moved to their death in orderly fashion; then there was the block curfew for "camp selection." That curfew was announced with a shrill whistle and every inmate, her heart frozen in her breast, ran to her bunker, standing at attention. SS drove through the camp, burst into barracks, selected hundreds of victims for the ovens.

No budding trees announced the coming of summer; only oppressive heat gave evidence of the change of season. The black smoke from the crematoria hung over the camp;

the stench of burning flesh permeated Fania's nostrils. It was summer in Auschwitz-Birkenau. Sometime during that summer, the SS commanded Alma to prepare a special concert for a high ranking SS visitor. The orchestra practiced intensely. The camp roads were being filled with gravel to keep the visitor from sinking into the Auschwitz mud. Who was expected in this place of death?

Heinrich Himmler, second in command to Hitler himself, the man in charge of Germany's "solution to the Jewish question," architect of this camp was expected. Himmler, coming to inspect his work! And the orchestra was to play for him! As Fania stood before the benign-looking monster, she vowed again to outlive her tormentors so that she could tell the world of the infamy that was Auschwitz.

On November 2, 1944, on a cold, wet evening, Fania, Clara and some of their friends went to the Sauna at the end of the camp to take a shower. Fania was suddenly aware of how thin the formerly chubby Clara had become; Clara remarked that Fania's hair had grown back — snow white. On the way back to their barracks, wet towels on their heads and shivering in their rags, they were stopped by SS men who were snug in their warm uniforms, guns drawn. The women were marched to the railroad platform near their barracks and pressed into waiting boxcars. Overhead planes seemed to be flying in the dark sky; bombs exploded in the distance.

Two days later, still standing up crushed together in that wet train, without having had anything to eat or drink or a chance to relieve themselves, they were ordered out. They were in a forest. Those who could walk stumbled for two hours in the freezing rain until they came to a desolate place, their "new camp." Fania looked around. She saw nothing; no camp, no barracks, not even the SS. Only some

Wehrmacht soldiers were standing around. One of them gave Fania and her group a tarpaulin tent and told the women to use it as their shelter. He said that they were now in Bergen-Belsen. Nine improbable hours later, after the tent finally stood, they crawled into it, exhausted and hungry. When they woke up in the morning, they realized that only eleven members of the music group were there. Frightened, they vowed to cling together.

They got wooden planks and had to build their own barracks. They labored day and night until something with a roof was finished. After a while "their" SS showed up: Kramer, Grese but not Mengele; here at Bergen-Belsen death made his own "selection." Typhus, hunger, cold killed the inmates. Those who could still walk were marched to work, barefoot, either to dig ditches in the forest or do heavy labor in a nearby factory. Overburdened, without food or sanitation, they slowly became animals. And the winter dragged on. Christmas, the first since Drancy, they celebrated with a turnip that someone had stolen from a passing truck.

By April Fania too had typhus. She laid semi-conscious in her excrement, her head a mass of pain. She heard faraway voices. Was she dead already? The voices persisted:

> *"Stirb nicht!"* don't die.
>
> The German voice made no sense; it had no power to pull me out of the black gulf into which I was sinking more deeply every second. For days now I had no longer possessed the strength to keep my eyes open. I wasn't sure whether it was my urine or the fever which alternately warmed and chilled me. Typhus was emptying me of life. I was going to die.
>
> My head felt terrible. The girls' wailing and sobbing and groaning shattered into needly-sharp fragments, little scraps of broken mirror which sank razorlike into my brain. I

ordered my hand to pull them out, but my hand was a skeleton's claw that didn't obey. The bones must have broken through the skin. Or had the hand actually come off? Impossible. I must keep my hands to play the piano. Play the piano. . . those knuckle-bones at the end of my arm might just manage *Danse Macabre*. The idea actually made me laugh. I was horribly thirsty. The SS had cut off water. It was days since we'd had anything to eat, but longer since I'd been hungry. I had become weightless. I was floating on a cloud, I was devoured by quicksand. . . no, flying in cotton wool. Odd. . . .

A trick I'd found to cool myself was to wash in my urine. Keeping myself clean was essential to me, and there is nothing unclean about urine. I could drink it if I was thirsty — and I had done so.

I didn't know the time but I did know the date — the girls kept track of that. It was April 15. What did that matter? It was just a day like any other. But where was I exactly? I wasn't at Birkenau anymore. There, there were 47 of us, the "orchestra girls." Here in this windowless shed, there were a thousand of us — burgeoning corpses. What a stench. Now I remembered. Bergen-Belsen. We had arrived here on November 3, 1944.

My head was in such chaos that I was no longer sure whether it was day or night. I gave up, it was too painful. . .I foundered.

Above me, over my face, I felt a breath of air, a vague smell, a delicious scent. A voice cut through the layers of fog, stilled the buzzing in my ears. "*Meine kleine Sangerin.*"

"Little singer," that was what the SS called me.

"*Stirb nicht.*"

That was an order, and a hard one to obey. Anyhow, I was past caring. I opened my eyes a fraction and saw Aufseherin Irma Grese, the SS warden known as *Engel*, the Angel, because of her looks. The glorious fair plaits, which surrounded her head like a halo, her blue eyes and dazzling complexion were floating in a fog. She shook me.

"*Stirb nicht! Deine englischen Freunde sind da!*"

Could it possibly be? The valkyrie had an amused glint in her eyes as though the whole thing were a mild joke. I closed my eyes again; she was a wearying creature.

"What did she say?" asked Anny and Big Irene.

I repeated the German sentence. Irritated, they insisted: "Tell us in French, translate it."

"I forget...."

"But you just said it in German."

More exhausting people; I retired from the fray, defeated.

"Come on." They were pleading. "Don't die."

That triggered it off; I repeated automatically: "Don't die. Your friends the English are here."

They were disappointed.

"Is that all?" muttered Little Irene.

Florette joined in. "The usual rubbish! We've had that with the Russians, the English, the Yanks. They fed us that dozens of times in Auschwitz."

I heard Big Irene's calm voice: "What if it's true?"

Anny spoke dreamily: "If only one could believe it and it could all end, now, just like that...."

I wafted off and most of Florette's colourful rejoinder was lost on me. God, how hot I was. My tongue was a hunk of cardboard. I felt myself drifting. Then familiar voices reached me, as if from the end of a tunnel: "Look, Irene, you can see there's no hope. She's stopped breathing, there's no mist on my bit of glass. This really works, they even do it in hospitals."

"Try again, you never know."

I wondered who was under discussion. Me? How infuriating they were. Admittedly, I had a pretty bad case of typhus, but I hadn't yet given up the ghost. I had to know the end of the story. I would bear witness.

Outside, superficially, all seemed normal but, if one concentrated closely, one could hear new sounds: running and calling. I was completely baffled. My head was swelling until it seemed to fill the whole barracks, to hold all the din within it like a reservoir. I had no more thoughts, I was sinking into the noise, it absorbed me and digested me. I was an echo chamber. I dreamed of silence.

No, I wasn't dreaming; the silence was real. The machine guns had stopped. It was like a great calm lake, and I let myself drift upon the waters.

I must have fallen asleep again; suddenly, behind me, I heard the familiar sound of the door opening. From the remotest distance a man was speaking. What was he saying? No one was answering him. That was odd. What was going on? Strange words reached my ears — it was a language I knew. It was *English*!

Tumult all around, women clambering down from the cojas. It couldn't be true, I must be delirious.

The girls, those girls of whom I'd grown so fond, threw themselves at me, shaking me.

"Fania, wake up! Do you hear, the English are here. You must speak to them."

An arm slipped under my shoulder and lifted me up: "Say something."

I was only too eager, but how could I with that leather spatula in my mouth? I opened my eyes and saw dim figures through a fog. Then suddenly one came into focus: He was kneeling down and thumping his fist on his chest, rocking to and fro repeating: "My God, my God!" He was like a Jew at the Wailing Wall. He had blue eyes but it wasn't a German blue. He took off his cap, revealing enchanting read hair. His face was dusted with freckles and big childlike tears rolled down his cheeks. It was both awful and funny. "Can you hear me?"

I murmured, "Yes."

The girls shrieked, "It's all right! She heard, she answered!"

Madness was unleashed around me. They were dancing, lifting their thin legs as high as they could. Some threw themselves down and kissed the ground, rolling in the filth, laughing and crying. Some were vomiting; the scene was incredible, a mixture of heaven and hell.

There was a flurry of questions: "Where have they come from?" "How did they get this far, to this hellhole?" "Did they know we were here? Ask him."

"We found you quite by luck," he answered. "We didn't know there was a concentration camp here. Coming out of Hanover, we chased the Germans through these woods and we saw some SS coming towards us with a white flag."

"Did you slaughter them?" someone chipped in.

He looked uncomprehending. I translated.

"I don't know, I'm just one of the soldiers."

Around us, the girls were clamouring. "You must kill them, you must kill them all. All." I was upset by this outburst of hatred, deeply though I felt it; I too wanted to shout, and tried to sit up, but flopped back, too weak. For the first time now I felt myself slipping. Everything became a haze. Yet I smiled, or at least I think I did. I would have been liberated after all. I let myself drift.

Irene noticed, and shouted: "No, no, not her, it's too unfair."

The "unfair" struck me as wonderfully comical.

"Sing, Fania, sing!" someone shrieked. The order galvanized me; I opened my mouth desperately. The soldier thought I was at my last gasp; he lifted me out of my filth, took me in his arms, showing no sign of disgust. How comfortable it was, how light I must feel (I weighed sixty-two pounds). Held firmly, head against his chest, drawing my strength from his, I started on the first verse of the *Marseillaise*. My voice had not died; I was alive.

The fellow staggered. Carrying me in his arms, he rushed towards an officer, shouting, "She's singing, she's singing."

The air hit me like a slap. I choked and was reborn. The girls ran out behind us. Technically no doubt I still had typhus, but the moment I found the strength to sing, I felt I'd recovered. The mists cleared; once more I could look around me and see what was happening. And it was well worth observing: Soldiers were arresting the SS and lining them up against the walls. We had savoured the thought of this moment so often and with such passion, and now it was a reality. Deportees were emerging from every shed. The men from whom we'd been separated for so long were coming towards us, desperately seeking out relatives and acquaintances.

Then I was in clean surroundings, in the SS block. I was bathing in a marvelous sea of khaki, and it smelled so good; their very sweat smelled sweet.

We had been liberated by the infantry, and now the motorized units were arriving. Through the window I saw the first jeep enter the camp. An officer jumped out, a Dutchman. He looked around dazedly and then began to run like a madman, arms outstretched, calling "Margrett, Margrett!" A woman staggered towards him, her striped tatters floating like rags tied to a pole — his wife, three-quarters dead, in a frightening state of filth and decay; and he hugged her, hugged to him the smiling, living wraith.

Someone handed me a microphone.

It was strange. The process of breathing exhausted me, my heart was positively economizing on its beats, life had become a remote possibility, yet I straightened up, galvanized by joy, and I sang the *Marseillaise* again. This time it emerged with a violence and a strength I had never had before and which I shall probably never have again.

Clearly moved, a Belgian officer sank his hand into his pocket and handed me the most marvelous present: an old lipstick. I couldn't imagine anything lovelier, three-quarters used as it was and despite its uncertain pedigree.

The microphone holder insisted: "Please, miss, it's for the BBC."

I sang: "God Save the King," and tears filled the British soldiers' eyes.

I sang the *Internationale* and the Russian deportees joined in.

I sang, and in front of me, around me, from all corners of the camp, creeping along the sides of the shacks, dying shadows and skeletons stirred, rose up, grew taller. A great "Hurrah" burst forth and swept along like a breaker, carrying all before it. They had become men and women once again.

PART V
Eastern Europe

SEVEN

The Balkan Countries

After France was defeated and divided, only two great powers were left in Europe who frustrated Hitler: Great Britain and Russia. He believed that he could conquer both of them and then be master of all of Europe. He expected to rule the new Thousand Year Reich from the Reich's Chancellory in Berlin and impose a "New Order" on Europe: Aryans would be the master race. Some Slavs and Serbs would be kept alive to do slave labor, but most Slavs, Serbs and all Jews and Gypsies would be killed, either directly or by planned starvation.

Hitler's immediate plan was to be in London by August 15, 1940, and to crush Russia before the winter set in. The English plan was coded "Operation Sea Lion" and the plan to break the mighty Soviet Union, "Barbarossa." Hitler initiated "Sea Lion" by trying to intimidate the British with predictions of their doom in his speeches which, he knew, were heard in London. But the newly appointed Prime Minister, Sir Winston Churchill, declared on London radio for all the world to hear: "We have become the sole champions now in arms to defend the world cause. . . We shall fight on unconquerable until the curse of Hitler is lifted from the brows of mankind.''

Hitler embarked on a program of ferocious air attacks, first on the British Navy and the Royal Air Force. Then, after the RAF had made a strategic air raid on Berlin in September, 1940, Hitler turned from the British war machinery and mercilessly bombed British cities, primarily London. But he received no sign of submission. On the contrary, the *Luftwaffe* met a skilled and fearless opponent in the Royal Air Force and was up against the RAF's new invention, radar. Hitler continued the air war and added a naval blockade to starve the British and to weaken their spirit, but his attention was beginning to turn to ''Barbarossa.''

He planned the campaign against Russia for the spring of 1941, thinking that he could defeat Russia in three summer months. Once Stalin was subjugated, he believed Churchill would beg for mercy. For the time being, however, the RAF penetrated German air defenses and bombed Berlin all through the fall and winter of 1940 in ''cowardly attacks on women and children and the defenseless aged of the Reich.''

Now for the first time, maneuvers other than his own dictated Hitler's next move. His friend and ally, the Italian *Duce* Mussolini, sent his armies into Greece in October 1940, hoping to conquer Greece and her islands as effortlessly as he had conquered Albania in the Balkans a year earlier. But the Greeks resisted and got the British to help them entrap Mussolini's troops in the mountains of Attica. Hitler's attention turned from ''Barbarossa'' toward Greece: He resolved to help his friend and drive the British out of Mainland Europe at the same time. The German strength was ordered toward the Balkans.

Quickly, Hitler arranged for a few peace treaties with Balkan countries: he invited Rumania, Bulgaria and Yugoslavia to join the Tripartite Pact of Germany, Italy and Japan. Rumania and Bulgaria joined the Pact, hoping that cooperation would protect them from German aggression. Bulgaria even lent troops to Germany to fight against Greece; she was later rewarded for her assistance with a part of Yugoslavia.

Yugoslavia, the largest of the five Balkan countries, stretched for a hundred thousand square miles from Austria to the Greek borders, from the Hungarian Plains to Rumania in lovely passages of highlands and mountains. The country was a patchwork of six historic nations: Slovenia, Croatia, Bosnia and Hercogovinia, Montenegro, Macedonia and Serbia. The country, rich in grain and tobacco, had great deposits of lead and oil and was growing industrially at a fast pace. Her fourteen million people were a mix of Serb and Macedonian Orthodox, Roman Catholics, Moslems, and about seventy-five thousand Jews. Belgrade and Zagreb had the largest, most prosperous Jewish population.

Initially, Yugoslavia had stayed out of the Tripartite Pact but finally joined in March 1941. Such initial independence angered Hitler and when a coup d'état brought a Yugoslavian government, which the Soviet Union recognized, to power, Hitler resolved to ''ground Yugoslavia under quickly and unmercifully'' on his way to Greece.

In the early morning hours of April 6, 1941, German war power attacked Yugoslavia by ground and air. After ten days of fierce fighting, the Yugoslav cabinet realized that their country would have to surrender and their king, King Peter, to flee. King and cabinet took refuge first in Palestine, then in England. With Belgrade bombed to ruins, Yugoslavia capitulated on April 17. The country was carved up and divided between Germany, Italy and Bulgaria. Secret national resistance groups formed immediately under Colonels Mihailovic and Tito.

The Jews of Yugoslavia were hunted at once. More than sixty-thousand were caught and killed in Nazi concentration camps; others escaped to Italy and to neighboring Bulgaria for a short-lived safety.

Located in the eastern part of the Balkans on the Black Sea and south of the Danube Basin, Bulgaria bordered Yugoslavia on Rumania, Greece and the European territory of Turkey. This country was much smaller than the other Balkan countries, but it was the most industrious and one of the richest in coal and iron deposits. Much of its forty-three thousand square miles was fertile farm land. Its six million people were Eastern Orthodox Catholics, Moslems and Jews. King Boris III of Bulgaria was married to a daughter of King Victor Emmanuel of Italy and had been a Germano-Italian sympathizer since the 1930's. In December 1941 Bulgaria entered the war on the side of the Germans: King Boris III and his cabinet declared war on England and the United States, but, paradoxically, not on Russia. Equally paradoxical were Bulgaria's actions as far as her Jewish citizens were concerned.

Bulgaria had a long history of sheltering persecuted Jews in Europe. In the fifteenth century, when Jews were fleeing from the Spanish Inquisition, Bulgaria offered them asylum. The country can always point with pride to the fact that it was Bulgaria who granted temporary refuge to the great Kabbalist Joseph Caro. There was little anti-Semitism in the country all through the centuries. When Hitler requested anti-Jewish measures to be implemented in Bulgaria and her newly acquired lands, King Boris found himself caught between his own sympathies toward the Third Reich and his country's refusal to hand over the ancient and respected Jewish community of fifty thousand souls for Hitler's "final solution." The Jews did encounter social and economic deprivation, but every time a mass transport was supposed to take place, pressure was brought upon the king to call it off. Thus the Jews of Bulgaria were not mass deported and extinguished. But King Boris' refusal to sacrifice the Jews did not extend beyond Bulgaria proper. The Jewish population of Bulgaria-dominated Thrace and Macedonia was wiped out.

Boris, who had saved the Jews of his country in spite of the fact that he was under Hitler's domination, died suddenly in August 1943, apparently from a heart attack. The government was reorganized after his death and was less pro-German under the new leadership. In 1944 Bulgaria's new government announced its desire for peace with the Allies. On September 4, 1944, Soviet troops entered Sofia; German dominance over Bulgaria had ended.

Rumania, the easternmost of the Balkan Five and the second largest of the countries, bordered on the Soviet Union and Hungary, on Bulgaria and Yugoslavia, and had access to the Black Sea. Country of Carpathian Mountains and Danube valleys, Rumania, too, was productive in agriculture and rich in gas, oil and coal deposits. Her sixteen million people were a mix of Germans, Hungarians, Serbs, Croats, Jews and Gypsies. The Rumanians, or Romanians as they like to call themselves, trace their origin back to a settlement of Roman legionnaires in the first century; later the region became a province of the Roman Empire and over the years expanded to include Transylvania, Bessarabia and Bukovina. To the present, the country considers herself a Latin island and is proud of her Latin-based language.

Like her neighbors, Rumania feared for her independence. In June 1940 Russia claimed Bessarabia and Bukovina; later that year, Germany took away Transylvania and gave it to Hungary; to avoid further decimation, Rumania's King Carol appointed a pro-German cabinet and abdicated. His son, King Michael, formed a new government under General Ion Antonescu, who joined Rumania to the Tripartite Pact in November 1940. German troops immediately occupied Rumania "for the protection of the country's oil fields."

General Antonescu brought Rumania into the war on the side of Germany. His army fought side by side with the *Wehrmacht* at Stalingrad, even when German fortune turned in February 1943 and Soviet forces pushed the enemy back to the gates of Bucharest. The Rumanians switched sides and overthrew Antonescu just as the Red Army started to liberate Rumania from German "protection" in August 1944.

Liberation came too late for two hundred seventy thousand Jews whom the Germans, with help from the Rumanian populace, hanged, burned and shot. The whole Jewish community was devastated. In one three-day orgy that began on October 23, 1941, twenty-seven thousand Jewish people died. Twenty-seven thousand men, women and children were machine-gunned in just three days.

Nestling between Yugoslavia, Greece and the Adriatic Sea, Albania had been invaded by Mussolini in 1939. The tiny Balkan state served the Italians as a base for their invasion of Greece in 1940. Hitler, too, used Albania, despoiling the country and harassing the Albanian Moslem peasant population. From there he invaded Greece.

Storied Greece, the Mediterranean member of the five Balkan states, with her mystic islands in the Aegean and Ionian Sea, land of bright villages, of ancient marble ruins; industrious Greece, with her fishermen and vintagers, fought off the Italian invasion with British help. Greece and Great Britain were the only countries in Europe in 1940 who dared to oppose the powerful German-Italian axis. Together they had been able to cope with one of the powers, but they could not hold off both of them.

The Germans, replete with victories in Yugoslavia and Albania, charged Greece full force on April 10, 1941 — very early in the morning, as was their method. The Greek's Macedonian front collapsed within days, and the Greek Second Army surrendered. Under the onslaught of German panzers and the assault of the Stukas, the British withdrew their troops from Greece by April 17, from the islands by April 30. The Germans, meanwhile, had penetrated to the Isthmus of Corinth by means of parachuted troops. In the east they had captured Salonika on the Aegean Sea and had begun to occupy the islands off the coast of Turkey. Hitler had hoped to induce Turkey to join the axis and had intended to offer the islands to Turkey as security against Italy.

On April 27 the triumphant Germans drove through deserted streets in Athens and arrogantly hoisted their swastika over the Acropolis. Proud Greece was forced to surrender, and a German rule set in that lasted for three harsh years. The misfortunes of the Greeks under German oppression reached a state of national disaster. Three occupying armies encamped: the German, the Italian and the Bulgarian troops all demanding to be housed and fed at the Greeks' expense. Before long the Greeks starved. In Athens people fainted in the streets from lack of food; many died, leaning against the corner of a building, simply too weak to go on. There was no fuel in the city either, no warm clothing, no leather for shoes. Children cried in schoolrooms from the bitter cold; people used paper wrappings to protect their hands and feet. The young and healthy were sent to Germany to labor; the Jews were deported and gassed. But the conquerers lived in comfort.

King George and his government had fled Athens and

had set up an exile government in London, supporting and financing Greek resistance organizations. Determined as these patriots were, they could not stem the destruction. More than a thousand villages were totally leveled; the peasants killed or displaced; an estimated half million Greeks died from cold, hunger and bombing. Whole Jewish communities were shipped to Auschwitz and burned to death on arrival. Proud and innocent people, they walked into the gas chambers still wearing their colorful native costumes, never comprehending the German barking.

On May 20, 1941, German troops parachuted onto the island of Crete. For the first time in the history of warfare, a full fighting force was air-dropped onto the scene of action, men and machinery, ready to do battle. The British inflicted over six thousand German casualties and fled; the Cretes were shocked into confusion. Ten days after the troops had landed, Crete surrendered to Hitler's force.

EIGHT
War With Russia

In the eighth year of his rule and at the zenith of his power, right after his successes in the Balkans, Hitler gave orders to attack Russia and to lay waste to her land and cities. On June 22, 1941, in the third year of the war, the German host converged on Russia.

The behemoth that is Russia encompasses nearly nine million square miles of territory that changes from frozen tundra in the north to citrus-growing valleys in the south. The enormous country stretches from the Baltic Sea to the Bering Straits and from the Arctic Ocean to the Pamir Mountains at Afghanistan. Russia's huge population of one hundred seventy million Caucasians, Armenians and Mongols had been united since 1917 into the Union of Soviet Socialist Republics, the Soviet Union, and were, by 1940, fully governed by totalitarian rule. Since 1927 Joseph Stalin had shaped the country into a huge concentration camp by means of forced labor for his country's surging industrialization and by collectivizing her farms and agriculture. Atheism became the official policy of the state, but many communists remained members of the Russian Orthodox Church, and there were many Jews,

Moslems and Buddhists in the vast country. Hitler wanted and needed Russia's iron and coal, her fur and timber. He did not want her cities nor her people. He gave orders to level the former and to starve the latter: he coveted the land as *Lebensraum* for his future German State.

His war plan called for intense action by all three army groups at once: Army Group South under General Rundstedt was to drive toward Kiev from the Polish Pripet Marshes; Army Group Center under Bock was ordered toward Moscow with full use of panzer groups under Guderian and Kleist coming in from Warsaw; Army Group North under Leeb was to advance on Leningrad by way of the Baltic Plains.

Early advances were followed by severe defeats as the winter set in, but from Army headquarters in Berlin, Hitler demanded that Russian positions be held at all cost. The generals chafed under Hitler's battle orders and were blamed for reverses. One by one they were replaced. The new military leaders understood that they could not change or modify the *Fuehrer's* strategies.

The war in Russia lasted for three years. Fighting with the Germans were two Rumanian armies and a division of Ukranian soldiers; fighting with the Russians were the savage Mongols. The Germans were hindered by relentless partisan action in the Ukraine and Belorussia; the Russians were helped by the harsh winters in the Steppe. What gains the Germans made in their spring-and-summer offensives were lost in winter battles; what lands they occupied were at long last taken back. By the beginning of 1945, the Russians were driving the Germans back over their own borders and pursuing them toward Berlin.

Lithuania, the small state wedged between Poland and Russia, neighbor of Latvia and the Memel Region on the Baltic Sea, had been under Russian occupation since 1940.

In 1941, on his way toward the Soviet Union, Hitler invaded the tiny country which lay directly in his path to Moscow and to Leningrad. German troops swept the Red Army out and settled into Lithuania for four long years. Ruthless damage was done to cities and countryside; Lithuanians were terribly abused, whether they were Jews or not. Countless men, some with their families, others alone, were sent to German labor camps; those who survived the ordeal never forgot it.

A Child's Vision of Hell: Alain's Story

In the cosmopolitan city of Kaunas in the center of Lithuania, the Stanké family owned and operated the city's official radio station. The family lived on a large estate in one of the suburbs: There was father, a handsome, bearded man born in France; mother, of White Russian ancestry; Aunt Lyudunia; the two boys: Lyudas, called Lus, age ten; Aloyzas, called Alys, age six. The Stanké's were pious Catholics.

In June 1940 the Russians occupied Lithuania, and the advancing soldiers shot first and asked questions later. Most Lithuanians stayed at home with fear and resentment against the Russian occupation in their hearts. But one day that summer Aunt Lyudunia took the boys out for a drive in the radio station's chauffeur-driven limousine. Surely no one would harm a lady with two small boys. And the chauffeur wouldn't permit them to get into a dangerous situation anyway.

Auntie had underestimated the Russians: The car was stopped, all four occupants ordered out and lead toward a gully. The soldiers at their back clicked their rifles, and Alys heard Aunt Lyudunia murmur a prayer when someone shouted a Russian command to stop: The car's official license plates had saved them. They were taken hostage and driven home with the ultimatum that the radio station was to be handed over intact in exchange for the two boys.

Within days the whole Red Army seemed to set up camp on the Stanké estate. Tents mushroomed on the lawns around the house; the soldiers camped on the tennis courts, stomped through the fruit and vegetable gardens and ravaged every room in the house. Alys could see them stealing silver and wrecking his toy train. Why didn't his father stop them? Why didn't anybody lash out at them when they shot his dog? And why did he and his whole family have to remain inside the house all day in spite of fine weather?

Alys yearned to sneak out to meet his friend Lazarius at the fence. Lazys was a Jewish boy, also six years old, but always full of information that was new and exciting to Alys. At secret moments at the fence, Alys learned that the soldiers on his lawn were Bolsheviks, heard about Siberia and why Lithuanians were being sent there in those box cars that he had seen at the railroad station. Alys knew the difference between the weapons and machinery the soldiers were using and all kinds of other news. But neither boy could understand why their parents were so afraid of these Bolsheviks. They seemed quite approachable to Alys as long as he ran their errands and brought them sausages and butter.

A few days after the boys' conversation, the soldiers allowed the Stanké family outside their grounds, but mother warned her sons sternly not to go into town alone. For a while, Alys played with Lazys around the estate, but one day Lazys suggested an excursion to Vytauto Park, and Alys ran with his friend into town. As they neared the park, they could hear a pack of horses approaching from the far side of the street and could hear the wild shouts of the riders. They hurried toward the park entrance and reached it at the same time the advancing riders did. Terrified, they hid behind a tree.

The horde stampeded past them, filling the wide street, trampling to death men and women in their path. Wild-eyed, foaming horses stomped so closely by the tree that Alys and Lazys could see the short, dark-skinned men who rode them, could see their slit eyes, hear their sabres clanging and smell the sharp odor of men and horses. Terrified, the boys clung to each other. "Mongols!" whispered a man near them. It was late before they dared to leave the safety of the tree and run home.

The vision of the Mongols followed Alys into his dreams. He became pale and fearful. It did not help much that mother assured him that the Mongols were only a small part of the Red Army; they stayed in the region disrupting Alys' days and nights, doing unspeakable violence. Once he saw two of these monsters drag a naked woman between their horses, leaving a trail of blood on the quiet street. The soldiers camping in his garden seemed almost like friends compared to these demons.

As the fine weather changed to cool days and cold nights, the soldiers made plans to move into the house. They gave the Stanké family notice to vacate in six hours. Six hours to find another place, pack and move! Depressed and angry, father went into town to look for quarters while mother and Aunt Lyudunia bagan to pack boxes and bags with their necessities. All their handsome furniture, the silver and the paintings, all the boys' books and toys had to be left behind.

In feverish haste they loaded their boxes and bundles onto a rickety horse-drawn wagon. When father returned from town with news that he had found a place for them at 3 Minties Ratas, they said good-by to the servants and walked behind the wagon into town. They were together. This was reason enough to be grateful and optimistic.

The war dragged on. The people in the cities were cold and hungry; the Stanké's, too, had changed. Mother became thinner and grayer, father more brooding, Lyudas quieter. But it was Alys about whom mother worried most. He had become so pale and thin that she decided to send him to Aunt Vale, her sister, who lived in the country at Pazailis. Too weak to protest, Alys was packed off to the country estate and for a short while lived the carefree life of a seven-year-old boy. He picked berries, went for walks with Mr. Petras, the caretaker, and listened for hours to Mr. Petras' singing and storytelling. Mr. Petras told him the proud history of their country and about the brave men who now risked their lives to free it from the Russians. He called them partisans, and he knew many of them by their first names. They were his friends, and they were doing dangerous work. Alys was proud that his new friend told him about the partisans. He knew instinctively that he must keep his knowledge about them to himself. On their hikes through the forest, Mr. Petras left parcels for his friends under certain trees and explained to Alys that the partisans came under cover of night to pick up the extra food and the letters from their wives.

One day Mr. Petras did not go the regular route through the woods, but turned toward an old cemetery outside of

Pazailis: He said he had seen tire marks around the area and wanted to investigate what was going on there. If there were Russians in the area, he needed to warn his friends.

It was a long hike to the cemetery. They sang and talked all the way, keeping a sharp look-out at the same time. Finally they entered the cemetery.

> Mr. Petras scans the horizon for Russian soldiers. Not a soul. He takes my hand and we enter the dismal place, almost on tiptoe, as if it were out of bounds.
>
> "Look, tire marks. . . ." His voice is shaky as he spots the trail and points it out with his finger. We follow the tracks carefully to the bottom of the cemetery where there's a clearing like a flower-bed. The tire marks are intertwined. The flowers are crushed. Mr. Petras starts searching. I'm looking at the same time, but I don't know what for. He bends over the tiniest objects, raises his eyes to the tall trees which border the graveyard, but he sees nothing. The place is quite sombre and dusk is starting to fall.
>
> "What did they want here?" Mr. Petras asks aloud, still searching for an explanation. In a voice flat with fatigue he adds, "There must be a reason. . . ."
>
> Suddenly the noise of a motor makes us jump. It comes from the road. Mr. Petras strains to hear. "It's a truck."
>
> His cheeks are burning, his large nostrils quiver.
>
> "We mustn't take needless risks," he snaps. We run to a tree, he grabs me and sits me up on a branch with the agility of a monkey.
>
> "Hang on, I'm coming too!" His reflexes are good. One move, a twist, and he's beside me in the lookout.
>
> "It's a Russian truck. Coming here! We'd better hide — let's climb up."
>
> I love climbing trees but I'm not very good at it due to lack of practice. You tear your pants and they scold you, and the grownups have this way of discouraging you forever by

raising points which aren't really relevant: "It's not your pants, but what if you fell and broke a leg?" No matter what happens, fear will take over and hold you back.

And here in the cemetery with Mr. Petras fear is the dominant emotion. I must pull myself together and cope with this unknown danger. My companion pushes me, and then when he sees I'm exhausted, climbs above me and hauls me up to his level.

The green truck reaches the cemetery entrance as we near the top of the tree. We can't go higher, the branches won't hold us. The motor noise is becoming more and more irritating. I wish it would go away. We stare down, trying to figure out its route.

Bad luck! With a quick turn the heavy vehicle takes the central route through the cemetery. It's heading right for us. I'm shaking with fear and Mr. Petras' face is a mirror of despair. He signals me not to move. I cling to him, making an effort to control my breathing.

Below us the truck stops at the foot of the tree. If the branch breaks we'll make a direct hit onto its canvas roof.

Three soldiers get out. They lower the rear panel and a lot of armed soldiers jump out. Some wear a kepi with a wide brim, others a plain cap. The driver has an iron helmet.

As they climb out, two of the armed men walk to the cemetery gates where they take up their posts, to keep intruders out.

Now a man in civilian clothes gets down. He has a red armband. They surround him. Orders are shouted in Russian.

Tucked under Mr. Petras' arm, my legs stretched along a branch, I listen to the duet of our thumping hearts. We're not moving — hardly breathing.

Now we see four unshaven men in shirtsleeves, their arms tied behind their backs. The soldiers shove and kick them. The four prisoners don't protest, they walk quietly around to the front of the truck and are told to keep still.

My friend's shirt is dripping with sweat. His flesh is burning hot, and a nervous twitch starts my body shaking too. I'll never forget that incident. It can never be blotted out of my mind.

They drag one of the four men to the foot of the tree. They bind him to it, while the man with the red armband asks questions I can't catch. He shakes his head. He doesn't know or he can't. . . . He screams. The interrogator kicks him violently in the stomach, punches him in the face. There's a stream of blood from his ear down to his mouth. The blood covers his face, pours down his neck and soaks his shirt.

It's getting dark. One of the soldiers turns on the lights of the truck and the other three prisoners stand facing it, watching their comrade. He's being used as an example, or perhaps they just have to wait their turn.

Back to business. Now the poor man is moaning like a whipped cur. Another burly soldier comes up to help. He brings his rifle butt down on the man's head. The man screams with pain and fright. The beating continues; the blows rain and vibrate through the tree, filling my entire body. Bloody scraps of flesh hang from his cheeks. His face and chest are criss-crossed with scarlet tracks. His body slumps. I can't take my eyes from this terrible scene. The prisoner is silent now. By the time the awful man with the red armband takes out his long knife, the prisoner must already be dead. He rams it into his victim's body with vicious force, then jerks it upward with a single movement as if he were dissecting a rabbit. My nails bite through the skin of my clenched fists, and an indescribable sick panic envelops me. My whole body goes stiff. My heart pounds against my ribs and a bloody mist swims before my eyes. I wish I were somewhere far away. I wish I could pluck the scene from my brain and forget. I may be on the verge of falling down onto the truck. I burrow under Mr. Petras' arms and he holds me tight.

I hear shouts, footsteps, then bullets. More shouting. What's going on? Has someone shot the soldiers or did the prisoners try to break loose? I'll never know. My friend's arm holds me too tightly, no doubt to stop me seeing. He's right but it doesn't help because I'd have to be not only blind but deaf, and I can't put my hands over my ears because I need them for holding on. No matter what Mr. Petras does, he can't stop this horrible incident from pursuing me through my dreams.

There are thuds and blows, more blows, constant blows, and terrible screams which are loud or soft, like a tide. I grind my teeth. I try to stretch my back without breaking the branch. I want to fight this discomfort. We've been up here for hours, half sitting and half crouching, and it's getting painful.

One more thud, then a sudden quiet spell in which we hear whispers, vague words, steps, the sound of digging.

The blood rushes to my head again. My legs are frozen with fear. I wish I could cry, but my eyesockets are dry.

A dreadful pause.

Then a flood of petrol makes the motor belch. The panel swings back, the doors slam. The truck starts up, the wheels turn, it moves, it goes away. The sound fades and changes tone: the vehicle has reached the paved road. Then it disappears completely.

Mr. Petras lets go of my head. We stare at each other in silence. He helps me down from the tree, breathing hard as if he'd been running. Now we're on the spot where a few minutes ago...

I cling to him, "Oh sir, sir...."

He scoops me up and runs toward the road.

I don't know how we reach home. I remember Mr. Petras stopping a few times and throwing up. He has convulsive spasms. Tears pour down his cheeks, and now I can cry too. It calms me.

Mr. Petras tries to speak. He opens his mouth wide, I can

see his teeth, his tongue, and his tonsils. But not a word comes out.

"Talk, talk!" I beg him. He makes a superhuman effort, but to no avail.

This terrifies me. I beg him to try again. He gazes at me in despair. My friend has been struck dumb!

"Where were you?" asks Aunt Vale, tortured by anxiety.

She knows something terrible has happened from the way I rush into her arms. "What happened? Tell me quick!" she asks my friend.

He opens his mouth again, and his tongue quivers like a snake; he sighs deeply but can't bring out more than a long, miserable gurgle.

Emotion overwhelms Aunt Vale. She doesn't know what to say. She keeps repeating, "Mr. Petras, Mr. Petras," sorrowfully.

I am full of hatred for the monstrous trick of fate which caught us in its coils. I want to lie down and stop thinking, to hide myself in oblivion.

"Will he never talk or sing again?"

My aunt tells me to be quiet. Mr. Petras gurgles again, and, as if the sound frightens him, turns on his heel and leaves us alone with the salty taste of fear.

During the winter of 1940, Alys went back to Kaunas. Nothing had changed: The days were full of hunger and fear, the nights filled with visions of hell. Alys and Lyudas went to a crowded, cold school where they had to wear blue shirts with red kerchiefs and greet the comrade teachers with a raised fist. The teachers promised them "nice rewards" if they would tell what their parents and relatives said at home. Stalin's picture was put in place of the crucifix and red flags hung everywhere. They were Communist youths now. The only good thing about school was that Lazys was there too.

All through the winter and the following spring, fear of deportation haunted Alys and his family. Men were rounded up on the streets, routed out of their homes, tortured and sent to forced labor in Siberia. Often whole families were sent along. Alys laid awake at night, listening for the collection trucks. One night a truck stopped in front of his house, right under his window. He stiffened with fear — and yet he felt hope well up in his chest at the same time. He understood then the awesome attraction of life when death seems close.

In the summer of 1941, incredibly, the Russians left. Was the war finally over? Was Lithuania free again? In answer to Alys' unspoken questions, a new army arrived: handsome, clean young men in shiny boots and snug uniforms. The people of Kaunas lined the streets, greeting their conquerors as liberators, throwing flowers, shouting "Victory! Bravo!" Alys, too, shouted excitedly. Perhaps his nightmares will stop now? Euphoria lasted for three whole days.

On the fourth day the SS arrived and settled in the country as the new usurpers, making their presence felt everywhere. At school Stalin's picture was replaced with Hitler's, the raised fist salute with the outstretched arm. And there were changes in the town too: It was now forbidden to use certain streets, to leave town without permission or even to leave one's house overnight. Anyone wearing sunglasses was subject to arrest, and anyone carrying a parcel had to expect to have it inspected or even taken away. Men had to shave off all beards, and boys were forbidden to run, a decree which Alys minded the most.

The Jews had their own set of regulations, the most obvious of which was the order that they had to mark themselves visibly with yellow Stars of David which they had to sew onto their clothing, both in front and in back. Alys was grateful that his friend Lazys and his family had turned

Catholic; surely they wouldn't have to wear that conspicuous thing? And surely they wouldn't have to be rounded up like the real Jews in Kaunas and forced to move to a separate part of the city called Vilijambol?

Alys knew that area well. His aunt had owned a house there which she had to give up to the Germans when the area was enclosed. It was now called a ghetto and was crowded with Jews. Alys heard that his friend was arrested and forced to live there too, and he went and stood at the barbed wire enclosure and scanned the crowded ghetto streets. He saw only old rabbis with their long robes and a lot of mothers holding babies. He wandered away with a heavy heart. He came again to see his friend, but instead he saw a blanket of smoke hanging over the ghetto, smelled the awful odor of burning houses and burning flesh, heard the moaning of the unfortunate Jews. Was Lazys in that inferno? Alys wept in powerless anger. At night he dreamed of the burning ghetto and saw red flames lick at his friend.

Air-raids interrupted his sleep. Almost nightly now, the Russians dropped bombs and dropped parachutists as well. All too often, they were caught and the Germans hanged them in public at Azuolyno Park, ordering the citizens of Kaunas to watch the hanging. Children had to attend these grim spectacles as well, and Alys had yet another terrible nightmare to cope with. He knew nothing but war and killing.

One afternoon while waiting for his aunt at the fortification near the University clinic, he climbed up on the embankment near Fort 7. A little ways off he noticed a group of men digging a ditch. He saw them put away their shovels and line up in a row facing their ditch. As he watched and listened in growing panic, he heard a shouted command, rifle shots and saw the men drop into the pit. A new group stepped forward, covered the grave and proceeded to dig its own. Alys was terrified. An SS man strolled up to him and motioned him away, saying lightly: *"Nur Juden!"* Despite the ban on running, Alys dashed into the clinic, searching for his aunt.

The war became grimmer, the nightly raids more devastating. The Germans took possession of the houses as yet intact, and one day they told the Stanké family to leave — immediately. Taking a couple of mattresses and the clothes on their backs, they moved into the trade school: miserable, desperate but still together.

Years went by with nothing but cold and hunger. Father looked lined, haggard; mother grey and wrinkled. Alys, only ten years old, was no longer a child. All around them, men were rounded up and sent to forced labor, whole families taken away in street raids.

In the summer of 1944, in a house-to-house roundup, the Germans took the whole Stanké family prisoner.

> Being a prisoner isn't so hard; you just have to take what comes. Climb into the truck when they tell you, be quiet, sit down, stand up at the whim of the guards. Behave as if your will was controlled by someone else. You don't make decisions, you just obey. Up to now it's been bearable.
>
> Then they discharge us in a woodlot full of other prisoners, who show neither joy nor sorrow nor astonishment at our arrival. The soldiers are a lively bunch. They cavort around in front of their superiors, describing the chase, mimicking our fears and our confusion with scorn. Someone barks an order and they all shoot their arms up; they're making fun of us. My lips tighten. A flood of saliva collects under my tongue and I swallow it because I don't dare spit it at them. Now they're thumping each other on the back, congratulating themselves. Some of them are bound to get medals. They make me sick.
>
> Things quiet down. It's not silence, just a lack of voices or

laughter. I can hear rasping breaths all around me. It sounds like the wind in the trees. Officers are approaching. They stare spitefully at us. The soldiers feel our muscles and examine our teeth, as if we were farm animals on exhibit.

A meaningful glance, a nod, a few muttered words . . . and our fate is sealed. Separated from my family for a moment, I feel myself floundering, drowning in anxiety. What will happen to us? I rush into Mother's arms, but the officer brushes me off with a sneer. No room for emotion here!

Father can't keep quiet any more. He asks questions, twisting his tongue around the unfamiliar language:

"Was? Wohin? Sie machen mit uns?"

The officer mumbles something incomprehensible, in which Father picks out two words: *Arbeiten* and *Deutschland.*

"We're going to a work camp in Germany," he says.

And so, on July 29, 1944, around 6 p.m., together with twenty other damned souls, we are transported to Germany on a train closely guarded by armed soldiers.

We reach Königsberg (Kalingrad) at midnight. Everyone has to get out, we're spending the rest of the night. It's unseasonably cold. We have to warm each other, bundled together like piles of wood on the cement platform.

The next morning, stiff and empty, they put us on another train. At the Marienburg stop they give us food, handed out by English prisoners with chalk-white faces who talk to us in their language. Unfortunately, no one understands. I smile with my eyes, cheeks, lips. I keep smiling. My face aches, but it cheers me up.

The Englishmen stay by our carriage a while. They communicate by signs making incredible gestures. I catch a few numbers, ideas, feelings. They wink and wave their arms, open their mouths and whistle. It's a frantic, visionary conversation. One of them makes a noise like a plane, glides with one hand and points at himself. We signal that we understand. We shake hands as the train pulls out. The English stare after it glumly. I wonder what they're thinking. Do they pity us? Envy us? Is there cause for envy? I'll never know.

The rest of the trip, at least for me, is a state of numbness, half fantasy and half real. We reach Berlin late at night. We get out. Some of the group must have left en route, because the number is smaller.

"If only we could be near France," sighs my father, who grew up in Paris.

He takes the opportunity of reminding us of a few things. If we are separated, "head for the nearest of the addresses on the document hanging around your neck!"

There's not much choice. I have two addresses: Mother's brother who is a priest in Poland, and Father's brother, who has lived for years in Marseilles. I finger the little packet. Still there round my neck. But what if I lost the addresses, or they take it away? Better learn them by heart, starting with the Marseilles uncle: 24 Malmousque Street. I say it over and over, like a parrot, until it's engraved in my mind along with the prayers, poems, and songs of my childhood. Father approves of my foresight.

"You'll see, we'll visit your uncle very soon!"

He's very confident. He's longing to see his brother. It'll be fun to see them together, Alec and Alexander...

Now our guards are replaced by two men in civilian clothes. The absence of uniforms and guns is reassuring. The new guards, who are also our guides, make us take the Berlin streetcar. I'm quite pleased to see this city, which they say is the centre of the world. Still, the world isn't seeing it the way I am. Perhaps it's because I'm still distracted, but Berlin doesn't look like the centre of anything. It's nothing but ugly ruins and desolation.

After the streetcar there's another train, then another, I've never traveled so much! We reach Storkow around midnight. A tractor and a wheelbarrow are waiting. Two long hours along the tree-lined road. Then, exhausted and famished, we reach a tiny village called Bugk where we gulp down some warm soup. This is the end of the road for us. They point to a hovel and we go inside.

We fall asleep, overcome by fatigue. The next morning they wake us with "Aufstehen!" Obviously this isn't a vacation. It's a work camp. I open my eyes and realize that we've been sleeping in a dilapidated boathouse. It's a depot for the last to arrive: the Lithuanians. The other prisoners are housed in huts. We get acquainted with the inmates, who seem happy to see new faces. Our new companions include four Frenchmen — one civilian and three soldiers — two Belgians, some Poles, Czechs, several Russian soldiers, and others of indeterminate origin. Very few women and no youngsters, except for a boy around Lyudas' age. I'm the youngest.

We only see our fellow-prisoners at mealtime, when we all eat together in a shed down in the woods. Family life has ceased a long time ago. I have to learn to fend for myself in everything except obeying orders. And of course the orders don't come from my parents.

The Germans are rebuilding houses at the edge of the village for themselves. They are relocating people who got bombed out. My father and brother are assigned to the installation of electric cables. They leave early in the morning, and I'm not allowed to go. Mother also leaves early, in fact she's the first out. She works in the prisoners' kitchen. She comes home after dark, I hardly ever see her. I sneak into the kitchen at mealtimes. Mother waves surreptitiously. But I always stay too long, the German wardresses kick me out, barking insults. My legs are black and blue from beatings.

I'm too young to work, so the Germans decide to send me to school. I learn to write the Gothic script, to sing "Oh Tannenbaum," and *"Deutschland, Deutschland uber Alles."* I try hard to please them, but none of the students

want to play with me. They call me "*Auslander.*" They only
stop during classes. The recesses soon become nightmares
for me. I'm always being beaten up. I never fight back, but
the venom swells inside me. I secretly envy a little one-eyed
boy, because they never call him "*Auslander,*" since he's
German. Horrible word! Why couldn't they stick to
"*Dumkopf*" or "*verruckt*" instead of that awful nickname
which keeps reminding me how far I am from home?

One day, after recess, the teacher asks if I'd like to join the
Hitlerjugend. I say "*nein*" without hesitation. The big man
swallows this affront without reaction, but from now on I
feel a hostile overtone in his polite voice. He spies on me,
waiting for his chance while his anger mounts.

In our little school at home we used to make the sign of
the cross at the beginning and the end of each lesson. Here
the gesture is replaced by a lifted right arm and a chorus of
"*Heil Hitler!*" I always abstain, hidden in the mass,
without him noticing. But now it's different, he has his eye
on me. I watch him: he's observing me closely, but I don't
change my ways.

It's "*Heil Hitler*" time. Everyone yells it out except me. I
remain silent. The great lout comes down from his platform
to face me.

"You didn't say '*Heil Hitler!*'"

"No."

Stiff, with clenched fists, I feel invincible.

"Why?" the pig asks sharply.

"Because I'm an *Auslander!*"

The explanation produces a violent reaction. A nasty
crack across my face. Hardly time to recover before a hefty
punch doubles me over.

"*Geh raus, du Schwein!*" he screams, pointing at the door.

No need to ask twice. I lurch out, quite happy to have spat
my defiance. In fact, I don't remember ever being so proud
of myself. They're punishing me by throwing me out, but I
wasn't so enthralled by the idea of the *Hitlerjugend.* Still,

214

school was good for one thing — in just a few weeks I learned to speak German fluently, without an accent.

With the cold weather Lyudas changes jobs. He's in charge of the transport and distribution of heating fuel. He spends his time walking from one hut to another with a barrow full of coal. The daily ration is seven lumps per hut. Lyudas obeys scrupulously...for everyone else. But when he passes our shed he empties the barrow and hides the coal under our beds where the inspectors won't see it. At night the heat is so oppressive that we have to leave the windows open. When that job is over, Lyudas cleans up the garbage. He doesn't enjoy that much.

As for me, now that I'm out of school, I do odd jobs. I spread gravel in the stonemason's cart, and I carry stone and bricks which are used to build shelters. I develop muscles.

The winter of 1944 was a hard one on the prisoners of war. Although they were able to keep warm inside their barracks, they were totally unprotected outside. They had no coats and no shoes, though they received wooden clogs to work in. Father wrapped brown paper around Alys' feet to keep them from being frostbitten. The paper didn't help very much. Alys tried to stay indoors as much as possible, finding odd jobs to do around the kitchen and managing to stay close to his mother. He got a little extra food that way too. But the food was depressing. Alys often thought that he gave his dog better looking meals than he was eating now.

The war just dragged on and on. Air-raids intensified, but nobody worried about those any more. Apathy set in and lasted throughout that long winter and into the next one. Early in 1945 Alys heard the grownups say that the front was moving closer. He heard that all schools were closed and that the students had organized into a home guard and had to defend the city against the advancing Allies.

Then suddenly one cold day in January the prisoners of war were moved on. They traveled for days, stacked up against each other in an overcrowded train. They stopped for air-raids and then many of their fellow prisoners escaped into the dark night. Father, too, considered escape with his family, but where would they go? How far would they get, weak and tattered as they all were? When they finally arrived at their destination, they were at Camp Grube Theodor at Holzweissig near Bitterfeld, a camp where, it seemed, half of Europe was represented: There were Poles, Czechs, Frenchmen, Italians and more Lithuanians. Was it true that this was the place from which the Germans selected people for their medical experiments? Father turned pale when, a month after their arrival, they informed them that they would be moved again.

They rode in an open truck for two days and two nights over the Autobahn, seemingly going south. Airplanes were striking the Autobahn day and night now, forcing the prisoners to hide under the truck in the deep snow. Already Alys was coughing with a steady cough that hurt him, and he felt both hot and cold all at once. At long last the truck stopped. They were on the outskirts of Wurzburg in southern Germany. The Germans ordered them out and into a stable. Alys fell asleep in a pile of hay. The smell of horses drifted into his dreams.

In the morning they were ordered to build bunks for themselves where once the horses stood and build quarters for the SS in the stable loft. They worked as hard as they could, grateful that the rumors of Camp Grube had not come true.

On March 16, 1945, leaflets were dropped from airplanes onto the city of Wurzburg. Alys read them to his parents in his flawless German: The city will be bombed! But the SS only laughed and declared the announcement enemy propaganda. They stopped laughing and were the first to head for the small cellar under the stables when the first low-flying formation appeared on the horizon. American planes! Alys' heart rejoiced. And when the first bombs started to fall, he too sought shelter. He could still hear the whistle of the bombs, could feel the walls of the stable above him shake. Soon it seemed as if the very foundation of the earth was shaking as bomb after bomb crashed and burst. Alys shook as much as the walls around him. What irony, he thought, to be killed by the liberators! The fear of death gripped his heart.

It seemed a long time before the drone of the planes began to fade and the all-clear siren wailed. Alys crawled out of the cellar into a smoke-filled dawn: Below him Wurzburg stood in flames. The castle, the beautiful *Schloss*, lit from the inside by fire, crumbled as he watched. People black with soot streamed out of the city toward the hill on which the stables stood, begging for help. Only yesterday these people were the masters; today they were beggars: Alys suddenly understood the absurdity of war.

Alys and Lyudas took advantage of the chaos all around them and ran into town. They had to climb over fallen walls and run to avoid walls still crashing down; they saw twisted and mutilated bodies in the ruins and pressed through throngs of dazed people in once wide and tree-lined streets. Someone distributed food and the two boys, hungry as they were, eagerly stood in line. With sandwiches in their pockets, they ran back to the stables and shared them with their parents. And even before they could get back, the sirens sounded again.

The planes pass right overhead, bombers dropping their loads. They spin as they come down on the field. I drop flat on my face, arms over my head. The ground trembles. What was it Lus said?

"If you're ever caught in a raid, climb into one of the bomb craters, it's the best shelter because no two bombs will ever land in exactly the same place."

I sight a hole and dive in headlong. A little further down, near the solitary tree, a man does the same thing. I watch him run, then disappear feet first into the crater. New planes reach the fray as I reach mine. The hole is still warm. I hunch down, breathing the bitter odor of scorched earth. Shattering, deafening, maddening noises burst around me. Then comes the long whistle before the blasts. At each explosion, a lump of earth falls on top of me. An awful, invisible pressure, like the breath of an infernal monster, seems to push me deeper at each blow. It flattens me painfully at the base of my crater. If I open my mouth to relieve my eardrums, it fills with earth. I cough hard to free my throat, and through the suffocating dirt I scream incomprehensible words. Fright, anger and pain are mixed; I sound like someone who's been skinned alive, and I can feel myself going mad with fear. If only my cries could reach God! Or even the planes which are terrorizing me!

Now everything is quiet. They've heard my prayer. The explosions stop. The planes are slowly leaving. The noise of motors is muffled by the beating of my heart.

I climb out and look first at the stable. Still standing. Then a glance at the tree, where the unknown man took refuge. All I can see is two other holes like the first one which isn't visible any more because the tree is resting on it, like a bouquet on a grave.

Wounded soldiers emerge from the woods and run in all directions. I rush toward the stable because I feel that if you're going to die, it's easier to do with other people. The building is badly damaged. Gaping black scars have split the walls. Bombs have plowed up the courtyard. My pile of wood has disappeared, and all the chickens are dead, flattened like pancakes by the air pressure of the exploding bombs.

I don't recognize the place any more. Not a living soul around. I run outside and shout. Muffled, distant voices come from the cellar — they're there! They're alive! I go down to find them. Two German soldiers arrive a few minutes later. One carries an almost severed right arm in his left hand. Blood is spurting from the terrible wound. He whimpers, twisted with pain. The other, really a Hungarian militiaman, has a grenade slung from his belt. We protest this and beg him to unload the weapon if he wants to share our hospitality. He refuses. It's his last piece of ammunition, and he won't give it up. Our stronger companions grab him and turn him out. There are no Germans in the stable, no one left to protect him. His wounded comrade is useless.

"I'll blow you all up!" he shouts.

Misera and Kvorek have an answer for everything.

"Poor bugger! If you let it off now you'll have nothing left to defend yourself with when they come to hang you!"

We squat anxiously inside the cellar, waiting to see if the uninvited guest will throw the grenade. He must have taken pity on his comrade inside; nothing happens.

The menacing buzz of the bombers starts again. It's louder now. The noise of the motors is so strong that we can't hear ourselves talk. The planes start another downpour on the town.

A light flashes, then another. Suddenly, the cellar is dark. A huge mountain of earth covers the tiny window. A soggy mess descends over all of us. Once again I am terribly and calmly certain of dying. My jaws are stiff. I shut my eyes, trying to clear my head and chase out the dizzying sequence of thoughts.

"We must get out of here!" orders Lus.

His voice brings back my courage. I start feeling around me. My clumsy hand brushes the wounded soldier's arm and he groans. Then I pat the walls, like a blind man. My

sense of touch improves after a few minutes. We push through the earth with our hands, like animals who burrow with their paws.

"Faster, we're suffocating here," someone complains in Polish.

I don't even know which of the three the voice belongs to. I don't know how long it takes to reach the opening but I know we're fighting all the time and praying for a miracle.

At long last the daylight filters in. We've made it. We extricate ourselves from the communal tomb, frightened to death, exhausted from the battle against the earth. My companions look like disinterred corpses, and no doubt so do I. They are all black as soot, their eyes sunken with fear.

The bombing of Wurzburg continued for two weeks. Alys, recovered from his fear of dying as soon as the shelling stopped, continued to run into town for food. Now he was glad that he had learned to speak German, even German with a Berlin twang. He simply posed as a displaced German boy who begged food for his bombed-out family. Only once did a woman identify him as the *Auslander* he was, and he rushed away from her on a chase that very nearly cost him his freedom. At this late date he definitely didn't want to be caught by the Germans. It was the Americans he wanted to see now.

In the early morning hours of April 3, 1945, Alys finally saw his liberators approaching. His heart thumped with joy as he watched American tanks drive through Wurzburg and up the hill to the stables. And then one of the Americans planted the American flag in the stable yard! The wind played with it. Alys stood hypnotized by that waving flag. So this is what freedom looks like, he thought.

The people in the stable were soon taken away, only this time they rode in American trucks. Alys got to ride next to the driver. The new camp was a huge compound where the liberators gathered prisoners of the Germans from all the countries of Europe and fed and clothed them. Alys was the youngest inmate there and soon the favorite of the Americans. They outfitted him in a green shirt just like their own, new shoes, and — dream come true — a helmet! In all his young life he had never been happier. He left planning for the future to his father.

Father did not dare to return to his home in Kaunas, nor did he care to live under the rule of the Soviets who had liberated Lithuania from the Germans. Most likely his radio station was destroyed. He asked to be repatriated to France where he had been born.

On April 30, 1945, the Stanké family was taken to the French border.

Biography of a Partisan: Bryna's Account

The Ukraine, the large territory between Poland, Rumania and Russia, open to the Black Sea on its southern border, was another country which became a throughway for German troops on their way to Moscow. In the five years that the theater of war played itself out there, the country was ravaged. But because of her thick forests and her proximity to Russia, the Ukraine became a stronghold for anti-German partisans who took their orders from the Red Army. They hindered the Germans and plagued them whenever and wherever they could. German wrath was fierce in return and few partisans lived to tell the story of their fight against the Germans.

Among the partisans were many Jews who had fled to the woods to save their lives. These freedom fighters were in particular danger, and not only from the Nazis: They were neither loved by the Ukrainians nor by the Russians. It is a wonder that even one of them lived to tell her story.

Bryna was born in Baranowicze in 1925. At that time Baranowicze was part of Poland, lying in the northeastern section, close to the border of Russia. Before she was five years old, her parents had bought an old grain mill in the *shtetl* of Byten and had moved there with their four daughters: Yentl, Henia, Dalya and Bryna. An older son, Nathan, had already left Poland for America; a younger son, Chaim, was born to them in the *shtetl*.

A village predominantly inhabited by Jews, Byten was about 35 miles north of Baranowicze. Life there, if isolated from the rest of Poland, offered the Jews a sense of identity and security. The activities in the *shtetl* reflected Jewish laws and customs. The mode of living, though simple and poor, confirmed a rich Jewish heritage. On Friday evenings shops and workrooms closed; the Jews rejoiced in the Sabbath; strangers shared their *gefilte fish* and *cholent*; Sabbath prayers and singing resounded in the synagogue and in every house.

The only gentiles in the *shtetl* were the mayor, the postmaster, the police and the teachers. The only outside contacts were the farmers who brought their produce into the *shtetl* on market days. After their wares were sold and before going back to their farms, the peasants would get drunk and insult and harass the Jews. Thus the Jews of Byten were well aware of Polish anti-Semitism.

On the first of September 1939, Hitler invaded Poland during the early hours of the morning and immediately disbanded the Polish government. The Jews of Poland trembled with fear. The Jews of Byten took in hundreds of fleeing refugees from central Poland and listened to the stories of German cruelties — listened, but did not comprehend. They did not even believe that the Germans were only 30 miles from Byten.

But before the Germans could get there, the Russians arrived with tanks and trucks and set up a local government and a secret police in the *shtetl*. Outside the village cattle cars stood ready to take any anti-Russians to Siberia. In the *shtetl* all Jewish organizations were dissolved; all social and cultural life stopped. The Jews, at first so glad to see the Russians instead of the Germans, were now afraid. For two years they lived under Russian occupation, under constant fear, but when they saw the Russians leave Byten on June 22, 1941, and saw German troops and war machinery come in their place, chaos broke out: Germany at war with Russia! What was to become of the Jews of Byten?

On June 25, as the last remaining Russians fled in haste, German patrols goosestepped down Main Street. Within hours they established a local SS government and proclaimed their anti-Semitism. The Jews of Byten hid in their houses.

But immediately they were ordered out for road repairs. Every day a quota of men had to report to the SS in the village square: If the quota were not complete, the SS went into the houses and dragged out whoever they found. Thus Chaim, Bryna's younger brother, was taken to forced labor, although he was but a child. Soon the SS did not bother to collect the Jews themselves: They ordered the Jews of Byten to set up a *Judenrat* instead whose task was to supply the daily requirement of workers. Harder and harder they had to work, longer and longer hours while their rations became smaller.

The *Judenrat's* next duty was handed down to them

within days: The Jews of Byten had to give up their gold and rubles, their furs and clothing. Ever larger ransom was demanded of them until every wedding band, every treasured heirloom was purged. And then they had to wear a white armband with the yellow Star of David to work and the yellow *Judenstern* on the front and back of their clothing, even inside the *shtetl*. The Jews were poor and hungry and exhausted. And now they were also marked.

A young gentile, delivering goods from neighboring towns, told the Jews of Byten that the SS made farmers of nearby villages dig huge pits. Then they rounded up the Jews and gunned them into the pits by the thousands, but who could believe such a thing? In November 1941 the stories were more specific yet: The Jews in the ghetto of Slonim had been herded to an abyss on November 14, and more than nine thousand of them had been killed in a single massacre. Now the Jews of Byten began to comprehend that any day might be their last.

By early spring 1942, the Jews in the *shtetl* were no longer permitted to live in their own houses. Instead a ghetto was staked out, consisting of forty-eight small wooden houses and enclosed with barbed wire. Into this area all twelve-hundred Jewish inhabitants of Byten had to move, as many as 20 people to a single room. That spring rations were cut again. Every person got four ounces of bread a day. Bryna, who by this time was part of the forced labor, walked back and forth to the highways near the railroad station of Domanovo. On the way she stole a few leaves of spinach or some berries for her family. Her father was skeletal and hollow-eyed; her mother, once stout, was thin and drawn. But it was the children of the ghetto who suffered most from the lack of food. For a while, the grown-ups gathered them in courtyards and gardens in an improvised school or kindergarten to make them forget their hunger for a few hours, but the ss found out and forbade this activity.

The news from Europe that leaked into the ghetto was depressing: almost every country in Europe was under German control! Jews being deported to Poland by the millions! Rumors spread of a Russian counter-offensive and of German losses. Indeed, the Jews of Byten saw some German soldiers straggling along the country road, confirming a German defeat, but this news did nothing to lift the mood in the ghetto. Everyone was sure that liquidation would start soon; everyone prepared some sort of hiding place: an attic space, an underground storage cellar, a barn crawlspace. In every house one person stood guard day and night to sound the alarm should the ss approach.

Friday, July 24, 1942, was the day after *Tisha B'av*, during which everybody had fasted. The young people had left the ghetto to work with their groups, and the older ones were sitting in the yards under the shade of the trees, for it was very hot. Those who still had a little barley and beans prepared the *cholents* for the Sabbath — *Sabbath Nachamu*, the Sabbath of consolation and comfort.

When the workers returned they brought news that the local police had gathered farmers from three nearby villages and were forcing them to dig pits. The panic in the ghetto was overpowering. Each family inspected its hiding place. Rabbi Jaffe and Rabbi Lieberman conducted Friday night services as usual and chanted the part of the Torah that says: *"Nachamu, nachamu, ami"* ("Be comforted, my people"). Suddenly several young men burst in, agitation reflected in their faces. They told the congregation to go home and prepare their hiding places. Our ghetto had been scheduled for liquidation.

Everybody slept fully clothed that night. As usual, father, Chaim and I were stretched out on straw sacks in the barn. Henia stood watch. At 3 a.m. she woke us up. "I hear

226

walking and running in the yards,'' she said. Leaving the
barn we saw that the whole ghetto had been aroused; it was
surrounded by police.

In our barn there was a hiding place for about ten people,
camouflaged with firewood. My brother-in-law grabbed
Yentl and their two children and forced them into it in spite
of the objections of others that there was not enough room.
He put back the lid of the hiding place and threw firewood
over it. He himself had no chance to hide; German police
and Lithuanians were already inside the ghetto. He ran for
cover between the vegetable beds where he was discovered
by a gendarme and shot. Lejba was the first in the ghetto to
be killed.

My father refused to hide. In his sheepskin jacket he
stood in the doorway of the house like a corpse — his face
the color of river mud, his eyes unfocused. On that hot
summer day of July 25 he shivered with cold, waiting to be
delivered from the shackles of the tormenting life of the
ghetto.

Mother, Henia, Dalya, Chaim and I climbed to the attic
where fifteen people were already hiding. In the attic we
had stored Passover pots, pans and dishes all covered with
rags. Henia came over and told me to lie down among the
dishes in the narrow space where the roof touched the walls.
I did, and she covered me with rags. She herself was highly
sensitive and confinement nauseated her. Unwilling to
cover herself up, she, mother and Chaim watched from the
attic window and saw people being dragged from their
homes, gardens and hiding places. They were clubbed over
the heads and forced to climb into trucks formerly used for
cattle. They saw father being led to one of the trucks.

After twenty minutes we heard knocking on the lid door
to the attic. Local policemen climbed the stairs to corral anybody they found hiding there. I heard Henia begging one
policeman, whom she knew by name, to leave her in the attic; she promised to give him money and jewelry. He asked

for it immediately, but she told him she had it hidden in the ghetto. She promised to give it to him as soon as things quieted down. He dragged her down the stairs by her hair.

The police failed to look where I lay hidden under the rags, paralyzed with fear and shock. I listened to the machine guns and prayed that my mother, father, sisters and brother would have easy deaths. (I was so shocked that I forever lost my memory of their faces. In 1947, when I arrived in the United States, I found at my brother's house an old picture of my family. In this picture I was about four years old. Now I remember my lost family only by that picture. In nightmares I am always hunted by murderers; as I run from them in fields, woods and mud, I am with my family, but I never see their faces.)

After the shooting stopped, I could hear horses and carriages in the ghetto and the voices of our White Russian neighbors who came to loot. They dug up every foot of earth looking for buried treasures. Like wild animals over their prey, our gentile neighbors threw themselves on the loot.

As it grew dark a deathly silence prevailed. Suddenly I heard a voice reciting psalms. I looked out and saw a very old man with a long white beard praying and crying. Then, miraculously, I saw my sister, Dalya, crawling out of her hiding place. I had been sure she was taken away with the others. I kept embracing her to convince myself I wasn't dreaming. She told me that at the very last minute Henia pushed her down in the crawl space among the dishes. Because of Henia both of us were alive; she had looked out for everybody but herself.

In a flood of emotions Bryna and Dalya ran to the attic to free Yentl and her two small children. The three sisters were stunned by their own unexpected survival and were desolate beyond words: Father, mother, brother Chaim and sister Henia were dead; of the twelve-hundred Jews in the ghetto only three hundred forty were left; the sisters knew that the SS would be back, that the killing would continue until they were all gone.

Bryna resolved firmly that she would not wait to be led to the slaughter, that she would escape before the hunters returned. For some time she had been hearing about a group of Jews who had escaped from the ghetto and had joined the partisans. She knew now that this was what she would do. At least she would die fighting. She told her sisters of her decision and begged them to join her, to be ready to flee with her at a moment's notice.

It was only a few days after the ghetto massacre that Bryna noticed some movement near one of the barns at the edge of the ghetto. She realized in a flash that a remnant of the survivors were preparing their escape. She ran to her sisters and told them to pack some essentials: diapers, milk for the children, some warm clothes into a rucksack and to be ready at the first sign of flight from the barn. On a hot August day in 1942 Bryna saw that sign: The escapees were getting ready to leave the ghetto. Quickly, she alerted her sisters and the five of them, Bryna, Dalya, Yentl and the two children, mingled with the group. Stealthily the leaders of the group cut the barbed wire that surrounded the ghetto and led the way through the narrow opening, out into barley fields. Bryna had to drag and carry little Rochele while Yentl held fast to her little boy; they dropped the rucksack with the precious provisions to run faster; they crawled through meadows and waded through streams; they ran with their remaining strength to the edge of the forest, fearing all the time that the Germans or the Polish Police would see or hear them and shoot them all.

At the edge of the forest two young men from Byten met them and took them to the partisans. Now they dared to breathe easier; they were in a Communist stronghold called Wolcze Nory, the Wolves Nest, a den of resistance in the dense forest in the midst of the German occupation.

Wolcze Nory was a fertile stretch of land divided into camps half a square mile to each camp. Every camp had a commanding officer and a leader who took his orders directly from the Red Army. Bryna began to understand very quickly that the Wolcze Nory stronghold was part of a larger Communist underground operation in the forests of Eastern Poland and the Polish and Russian Ukraine, in the dense woods that covered much of the territory of White Russia. Beyond the woods to the north lay Moscow from whence the orders to the partisans came. Among themselves, Bryna learned that the partisans exchanged messages and information between forest camps by messengers crossing the thick forest on footpaths and hidden dirt roads known to them alone. She saw that the partisans at Wolcze Nory were well equipped with guns and rifles and noticed cartridge belts hanging loosely over their shoulders.

Someone took the newcomers to an unfinished building which seemed to serve as a war commission office. The man who obviously was the leader of that office spoke sternly to them: If they had come to save their lives, there was no place for them in the stronghold, but if they were willing to help fight the common enemy, they would receive ammunition and a place to live. They would be welcome as member partisans. He told them that Jews from the ghettos of Slonim, Kosov and Iwacewicze had already joined up. The hundred or so Jews from Byten were eager to become part of the partisan movement.

The leader assigned them a place three miles from the main camp and showed them how to build huts from twigs and roofs from bark; he gave them guns in exchange for some boots; he advised them to go into the nearby village and barter for a cow and some cooking utensils. In time he told them, they — the hundred Jews from Byten and another hundred fugitives whom he expected shortly — would be charged with cooking and caring for the whole Wolcze Nory camp.

By early fall their number had swelled to three hundred fifty, all Jews fleeing from the ghettos to the woods. Young children were among them, and they were soon known as *Semejner lager*, the family camp. A Russian officer named Seryosha became their leader and instructor in partisan warfare.

In the fall of 1942 the Germans, desperate because of their defeat at Moscow, mounted an offensive against the partisans in the forests of Eastern Poland. On September 18 they ambushed the woods around Wolcze Nory in great numbers, harassed the resistance fighters with their low-flying planes and penetrated partisans' defenses with their tanks. The chief of staff at the Wolves Nest called a meeting that evening and told the partisans of directives he had received that day from Moscow: All partisans were to unite and prepare for a major attack; sabotage operations were to intensify; everyone was to be ready for duty, day and night.

Training was stepped up at Bryna's camp. Everybody knew what their assignment was in case of attack: Bryna was one of the guards. But when the first onslaught of German troops and armored vehicles crashed through to Wolcze Nory, all plans, all organization broke down: The central executive staff and the commander-in-chief left to set up defenses deeper in the woods; the partisans had to fend for themselves.

The people from Byten — three hundred fifty by now — left the camp to seek refuge in the forest. At night Bryna and a group of young people gathered dry leaves and urged the group to try to rest before they had to flee again as soon as the sun rose. During that first night, the nightwind carried the smell from their burning huts at Wolcze Nory up to their new hiding place, and they knew that they had left just in time to save their lives. They also knew that their flight had only now begun. Bryna tried to quiet her sisters and calm the two children, but she was in despair herself: How will they manage with these crying children; how will they feed them and keep them warm at night? Most urgently, how will they run through this inhospitable terrain with them?

The morning dawned hot and humid. As they fled deeper into the woods, they passed the bodies of their comrades: mutilated bodies under trees, in groves, everywhere. As she hurried past them, seeing their tortured features, their twisted or missing limbs, smelling their decay, Bryna sent a fervent prayer to Heaven: Let me and my sisters be shot, God! Let Yentl and the babies die, God, before we can be captured alive and tortured like this!

Yentl and the children fell behind; the children cried; the Germans seemed close. Seryosha, the leader, stopped the fleeing people and asked the mothers with their children to separate from the group. Six young women, their infants and children clinging to them, camped in a hollow where the children's wailing was somewhat subdued. There the group would fetch them the next day.

The next day, as Bryna rushed to the hollow to meet with the mothers, five mothers came toward her, five dead babies in their arms. Bryna, weak-kneed, searched for Yentl: What in God's name had happened? An ashen-faced Yentl told a story of madness: One of the mothers, in a fit of despair, took her shawl and slowly suffocated the infant at her breast and as if infected by an inexplicable hysteria, one after another of the mothers slowly smothered the babies in their arms. Yentl had implored them to stop, to come to their senses, but they did not hear her.

The lamenting of the fathers and mothers, the crying of the older children drew the enemy nearer. Shouts of "Halt, Halt!" echoed around them: They had to move on.

Yentl was hardly able to run. Stumbling along with the baby in her arm and Rochele beside her, she was at the end of endurance. Bryna quietly took the baby from her, pressing the little boy to her own bosom and firmly grasped Rochele's small hand. She urged the little girl along with kind words and little rhymes. Uncomprehending, the child ran alongside her, one shoe gone, feet and legs scratched and bleeding; the baby in Bryna's arms seemed asleep. Behind them, deep in the forest, Bryna could hear gunfire. She begged her sisters not to fall back; she grasped Rochele's hand more firmly and held the baby tighter. When the sun began to set, they had run fifteen miles. They were exhausted and terribly hungry. Bryna realized then with a start that the day was *Yom Kippur*, day of fasting and atonement. She fell onto some dry leaves, the baby still in her arm.

But the baby looked so still, so white. Bryna looked closer in the waning sun and felt her own blood turn cold: The little boy was dead. In her flight from the demons behind her she had suffocated him. She was without consolation.

That Yom Kippur night, in the dark of the early evening in the strange woods, surrounded by the enemy, the sisters buried the baby under a huge tree. Through their prayers they could hear gunfire deep in the forest.

> It was quieter the next day. We gathered berries, tried to dig for water with our bare hands and rested. We then set out to search for others of our people. What we found were corpses. Some were tied to tree trunks, their tongues torn

out, shoulders and arms wrenched from their sockets, hips bowed, knees turned inward, teeth clamped together, fingers bent in claws, faces contorted, eyeballs bulging, and their private parts burned by fire. By these signs we knew that some of them had been captured alive. What we saw made us pray that if we had to die, it would be by bullet and not by slow torture. Many partisans kept loaded revolvers and were prepared to shoot themselves rather than fall into German hands.

In our wandering we came across a dead deer. Flies and vermin swarmed over the carcass and the smell was terrible. Still, we cut out its liver and roasted it over a little fire. Yentl refused to eat it; the sight made her nauseous. All of my pleading did not help. Rochele's condition was almost as bad as her mother's. Her face was sunken, her body badly scratched by nettle weeds.

By Wednesday we were close to a highway that led to Moscow. About to cross, we saw some Germans trying to repair a tank. We lay flat on the ground and, miraculously, the Germans failed to notice us.

It seemed evident now, ten days after the attack began, that the Germans were leaving. Our group decided to go back to our old camp, to look for other people as well as food and clothes. As we walked, I kept my little niece close to me, holding her by the hand most of the way. Yentl, too weak to take care of her, kept stumbling and falling. But by now the whole group was moving slowly and painfully so we managed to keep up. We listened for voices, hoping we could find some other survivors and begin to reorganize in some way.

Wolcze Nory, when we finally spotted it, did not present the same vista we beheld when we first came into the woods. The farmers' houses had been burned to the ground. Bodies of men and animals lay in the ashes. Hoping to make it more difficult for the partisans to operate, the Germans had simply liquidated peasants who lived near the woods.

We walked on to the other side, a treeless hilly area where an abandoned Russian tank stood. It was some distance away, but my sister Dalya was farsighted. "There are partisans behind the tank," she shouted. "They are motioning us to join them. Finally we found friends!"

We were halfway there when Dalya appeared to freeze in mid-stride. Her words now sent shivers through us: "We are trapped, we are trapped! The men wear black uniforms. It is the police."

Turning, we tried to make a hurried retreat into the woods, but low, thick bushes made it difficult to run. The police started to shoot and throw grenades. Soil, splinters and even bushes flew into the air. It seemed as if we were in the core of a volcanic eruption. We kept running, but we could no longer see each other because of the smoke, dust and debris.

Within hours after the attack, I found Dalya and everyone else in our group except Yentl and Rochele. I prayed that they had merely wandered away or had met up with other survivors. I prayed in vain.

Six months later my worst fears were realized. Moshe Witkow from Byten told me that, alongside the roadway leading to the village of Kochanowo, he had seen seven corpses in a pile, some of them women and children. I asked him to take me to this place. Among the seven skeletons I recognized Yentl by the half-rotten fur collar on her coat. Only one of her legs still had flesh. My little niece I recognized by the high-laced shoes I had given her. It looked as if all seven people had been caught alive and burned on a bonfire.

Moshe helped me dig a grave. We buried all seven in one pit. As he chanted the *El Molei Rachamin*, I thought of the irony of that psalm which praises our merciful God. I stood there numb and without tears, feeling only that life means nothing. Life suddenly snatched away becomes only a troublesome dream, a persistent vapor. I raised my eyes to heaven; a burning sun was shining in undisturbed glory on an earth soaked with human blood. The ancient trees murmured tales of tragedies they had witnessed.

The terrible German attacks left the Wolcze Nory partisans depleted. In Bryna's group one hundred seventy people had survived. Bryna and Dalya mourned for their sister, for the children, for the many friends and comrades they had lost in the forest. And the Germans were not through with them yet. New fugitives arrived daily at the Wolves Nest, now mostly farmers fleeing from the German atrocities against them. They told the group that the danger was by no means over. And they blamed the Jews for this danger; it was because of the Jews that the Germans had attacked Wolcze Nory, they said. Bryna's heart was heavy. From the outside they had to fear the Germans, but now they had to fear the these anti-Semitic Poles from within.

It wasn't long before the leader of the partisans gave the Jewish members an ultimatum: Either leave the woods By the second day of November 1942 or stay and risk being shot.

One of the young Jews from Byten, Shmuel, a strong man with a good sense of direction, gathered a small following of members and urged them to leave with him. Bryna, Dalya and thirteen others chose him as their leader, and slowly and carefully they made their way through the woods back toward Byten. Some four miles from the *shtetl*, close to the railroad station of Domanovo, they found a thinly wooded area where they thought they could hold out during the winter months. Already it was getting cold. The first thing they had to do was look for cover. They dug a cave with their bare hands, camouflaged it with green moss. It was small, but it would protect them; if they all lay close together, it would give them extra warmth. They needed water before the ground froze. They dug a well. Then they foraged for food and found a potato field near-by. At night Bryna and a few other members would steal potatoes from there and cook them in their cave, hoping that the smell would not betray them. Once the snow began to fall, they took extra precautions not to leave tracks lest the Germans would find them.

All winter of 1942 they lived thus in hiding, taking in even two more Jews, two fugitives from Slonim who had discovered their cave by chance. Together they waited and prayed for an end to the war, to the German occupation, to this hiding and stealing and trembling whenever they heard human voices or saw a human figure.

In the early spring, in March 1943, two armed men approached their hideout. Everyone froze. Armed men could mean only one thing: death. But to their immense relief, the two uniformed men turned out to be fellow partisans in stolen uniforms who joined their little band. Bryna was glad to get some news after the long winter's isolation and became excited when the newcomers told her that seventy Jews of the Byten group were still alive and were again settled in Wolcze Nory. Bryna and the group quickly decided to join them.

In April 1943 they returned once again to the forest, not dreaming that they would have to remain there for more than a year before liberation finally came to the Ukraine. During that long summer they had to endure many attacks on the Wolves Nest and much hostility from their gentile member-partisans. But they were able to work together and harass the common enemy, the hated Germans.

At one time during that hot summer, a common foe of

237

quite another nature settled in the partisan camp: typhus. Many of the group lay sick and inactive, Dalya among them. Bryna nursed her sister and her comrades back to health and back to their activities.

Time now seemed to pass more slowly. We began to breathe freer, especially in the evenings. We could read between the lines of German newspapers that not everything was going well with the German armies. Naturally the Germans did not write about their defeats, but they didn't have to.

Frequently, Russian paratroopers descended into the woods, and underground activities perked up under their guidance. An airfield was built. Sometimes, when Russian planes were expected, we made fires to show them where to drop ammunition. The partisans, sensing their mother country was close to victory, became fretful about their reputation for hostility toward us. Communism preaches humanitarianism, equality and brotherly love. But the partisans' hatred for Jews was so deeply rooted that they still could merely tolerate us.

During this time, we were heartened to hear that an American-British-Russian conference was held in Moscow from October 19 to October 30, 1943, and that now the three nations were jointly planning their military campaigns.

On our front, partisan activities were increasingly effective. Hardly a night passed in which partisans did not derail trains, destroy miles of track, disrupt telephone service and harass the German garrisons. The railroad sabotage was especially fruitful because the Germans had to keep the trains moving to bring back frostbitten soldiers from the Russian front and to supply the front with new troops and food.

In March 1944, the Germans assailed our woods again and sent us retreating to a forest four miles away. As I ran through mud and snow, I felt my legs collapsing under me. My head was a flaming furnace. To keep up with the others, I threw away my patched coat. We were on the run most of the day, my legs unsteady every inch of the way. At dusk, when the shooting abated, we lay down to rest. We were afraid to make a fire, and to keep warm we lay in a row snuggled against one another. Burning and at the same time shaking with chills, I moved close to a man who wore a long sheepskin coat. Unbuttoning his coat, he put part of it over me to give me some protection from the cold. Dalya covered me on the other side.

The next morning my body was livid with red spots. It was typhus. Six months after the epidemic had passed — six months after my sister and everybody else had been struck — I had to get sick. And the only doctor was in another forest with the partisans. I couldn't even get an aspirin.

For 14 days I faced death. My fever remained high but I was not unconscious of what went on around me. My sister, who kept vigil over me, told me later that I did talk and sing in my sleep. Even on the fourteenth day, when the crisis passed and my temperature returned to normal, I was unable to get up. Like the other typhus victims, I had to take walking lessons. Fortunately, the woods were peaceful during my convalescence. In two weeks I could walk without my sister's help, but now my wavy, blond hair started to fall out by the handful. Soon I was completely bald. I was nothing but skin and bones; I had lost even my freckles. One of our people brought me a babushka, which I didn't remove from my head for a very long time. A year later when my new hair grew in, it was kinky, like sheep's wool. Within two months there was another scare. A rumor circulated that a special German battalion had been ordered from the front, and that they were bringing cadres of dogs trained to search and kill, leaving no chance for survival. Fear mounted in us at the thought of German dogs trapping us in our hiding places. We prayed that, if our time came, death would be delivered by bullets penetrating us while we were running. But we went on constructing better caves and hideouts.

Daily the mood of local German authorities and police became more somber and depressed. Strong walls were built around their station posts; barricades of sandbags went up. No German would leave his post by himself; for their safety they moved about only in groups. At the same time, the partisans became bolder.

In the early days of July 1944, multitudes of Russian planes darkened the skies. We knew then that the harassed Germans no longer had time to mount an attack on the partisans. At long last, we had the upper hand.

In July 1944 the woods were again full of German soldiers and those who collaborated with them, but now these soldiers used the woods as hiding places themselves. They were fleeing from the pursuing Red Army. Russian tanks were driving them toward Germany; the long German occupation in the Ukraine was over.

Twenty-seven Jews from the *shtetl* of Byten had survived the grim ordeal: Bryna, Dalya and twenty-five others. On the day a Russian colonel told the women, children and the very old partisans that they could go home now, that only young men needed to remain and were recruited into the Red Army, Bryna and Dalya embraced their friends and went back to Byten: They had to see the ghetto just once more, had to stand at the place where their parents were taken and throw themselves upon the earth outside the village that was now a mass grave. Cows and sheep were grazing nearby; the warm smell of summer hung over the place. There, beneath a mound measuring forty-eight meters in length and six meters in width, lay their people.

They tidied up the huge grave, erected a crude fence around it and prayed.

240

After much waiting, Dalya and Bryna emigrated to the United States, to Chicago and found their brother Nathan again.

PART VI
Italy and Hungary

NINE

Hitler in Italy and Hungary

Italy was one of the last countries to experience Nazi abuse. The country with the world's most prestigious history, birthplace of Dante, Leonardo and Michelangelo, land of grapes and olives, had been dominated since 1922 by the fascist *Duce* Benito Mussolini, who became Hitler's friend. Mussolini did not yield to Hitler's pressures for active anti-Semitism in Italy. In July 1943 the Italian Grand Council deposed their fascist dictator, and King Victor Emmanuel was once again Italy's sole ruler. Mussolini, by then hated and despised, was taken to a mountaintop hotel as prisoner of the Italians.

In Germany this fact was disguised as the news that Hitler's friend and ally had resigned for reasons of health. Hitler and his staff met at once to plan a rescue. On September 13, 1943, German gliders landed on the mountain, took the guards prisoner, stuffed the overweight *Duce* into one of the gliders and delivered him to Hitler's headquarters. The German plan had also called for the arrest of King Victor Emmanuel and his ministers, but the king, his family and the Grand Council fled from Rome to the safety of southern Italy and the presence of the Allies.

Hitler's personal bodyguard installed and guarded the *Duce* in a northern Italian village.

Meanwhile, German troops successfully fought against the Allies in the south of Italy, holding the enemy as far as possible from the Reich and placing the whole of northern Italy under German occupation. SS *Sturmfuehrer* Karl Wolff became Hitler's representative in Rome, and the Jews came under the power of SS *Sturmfuehrer* Theodor Dannecker, the deputy of Eichmann.

Roman Jewry had flourished in Italy ever since the Destruction of the Temple in Jerusalem in 70 C.E. Some of the richest and most ornate synagogues in the world rose in Italy, and the most respected rabbinical schools were established there. Jews were integrated citizens in modern Italy. When Hitler marched in the Jews were told what to expect, but they did not believe the reports of German inhumanities and very few of them fled their ancestral homes. In the two years of German occupation, aristocratic Jewish Romans were uprooted, their baronial homes, estates and gardens were taken over by the Germans. Their magnificent synagogues were smashed to ruins and their treasures taken away. In Pisa a group of ten Jews was murdered while gathering for prayers in a private home. In Rome the roundups were conducted with such cruelty that Christian spectators fled in horror. The terror stopped only when Allied troops entered Rome and took control of Italy on April 29, 1945. By then seventeen thousand of Italy's fifty thousand Jews were dead.

Hitler's fortunes had been declining ever since the battle of Stalingrad in January 1943 while the Allied forces had grown in strength. American armies come to Europe's rescue in June of 1944. But before they could smash the German steel and iron, one last country in Europe fell victim to the full force of Hitler's fury. Hungary, the land where Attila the Hun had held court fifteen-hundred years earlier, became the theater of Hitlerean action as late as March 1944. Magyar tribes settled there after the Hun left, leaving no other trace but his name. The Magyars built Hungary into one of Europe's most productive sources of grains and grapes, established some of Europe's most sophisticated cities, brought forth some of the world's greatest artists like Molnar and Liszt. Magyars also ruthlessly suppressed the Slavs and vetoed reforms in the Austro-Hungarian Empire. And in the 1930's, Hungary developed a fascist movement which followed the Nazi pattern of racism. Hitler brought her nine-and-a-half million inhabitants under Nazi rule in the last year of his power.

Already in 1940, the Hungarian regent Miklos Horthy had committed his country to Germany when he joined the Berlin-Rome-Tokyo Tripartite Pact together with Rumania and Bulgaria. A year later, Hungary allowed German troops to move through her territory toward the attack on Yugoslavia and, in June of 1941, joined Germany in the invasion of Russia. Hungary was rewarded for her alliance with the Reich by getting part of Czechoslovakia and territories in Transylvania.

But by 1944 Horthy was disillusioned with Hitler and tried to sympathize with Russia instead. Hitler summoned him to Berlin and informed him that he would have to accept the Hungarian Nazi, Dome Sztojay, as premier of his country, and that henceforth German troops would be stationed in Budapest and, furthermore, that he would have to hand over the Jews of Hungary for extinction. Horthy agreed to all propositions, but once back in Budapest he broke off alliance with Germany. He was promptly arrested, returned to Germany with his entire family under guard and imprisoned. Sztojay proceeded with Hitler's orders in regard to the Jews.

The yellow star was first. Then in April 1944 Jews in the provinces were forced from their homes and crammed into ghettos. From there they were shipped to Auschwitz and quickly killed. After the rural areas were free of Jews, Budapest with its large and prosperous Jewish community- was tackled. Roundups began, transports left, Jews were gassed and burned. Finally, the Hungarian government balked and supported one of its Jewish citizens, the influential lawyer Rudolf Kastner, in his efforts to save Hungarian Jews who were still alive. Kastner aproached *Reichsfuehrer* Himmler through Himmler's deputy Kurt Becher and, backed by his government and by the Swiss Joint Distribution Committee, negotiated for the release of the Jews.

He had a small measure of success. Himmler granted the release of three thousand Hungarian Jews to Switzerland. But two hundred thousand others, half the Jewish community of Hungary, died either in Auschwitz or on "death marches," driven ahead of the Allies from place to place in the early winter months of 1945. Isabella Katz of Kisvárda, Hungary, is one of the few survivors of those two ordeals.

Memories of Auschwitz: Fragments of Isabella

Main Street, Hungary.
Kisvárda was a small town in Hungary with a population of only twenty thousand. Yet it stands out in my memory as a very sophisticated "city" with visiting opera and theater companies, masquerade balls for the rich, cafes in which to while the time away trying to sound clever and worldly,

auto racing, and horse racing. Barons, princes, and rich landowners, with their high-class manners and designer clothes, pranced around town in their fancy carriages. These aristocrats put their stamp on the town.

Main Street in Kisvárda (St. Laslo Utca), I remember, smelled of French perfumes when I used to accompany my mother to the marketplace. The aroma would fill my nostrils as I'd watch my mother feel the force-fed geese to see if they were fat enough to nourish her six growing children — her bright, handsome, sensitive kids who would one day go out into the world well prepared by a mother whose intelligence and enlightenment were legendary and whose social conscience earned her my title "the poor man's Mrs. Roosevelt."

An avid reader, my mother marched her six kids off to the library every Friday to borrow the maximum number of books allowed to us, which she herself would devour before they had to be returned. And when my mother would buy fish for the Sabbath or holidays, she was incapable of throwing away the newspapers the fish were wrapped in before reading the smelly sheets first.

And I remember Teca, the gypsy, who used to come around to cast her sad eyes at my mother every day. Her source of sadness was always the same: "My children are hungry, Ma'am." and "Ma'am" would invariably fill Teca's potato sack with whatever she could spare. And anyone happening by at mealtime would automatically be invited to dine with us. "There will be enough. I'll put a little more water in the soup."

But mostly I remember the conversations my mother used to have with the many adults who came to visit us from other parts of Europe — business people, friends, relatives. The six kids stood around drinking in those very big words, those very big subjects — politics, art, books and always *man's inhumanity to man*. Sometimes I was resentful. Must she care about everyone in this world? Look at me! Praise me! I want to be more important! Why do you care so much about so many things?

But now, so many years later, I say: Thank you, Mother, for being what you were, for trying to develop me in every way.

Kisvárda was just a little town. It's where I began, where I yearned to be away from. I didn't think I could take a large enough breath there. Yet the memories of my teens are crowded not only with teen pains but also with precious hours spent with dear friends in a house so alive with interests, thoughts, activities, conversations, dancing, playing, and falling in and out of love that my house — the whole town — seemed to be bursting apart.

But there were other things, too — bad things. I cannot count the times I was called a "dirty Jew" while strolling down Main Street, Hungary. Sneaky whispers: "Dirty Jew." No, "Smelly Jew" — that was what I heard even more often. Anti-Semitism, ever since I can remember, was the crude reality. It was always present in the fabric of life. It was probably so everywhere, we thought, but surely so in Hungary — most certainly in Kisvárda.

They really hate us, I would think. It certainly felt that way. You couldn't hide from it. You couldn't run from it. It was everywhere. It was thinly veiled, when it was veiled at all. It was just under the skin. It was hard to live with. But we did. We knew no other way.

Each "Heil Hitler!" speech on the radio made things worse. And such speeches were on the radio constantly. Not many people understood German in my part of Hungary, but the radio was blasting away Hitler's speeches, and the frenzy of the incessant "Heil Hitlers!" made the Hungarian gentiles feel a camaraderie, a oneness, with the mad orator. It also made us Jews cringe in the very depths of our souls. It made us fear the people with whom we had shared this town for generations.

What could we do?

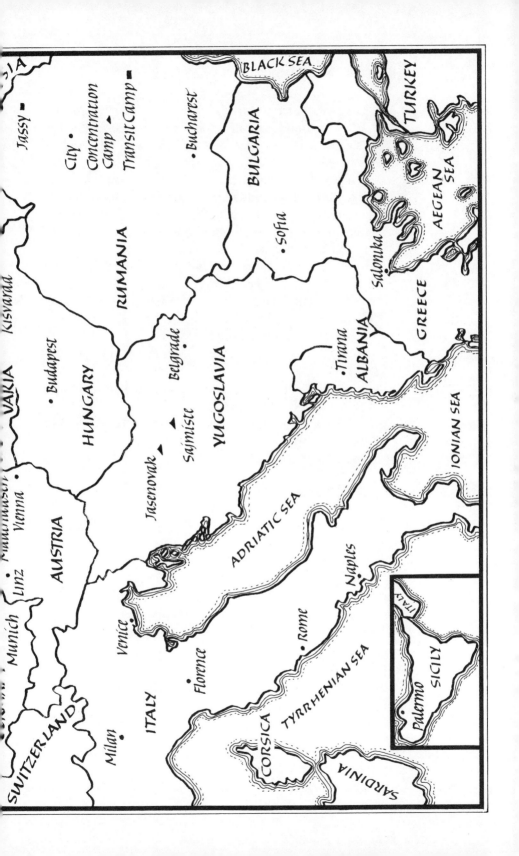

Give us a patch of earth that is free of anti-Semitism!

We were afraid. Our neighbors, we knew, would be Hitler's willing accomplices when the bell would toll. And the bell tolled.

On Monday morning, May 29, 1944, the ghetto was evacuated. Jews, thousands upon thousands of Jews — every shape and form, every age, with every ailment, those whose Aryan blood was not Aryan enough, those who had changed their religion oh, so long ago — dragged themselves down the main street toward the railroad station for what the Germans called "deportation." Upon their backs, bundles and backpacks — the compulsory "50 kilos of your best clothing and food" (which the Germans could later confiscate in one simple operation).

And the Hungarian townspeople, the gentiles — they were there, too. They stood lining the streets, many of them smiling their smiles. Not a tear. Not a good-bye. They were the good people, the happy people. They were the Aryans.

"We are rid of them, those smelly Jews," their faces read. "The town is ours!"

Main Street, Hungary.

Monday, May 29, 1944, on deportation day, cattle cars stood ready at the railroad station in Kisvárda, ready to be crammed with unfortunate Jews. The ss pressed seventy-five people into each car, boarded up the windows, bolted the sliding doors. There was no air, no water, no provision for a toilet or for help to the sick and dying in each car. The ghostly cargo rolled for two long days and nights until, on Wednesday, May 31, the train slowed and halted. The doors were unlocked; the people ordered out onto the ramp.

Isabella looked around: Auschwitz! They had arrived in Oswiecim, as the town was called; Auschwitz was the concentration camp that the Germans had created next to the town. She looked for her mother, her sisters and brother. They were still together: Mama Katz, Chicha, Rachel Cipi, Isabella, the child Potya and Philip, her seventeen-year-old brother, together for a few more minutes.

Ahead of them selection was taking place. Someone whispered the name of Dr. Mengele. They were shoved and pushed closer to that man. When they stood in front of the line, he ordered Mama to one side, Philip to the men's prison and, incredibly, Potya, the child, to be thrown into an open pit together with other children from the transport. Mama no longer saw this tragedy — she was already moving toward her own death by gassing and burning, but the four sisters were dazed. Could this be reality they were experiencing? As Isabella looked uncomprehendingly into the fiery pit, they were all pushed onward, away from the spectacle, to the far end of camp and into showers. With furious speed, they were lined up, robbed of their possessions, shaved even to the pubic hair. Hardly conscious of what was going on, Isabella searched for her sisters in the milling crowd and found them, shivering and naked, in the mass of women. They barely had time to embrace and vow to try to stay together when they were rushed to Block 10. They were still together; that was all that mattered.

Through the summer of 1944, the sisters managed to stay alive and cling to each other. They survived several selections; they were thin and ragged, but the will to live through this hell was powerful within each of them: Together they could endure; together they would outsmart their jailors. Hadn't they survived Mengele's devilish selections?

But Mengele was not content with selections at the gassing site. He came to their bunker time and again to collect fodder for the ovens. He stood at the entrance to Block 10; another SS stood at the exit: The women were trapped. Death became real for Isabella at that moment. She searched her two sisters' eyes and prayed for a miracle to let the three of them get out to join their other sister, who was outside the doomed barrack. Suddenly imbued with the will to live, Cipi, Rachel and Isabella started acting as if they were *kapos*: "Move!" they screamed into the crowd. "Don't move! This way, that way!" Will Mengele be deceived into thinking them on assigned duty and not order them outside?

In a few minutes the selection was over and the doors were bolted once more. And now, with sickening fear, the girls realized that they had fallen into a trap: This time Mengele had sent the "healthy" ones outside, and it was the "oven fodder" that he had locked into the barracks. Now one thought possessed the three girls: to get out! And with a force born of desperation they charged the door. The thin inmate guarding it stepped aside in confusion, the door gave way, the three girls were outside. And there, miraculously, was Chicha. They fell into her arms.

From time to time during that awful summer, the girls received smuggled messages from Philip from the men's prison. But those welcome signs of life from their brother stopped around November. Isabella wondered and worried about Philip: Was he still alive? Where had he disappeared to? The four sisters clung closer to each other, four in the midst of thousands. They knew instinctively that it was their combined and shared strength that kept them going, helped them endure the chicanery of their tormentors. Their combined willpower enabled Chicha to endure the wrath of Irma Grese, the blond SS woman who seemed to hate Chicha for no apparent reason; their strength lifted Chicha's arms out there in the *Lagerstrasse* as she knelt there, two heavy rocks over her head, until SS woman Grese called off the ordeal. And it was their combined strength that made them serene as they stood before the crematorium one night, waiting in line to be ordered into the gas chamber. Together they could face death.

But the SS changed orders and the long line was taken into icy freight cars and moved out of Auschwitz. A few days later, on a snowy December night in 1944, the train stopped near a small town in Eastern Germany, Birnbaumel. This new camp was smaller than Auschwitz. Isabella saw no smoke stacks, no electric fences. Dare she hope this would be a "good" concentration camp? The sisters renewed their pledge to support each other, to stay alive at all cost.

Camp *kapos* got a better deal than ordinary inmates and when the SS chose Isabella for that dehumanizing job, she was willing to take it: It would help her and her sisters endure Birnbaumel. With her stick she walked among her fellow prisoners, yelling and hitting, right and left, but she hit the walls, not the women. For two whole days she bore the wretched job and then she begged the SS to let her work with her sisters in the forest, digging anti-tank trenches. Twice a day now she and the other skeletal women walked through the town of Birnbaumel. They well observed the pedestrian life of the small town, but the citizens there did not seem to see the thin, ragged, barely human prisoners in their streets. Enraged, Isabella tried to carry out her own sabotage against the hated German: She dug at her trench only when the SS was looking her way and threatened to beat her. As soon as they were gone, she filled in the bit she had dug. Let the Russians come, let their tanks rumble smoothly into this arrogant town.

And the Russians came. On January 22, 1945, the Germans rounded up their prisoners to drive them away again, ahead of the approaching Russian armies. Now there was not even the luxury of a cattle car, but this did not deter the Germans. They herded the remaining inmates before them, weak and broken as they were, on long death marches through Germany. Isabella and her sisters lined up again. In rows of five they walked, stumbling through the snow. They were driven toward Bergen-Belsen in the northern part of Germany.

The sisters were so weak now that it took extra human effort just to keep walking. They were so hungry and cold that to lie at the side of the road seemed tempting. But those who did were shot — and the sisters had vowed to support each other. So for the sake of the others, Isabella stumbled on. Only when the column halted at night did they dare to fall exhausted into a haystack to sleep.

January 23, 1945.

Back in the line, the pitiful thousand, minus the few who did escape, the many who died, we are on our way to walk the indefinite distance to Bergen-Belsen. Our pact now is not spoken but fully understood. Any of the sisters is now allowed (meant in a deep emotional sense) to vanish, to die, to give up, to live. The faintest possibility of aiding each other morally or physically no longer exists.

Eastern Germany is now bitter cold in January. There is a blizzard. Rachel is coughing very badly. On one foot she has a torn leather shoe, on the other a Dutch wooden shoe. In the blizzard and with the uneven shoes, she can barely drag herself along. Between the four of us, we are missing one shoe, and whichever one tries to aid Rachel by giving up a shoe will be the one to die. In the past, we always found a solution — an abnormal solution in an abnormal setting, but still, some kind of solution. But we cannot crack this one. For one of us, death is hours away. What to do? Is the life force strong enough yet to make us act if there is another opportunity? Will instinct guide us to survival? We don't know.

We are marching in the blizzard in *Fünferreihe*. Always five in a row. For the four of us, this was a special problem, because to be five in a row was the prisoners' responsibility. And so we always had to find an unattached girl for our row. And when we found one, it was never permanent, for sooner or later she died, was taken on transport or to the crematorium, or attached herself to someone else. It was a continuous struggle.

But now we are marching in the blizzard on a silent, deserted road. SS guards are in front, leading the column, on both sides, and in the rear. We have just reached a tiny village called Jagadschutz. Suddenly, Chicha notices a little house to her right. It is covered with snow, and no smoke is coming from the chimney. Chicha is on the outside of the column. Rachel is next to her. I am next to Rachel, and Cipi is next to me. The side guards have gone to the rear because some prisoners have escaped. Only the guards in the front remain, and they can't see us from their position.

In a flash, Chicha is running toward the house. Then Rachel. Then I. There is no thinking on our parts. Not a word among us. Just one sister following the other.

Rachel and I run to a tiny doghouse behind the main house and crawl inside. Everything is totally silent, deserted. Deep snow blankets the area. The scene is reminiscent of Christmas — "Peace on earth, good will toward men."

Crouched in the doghouse, we are not breathing. There is nothing but silence and terror. When will they kill us? Where are they? Why did we escape?

Slowly, carefully, we inch our way out. We crouch behind the doghouse. Silence again. Where is Chicha? Where is Cipi? Silence. Only silence.

Suddenly there is the sound of crackling snow on the road. The *Oberscharführer*, with his dog, is coming back from the slaughter — we heard the shots. He is cursing the filthy Jews for slowing down the column by attempting to escape. He is utterly furious, mumbling to himself, in a hurry to catch up with the group. We can see him from our crouching position. He cannot see us.

But the dog will smell us. Rachel and I automatically grab our chests. What will it feel like — the bullet? Oh! Oh! Please, please don't do it. Will it be in the chest or in the head? Will it hurt terribly? Will we die immediately? If not, will he shoot again?

Till now, we have seen only other people die, and it was awful. But this will be us. It will be me. Now we are only seconds away from death, and it is terrible. It would have been better if we hadn't seen him, if our backs were to him. Then we wouldn't have to know in advance that we are going to be murdered. Cruel, ugly fate. At least not to know, not to see him point the rifle at us.

God! God, help us! This once. You have not shown us any mercy all these months. Have mercy. My chest feels awful. Something will rip it apart in a second. Can't you do something, God? Don't let us die. Not this way. Not here. Not now. Not ever. Death, go away — go! Please!

I have lived barely two decades. Rachel is only sixteen. Will nobody help us? Will this dog and this dog of a man just rip us apart in a second? Somebody, please help us! Isn't there anybody in this whole world who cares?

We haven't done anything. We have hardly lived. We have barely known anything but war.

Where is my mother? She will protect us. Mama, where are you? Somebody is trying to kill your children. The *Oberscharführer* is coming to kill us. He is coming closer...closer. He is right here.

He is gone.

What happened? Was the wind blowing our scent away from the dog? We are not dead. There is no bullet in our chests... We are alive... He is gone.

Thoroughly shaken, they crawled into the house. It was indeed empty, but, what luck, the refrigerator was full! And the pantry was laden! It looked as if the owners of the house had themselves just recently fled. Isabella wondered for a second whom they had run from, but then she and her sisters fell over the food. They ate and ate. They fell into soft beds with quilts upstairs and came down and ate some more. They worried about Cipi and ate more. There was a knock at the door and they thought Cipi had finally come, but the three prisoners that stood there knew nothing of Cipi. The three joined them, and together they continued eating. Only slowly did they understand that Cipi had not run for her life with her sisters. Why didn't she escape when she saw them running? Where was she?

Sobered, Rachel, Chicha and Isabella waited for liberation. Once a Pole knocked at their door and warned them to flee before the desperate Germans found and killed them, but they waited and ate.

On January 25, 1945, they heard rumbling outside their windows. Did the Germans come for them now? They carefully looked out into the street. Tanks were approaching, and trucks, and columns of soldiers — and flags, red flags! They were looking at the Red Army, at Liberation.

Later they heard that Cipi was dragged all the way to Bergen-Belsen and was liberated there by the British. But she was so weak that she died in their care. And much later still, they learned that Philip, too, was driven from camp to camp and that he was liberated by the Americans. Sick and drained, he also died in the care of his liberators. The three sisters, nursed back to life, together made their way to America.

World Highlights, 1945–1950

Nuremberg becomes the scene of the first international trial of war criminals. Pièrre Laval is executed in France. The black market flourishes in many parts of Europe. The General Assembly of the United Nations holds its first meeting. The Paris Conference estimates war devastation in Greece at 8.5 billion dollars. Italy becomes a republic. The Truman doctrine, aimed at curbing spread of totalitarianism to Greece and Turkey, is announced in March 1947. Tennessee Williams' A Streetcar Named Desire is produced. India becomes a sovereign state. The Marshall Plan introduces a recovery program for Europe. A State of Israel is proclaimed. The Allies supply blockaded West Berlin by means of an airlift. Following a disagreement over autonomy between Tito and Stalin, Yugoslavia is expelled from the Cominform. The transistor is invented. Count Bernadotte is assassinated by a Jewish extremist. Harry Truman, in his own right, is elected President of the United States. NATO is born. Cortisone is discovered. The first Russian atomic bomb tests take place. Chou En-lai becomes premier of the People's Republic of China. Indonesia obtains independence. North Korea invades South Korea.

TEN
Postscript

Officially the war ended on May 7, 1945, when Admiral Doenitz, Hitler's designated successor, surrendered to the Allied High Command at Reims, not very far from the fateful Compiègne, place of German *hubris* and German defeat. But the war had really ended the day Hitler committed suicide, April 30, 1945. On that day the Germans were at last released from his grip of madness and delusion. Hitler had kept the killing processes active to the very last: He had managed to wipe off the face of Europe six million Jews, six million non-Jewish, non-Aryan Europeans; had displaced no less than five million men and women and even children from all of mainland Europe to forced labor in Germany. In addition, millions of European soldiers were dead and some three hundred thousand American soldiers as well. Chaos reigned on the Continent, chaos and a surging sense of hope: The displaced were picking their way out of labor camps through the rubble that was Germany, back to a native country or away from it; the survivors of concentration camps were being nursed back to life by their liberators and were looking for their families; Jews in America and Palestine were besieging rescue committees for news of their people. The scene was the same for us all and yet different in every case. Let the people whose fate I have depicted here stand for survivors everywhere.

Alys Stanké, the boy-prisoner, went with his parents to France at the time of liberation. In time Alys, now Alain, came to Canada; he is now a writer and publisher. The Jewish survivors, all women, all in their early twenties then, heirs to the dead, were eager for life. Luba Gurdus and her husband settled in New York where Dr. Luba is an artist and art historian; they established a kindergarten for Russian children in memory of Bobus in Israel. Leesha Rose married one of her liberators and first moved with him to Canada, then to Israel. Leesha has two children who both have careers in psychology; Leesha herself divides her time between working at Yad Vashem Holocaust Center in Jerusalem and speaking engagements for the Jewish cause in America and Canada. Fania Fénelon, the French singer, made her career singing of the joys and sorrows of the world. Of Bryna Bar Oni I know only that she settled in Chicago. Isabella Katz, now Leitner, lives with her husband and two sons in New York. I, Gerda Schild, am married in Lewiston, Maine, have four children and three grandchildren. And when I tell now of the transition from Holocaust to serenity, I am sure that I speak for us all: Survivors we are and grateful to be alive, and the souls of our martyrs permeate our every day.

In 1945 when the Swiss gave us refuge in a camp in St. Gallen, the first thing I asked of them was pen and paper and postage stamps. I needed to record, while still so fresh, the experiences of the past twelve years, and I needed to find Father, have information about Mother and Friedl. As yet I had illusions that they had survived somewhere, somehow, as I had. I wrote to the International Red Cross in

Geneva, giving Father's last known New York address, Mother's date and place of deportation — November 9, 1941, from Munich — asking about Friedl's fate in Berlin; asking about relatives. The answer came a month later: I learned that Father lived at 701 West 179th Street, Apt. 62, a place which in my mind immediately took on all the properties of Acadia. But I also learned that there was no information about my dear ones. I knew that Grandmother had died a natural death in Regensburg, that Aunt Adelheid had succumbed to cancer of the stomach at the Jewish hospital in Fuerth, but where was the rest of my large family? Where was Aunt Berta and Edith; Aunt Thekla and her husband; Uncle Isaac and his whole family? Had all these pious people disappeared? Wasn't my mother alive somewhere? And my sister?

All around me in St. Gallen, the search for loved ones was duplicated: Eva found her mother in London; someone found a sister in Shanghai; a cousin in Sweden; a friend somewhere. And many, many others around me, many of the survivors, found no one.

My father in New York read my name in a published list of the twelve-hundred people who were liberated to St. Gallen. First he arranged for a silver Torah plate to be made, engraved with my Hebrew name, to be given to his synagogue, *Kehillath Yaakov*, in New York's Washington Heights section as his thanksgiving for all times. Alas, it was stolen from the synagogue twenty years later. Then he wrote to me in St. Gallen, but it was months before I received his loving letters in Les Avants sur Montreux where next I went. Since the Swiss charged me *Pensionskosten* for their hospitality at fr. 3.50 a day, I soon accepted the offer of a Jewish family in Luzern to take me into their home as a domestic and stayed with the Erlanger family until I could get to Father. Memories of the recent past began to dim in

Luzern because I was so happy there with Trude Erlanger and with old Ansbach friends who found me: Boya Stefansky now married in Basel; beloved Rabbi Elie Munk and his lively family temporarily living in Geneva. Eva too had left the Swiss refugee camp and went to live with a family in Zurich. Eventually she married Eric Hammel, a Jewish refugee from France, and settled with him in Périgueux.

The day came when I was able to leave Switzerland to rejoin Father. I had visualized him as aged and white-haired, but when I saw him again in Boston, I embraced a stately figure and kissed a youthful face framed by nearly jet-black hair. Only six years had passed since I last saw him, not the eternity of my perception. Clearly, I had some adjusting to do to get my inner pictures and the reality that lay before me aligned.

It proved to be both easy and difficult to adjust to the banalities that made up my happiness back there in 1946: good food and plenty of it; a bed with pillows; a dentist appointment; a permanent wave at the beauty parlor; a winter coat from Macy's with a fur collar, light and warm and chic. It was both easy and difficult to pick up the telephone: Did people really call just to say a pleasant "hello?" It took time to suppress the sudden fear, the impulse to hide, upon seeing a man in uniform, a policeman, and it took even longer to feel at ease when talking to an official behind a desk. It was easy and hard to go to synagogue: Was the God to whom I prayed in gratitude and in quest listening to me? How had he made His selection? Why was I saved and why was there still no news from my loved ones? The days were easy, but the nights were filled with fear and guilt — guilt at being alive and at being glad to be alive, guilt at not being able to mourn my people properly.

For slowly we had to admit the fact of their deaths. But

the comforts of *K'riah*, of *Shivoh* and *Kaddish*, of *Yahrzeit*, all rituals of mourning, were denied us. Wise Jewish sages had decreed these rituals to be observed upon hearing of the death of a blood relative or a spouse within thirty days: We tear our garment; we observe a week of deep mourning; we recite the *Kaddish*, the prayer for the dead, and, when the anniversary of the occurrence of death comes around, we observe *Yahrzeit* and visit the beloved's grave: rituals all to help us deal with our loss — and to return us, purged of grief, comforted, to normal living. But no such helpful exercises existed for us, mourners of the departed who had no death date, no grave. Our sorrow remained unreleased, our tears unshed, for the wisest of sages could not foresee the Moloch that was Hitler.

And so, not knowing what to do, Jews did nothing for many years. Then, slowly, men and women asked their rabbis if they could remarry, and eventually rabbis permitted survivors to regard themselves as widows and widowers. They declared *Yom Kippur*, the Day of Atonement, as the common *Yahrzeit*, and the Martyrology of the *Yom Kippur* Service became quite naturally the prayer which released our tears: *These I do remember and my soul grieveth within me in secret sorrow.* Slowly, lonely men and women found each other. Father married a kind woman who had lost her husband and son in Theresienstadt, another son in Holland. They healed each other's wounds, my father and good Flora Baer Schild.

I had meanwhile met Rudy Haas who had come to New York for a refresher course in medicine after his discharge from the United States Army. We were married in 1946 and settled in Lewiston, Maine. He, too, was quite bereft: His parents had died a natural death in Frankfurt. At least we had some graves and could observe some *Yahrzeits*, but his two sisters and their six children had become victims of the Holocaust: Our children would know no aunts, uncles or cousins.

It is customary to bestow the names of dear departed upon newborn Jewish children, and when our children began arriving, we had plenty of names to bestow: Leopold, Hedwig, Paula, Erna Haas live on in the names of our sons and daughters as do Paula and Friedl Schild. For me the two bleakest dates of the past were changed into two of the happiest when November 9 and November 11 became the birthdays of our two sons. In our daughters we began to see bearers of future generations. One of them has already fulfilled such promise. On May 11, 1975 — Mother's Day — Polly Haas married Jean Hammel, the son of my dear friend Eva and her late husband Eric Hammel from Périgueux. Jean and Polly have three children, three grandchildren for Eva and me: The grim past is at long last receding.

The guilt feelings, too, that claimed my nights for so many years are receding. A loving and compassionate husband and a perceptive psychologist helped me understand and resolve them. And when restitution made it possible to reclaim our properties in Germany, it helped to know that my husband's parental home, Weberstrasse 3 in Frankfurt, turned over by him to the Joint Distribution Committee, aided survivors less fortunate than I had been; that the money Father received for the ancestral house in Ansbach was used for a memorial to our loved ones in Israel.

Israel. On May 14, 1948, the State of Israel was proclaimed. It rose, phoenix-like, slowly, from the ashes of our people, and with it rose a new kind of Jew. Dispossessed and disinherited, the Jews of Europe had been incapable of resistance during the hopeless years of the Holocaust. But when these selfsame Jews had a homeland to protect, a metamorphosis took place. Now they gave their lives in reckless fighting so that their new state could live. And what do they look like, these insolent new Jews, offspring of Jews whom Hitler had described as the most ungainly of humans, yes as hirsute subhumans? Some look positively Aryan, blond and blue-eyed; some are olive-skinned and black-eyed; all are very beautiful. And what are their names, these children of the Holocaust? Their names are Sarah and Israel, and even Israela, names that Hitler had thought would so degrade us. And they wear their Star of David, these young Jews, men and women, their yellow star in gold or silver around their proud necks.

Today Israel is filled with memorials to her fallen people, both those killed in battle and those murdered in Europe. No monument can bring any of them back. All we can do now is remember our heroes and our martyrs.

ELEVEN

Sentencing

When the twelve years of German National Socialism ended in May of 1945, an inquisition into public guilt began. Righteous nations set for themselves the task of judging those who were responsible for war crimes and for crimes against humanity: An International Military Tribunal was created and held court at Nuremberg from September 1945 to October 1946; a British court sprang up at Lueneburg and dealt with the Nazis caught by English liberators; a *Volksgericht*, a people's court, formed in Vienna. Countries all over Europe, freed at last from the German presence, judged their oppressors; German courts, under Allied orders, embarked on denazification programs.

But many a corrupt German slipped through the net of justice, either to safety in South America or quietly back into the mainstream of life in Germany. Many Nazi officials, high and low, returned to desks and shops, to wives and children, never to talk, or perhaps even think, of the past. Like sheep these Germans had obeyed any order barked at them by their superiors, had done any performance upon command. And now they felt themselves guiltless: Let those who gave the orders be judged, not them, obedient servants, who drove the trains and stoked the fires and sorted the clothes and wrote the statistics.

Top Nazis had avoided the judges by killing themselves: Hitler was dead, so was Himmler and many other "high ranking" killers whose names do not appear in the pages of this book. Here I report only on the fate of those who appear in these pages:

Ion Antonescu, the pro-German Marshal of Rumania, was tried, sentenced and executed in his own country in 1946.

Werner Best, SS *Reichskommissar* for occupied Denmark, was tried before a Danish tribunal, sentenced to death in 1948; sentence changed to imprisonment; he was released in 1951.

Fedor von Bock, Commander of Army Group Center, was killed in an air raid in 1945 before he could be brought to trial.

Anton Burger, second Commandant of Theresienstadt and later transferred to Athens, was tried and executed by a Czech court in Leitmeritz in 1946 or 1947.

Alois (or Anton) Brunner, the man who taught Jewish self-destruction, first in Vienna, then in Berlin and subsequently in other occupied lands, was condemned to death by a *Volksgericht*, a people's court, in Vienna in May 1946. (Some sources say he was never caught and is still missing.)

Theodor Dannecker, SS *Sturmfuehrer* in charge of Jewish deportation in France, later in Bulgaria and Italy, is reported missing as late as 1967.

Adolf Eichmann of RSHA, Amt 4 (*Reichssicherheitshaupt-*

amt, office for the final solution of the Jewish question) fled to South America; was recognized and kidnapped by Israeli agents, tried and executed in Jerusalem in 1960.

Alexander von Falkenhausen, Military Commander for occupied Belgium, was sentenced by a Belgian court to twelve years in prison but was released in 1951.

Hans Frank, ruthless Governor General of occupied Polish territories and responsible for the death and displacement of Polish Jews and Slavs, was sentenced by the International Military Tribunal in Nuremberg and hanged in 1946.

Ferdinand aus der Fuenten, SS *Hauptsturmfuehrer* in Holland, received the death sentence; sentence commuted to life imprisonment.

Irma Grese, SS woman, administrator at Auschwitz and Bergen-Belsen, condemned to death by a British court; executed in 1945.

Heinz Guderian, Commander of Panzer Group 3 and Chief of General Staff, credited with originating armored warfare, lives in retirement.

Rolf Guenther, RSHA Berlin, is missing.

Hans Guenther, head of the Prague Central Office for Jewish Affairs, fled and was shot near Prague. His pockets were found filled with gold and diamonds.

Rudolf Haindl (or Heindl) SS deputy in Theresienstadt, was arrested while trying to flee in 1945; hanged in Leitmeritz in 1948.

Reinhardt Heydrich, head of RSHA and *Reichsprotektor* for Bohemia and Moravia, died June 4, 1942, of wounds received when his car was bombed by two Czechs.

273

Heinrich Himmler, *Reichsfuehrer* SS and chief of Police and Gestapo, committed suicide upon capture by the British at Lueneberg, May 23, 1945.

Rudolf Hoess, Commandant at Auschwitz, was condemned to death by a Russian court in Warsaw, 1947.

Ernst Kaltenbrunner, successor of Heydrich, chief of Security Police and *Sicherheitsdienst*, head of RSHA, was sentenced by the International Military Tribunal in Nuremberg; hanged in 1946.

Ewald von Kleist, Commander of Panzer Group 1, Army Group South, reportedly died in Russia.

Guenther von Kluge, Commander of Army Group Center, committed suicide in 1944.

Josef Kramer, Commandant at Birkenau, later at Bergen-Belsen, was condemned to death by a British court at Lueneburg; executed in 1945.

Georg von Kuechler, Commander of the Eighteenth Army and of Army Group North, was sentenced to twenty years in prison; sentence reduced to twelve.

Pièrre Laval, Premier of France during the German occupation, was sentenced to death and shot by a French firing squad in October 1945.

Wilhelm von Leeb, Commander of Army Group North, was sentenced to three years' imprisonment.

Maria Mandel, SS woman at Auschwitz and Bergen-Belsen, was presumably captured and sentenced by the British.

Joseph Mengele, camp doctor in Auschwitz, is still missing, probably living in Brazil or Argentina.

Rudolf Mildner, SS *Standartenfuehrer* in Denmark, prosecution witness at Nuremberg; released in 1949 and apparently not subsequently tried.

Heinrich Mueller, chief of the Gestapo and RSHA, disappeared after the war and was never found.

Henri Pétain, Premier of France to 1943, was sentenced to death by the French; sentence commuted to life in prison; died in 1951.

Vidkun Quisling, the Norwegian Minister during the German occupation, was sentenced to death by his own countrymen; executed in October 1945.

Karl Rahm, third Commandant of Theresienstadt to the end, was caught while trying to flee from there on a bicycle; sentenced and hanged in Leitmeritz, April 1947.

Hans Albin Rauter, Commandant of the SS and Police in Holland, was tried in The Hague; executed there in March 1949.

Walter von Reichenau, Commander of the Sixth Army and of Army Group South, died in 1942.

Karl von Rundstedt, Commander of Army Group South, was freed and pensioned in 1951; died in 1953.

Walter Schellenberg, of the RSHA and deputy to Himmler, was sentenced but not for anti-Jewish acts; released; died in 1952.

Siegfried Seidl, first Commandant of Theresienstadt, from there sent to Bergen-Belsen in charge of the camp; later sent to Budapest where he supervised the deportation of Hungarian Jews; was tried by the *Volksgericht* in Vienna; hanged in 1945 or 1946.

Artur Seyss-Inquart, *Reichskommissar* for occupied Holland, before that active in the Austrian *Anschluss* and in occupied Poland; was tried as a major war criminal by the International Military Tribunal at Nuremberg; hanged in October 1946.

Gustav Simon, SS Chief of Civil Administration in Luxembourg, was arrested but committed suicide before he could be tried in 1945.

Julius Steicher, founder and publisher of *Der Stuermer* in Nuremberg, was tried by the Nuremberg court and hanged in 1946.

Heinrich von Stuelpnagel, Commander of the Seventeenth Army and Military Commander of France, was executed in 1944.

Otto von Stuelpnagel, his successor as military Commandant in France, was arrested at liberation; imprisoned; committed suicide in 1948.

Sztojay, *Doeme*, Prime Minister of Hungary during the German occupation, was executed there in 1946.

Josef Terboven, *Reichskommissar* in Norway, died there in May 1945, presumably a suicide.

Karl Wolff, Chief of Himmler's Personal Staff and Commandant of Italy during the German occupation, was sentenced by a denazification court; tried by a British court and released in 1951; rearrested in 1962 and sentenced in Munich to 15 years of hard labor in 1964.

Works Consulted

Adler, H.G. *Theresienstadt, 1941–1945*. Tubingen, 1960.

Barber, Noel. *The Week France Fell*. New York: Stein and Day, 1976.

Bauer, Yehuda. *The Holocaust in Historical Perspective*. Seattle: University of Washington Press, 1978.

Cargill, Morris, ed. *A Gallery of Nazis*. New Jersey: Lyle Stuart, 1978.

Cavendish, Marshall, ed. *History of the Second World War*. Pts. 1, 4, 7, 17. U.S.A., London: Marshall Cavendish, 1973—

Dawidowicz, Lucy S. *A Holocaust Reader*. New York: Behrman House, Inc., 1976.

Fest, Joachim C. *The Face of the Third Reich*. New York: Pantheon Books, 1970.

Gilbert, Martin. *The Holocaust*. New York: Hill and Wang, 1978.

Hayes, Paul M. *Quisling*. Bloomington: Indiana University Press, 1972.

Hilberg, Raul. *The Destruction of the European Jews*. Chicago: Quadrangle Books, 1961.

Holt, John B. *Under the Swastika*. Chapel Hill: The University of North Carolina Press, 1936.

Kulski, Julian Eugeniusz. *Dying, We Live*. New York: Holt, Rinehart, and Winston, 1979.

Lederer, Zdenek. *Ghetto Theresienstadt*. London: E. Goldston, 1953.

Maass, Walter. *The Netherlands at War: 1940–1945*. New York: Abelard-Schuman, 1970.

Mau, Hermann and Helmut Krausnick. *German History 1933–45*. London: Oswald Wolff (Pub.) Ltd., 1962.

Melzer, Milton. *Never To Forget: the Jews of the Holocaust*. New York: Harper and Row, 1976.

Michaelis, Meir. *Mussolini and the Jews*. Oxford: The Clarendon Press, 1978.

Mitchell, B.R. *European Historical Statistics from 1750–1970*. New York: Columbia University Press, 1975.

Oakley, Stewart. *A Short History of Denmark*. New York: Praeger Pub., 1972.

Petrow, Richard. *The Bitter Years: The Invasion and Occupation of Denmark and Norway, April 1940–May 1945*. New York: William Morrow and Co., Inc., 1974.

Reitlinger, Gerald. *The Final Solution*. New York: A.S. Barnes, 1961.

Robinson, Jacob. *The Holocaust and After: Sources and Literature in English*. Jerusalem: Israel University Press, 1973.

Roussy de Sales, Count Raoul De, ed. *My New Order*. New York: Reynal and Hitchcock, 1941. (The Speeches of Hitler, 1922–41).

Shirer, William. *The Rise and Fall of the Third Reich*. New York: Simon and Schuster, 1960.

Smith, Bradley F. *Reaching Judgment at Nuremberg*. New York: Basic Books, Inc., 1977.

Snyder, Louis Leo. *Documents of German History*. New Jersey: Rutgers University Press, 1958.

_____. *Encyclopedia of the Third Reich*. New York: McGraw-Hill, 1976.

_____. *The War; a Concise History, 1939-45*. New York: Simon and Schuster, 1960.

Thomas, John Oram. *The Giant-Killers: the Story of the Danish Resistance Movement, 1940–45*. New York: Taplinger Publishing Co., 1975.

Woodhouse, C.M. *The Struggle for Greece, 1941–1949*. New York: Beekman/Esanu Pub., 1976.

Zisenwine, David W., ed. *Anti-Semitism in Europe: Sources of the Holocaust*. New York: Behrman House, Inc., 1976.

Documentary Material

General Record of the Department of State; Decimal File 1945-49. from: 840.48 FAA/1-145 to: 840.48 Refugees/2-2845.

Record Group No. 238, Nuremberg Interrogation, Testimony of Jean-Marie Musy.

Nazi Conspiracy and Aggression. 10 vols. Washington: U.S. Government Printing Office, 1946.

Trials of War Criminals before the Nuremberg Military Tribunal. 15 vols. Washington: U.S. Government Printing Office, 1951-52.

Map Citation

(All maps used are from the Cartographic Department of National Archives, Washington, D.C.)

Researched from Record Group 160, Records of the Armed Service Forces. NEWSMAP, Monday, October 18, 1943 (vol. II no. 26) week of October 7-October 14; 214th week of the war — 96th week of U.S. participation.

Newsmaps: September 11, 1944
    November 6, 1944 (2 maps)
    May 15, 1944
    April 3, 1944

Demographic statistics are from B. R. Mitchell, *European Historical Statistics from 1750-1970.* Columbia University Press, 1975.

For statistics pertaining to the Jews in Europe I relied on Raul Hilberg, *The Destruction of the European Jews,* Quadrangle Books, 1961.

Military facts are from *The West Point Atlas of American Wars,* vol. 2, Vincent J. Esposito, editor. Praeger, 1959.

For demographic details for European countries I consulted the United States Government Printing Office's *Area Handbooks,* 1971–1976.

Glossary

Adass Yisroel Schule, name of a Jewish school in Berlin
Amt, bureau
Anschluss, Occupation of Austria
Arbeiter, worker
Arbeits Einsatz Osten, work detail East
Auslander, foreigner
Ausweiss, Identification
Block, one section in a concentration camp
Blockowa, inmate in charge of a section
Buergermeister, mayor
Bundesrat, equivalent of upperhouse of parliament
Chanukah, Festival of Lights
Cholent, a Jewish dish
Devisenstelle, office of currency and foreign currency
Duce, the Italian leader
Dumkopf, dunce
Fabrikaktion, a hostile action against a factory
Fuehrer, the German leader
Funferreihe, in rows of five
Glimmer, a mica factory
Hanukah, see Chanukah
Hauptsturmfuehrer, high official in the German Nazi hierarchy
Hilfsverein, Jewish organization of Germany to assist in emigration
Hitlerjugend, Hitler Youth
Joodse Raad, Dutch Jewish Council of Elders under Nazi orders
Judenaeltester, (plural: Juden-aeltesten) the head of the Jewish council
Judenfrage, the Jewish question, the Jewish problem
Judenhass, anti-Semitism
Judenrat, (plural: Judenraete) German Jewish council of elders under Nazi orders
Judenstern, Jewish star

281

Juedische Kultus Gemeinde (J.K.G.), Jewish community center
Kapo, concentration camp inmate in charge of other inmates
Kaserne, military barracks
Kasernenhof, the yard of the barracks
Kennkarte, a Jewish identification card
Kleine Festung, a small fortress, a prison
Konzentrationslager (K.Z.), concentration camp
Lager, camp
Lagerkommandant, camp commander
Landstrasse, a country road
Lebensraum, living space
Magenonanie, stomach masturbation
Militaerbefehlshaber, German military chief of an occupied country
Mischling, a person with one Jewish and one non-Jewish parent
Moffen, the name the Dutch used for the Nazis
Musterprotektorat, model domain
Nationalsozialistische Arbeiterpartei, national socialist workers
   party (Nazi)
Nur Juden, only Jews
Obergruppen fuehrer, group leader
Oberschar fuehrer, group leader
Onderduiker, people who live in hiding in Holland
Ostjuden, Eastern Jews
Parteigenosse, party member
Pensionskosten, charge for board and room
Pflegerin, practical nurse
Rassenschande, intimacies between an Aryan and a Jew
Reich, empire
Reichsfuehrer, leader of the Reich
Reichskanzler, during the Nazi regime, the country's leader
Reichssicherheitshauptamt (RSHA) something like a secret police,
   but more powerful
Schleusse, checkpoint
Seuchensperrgebiet, an area of quarantine
Schutzstaffel (SS), at first Hitler's personal bodyguard, ultimately
   Germany's all-powerful policing force
Shtetl, a part of the city or village where the Jews live
Sicherheitsdienst (SD), arm of the secret police concerned with
   security

Glossary

Sicherheitspolizei (Sipo), the policing force of the SD
Stadtkapelle, the orchestra that played in the city square
Der Stuermer, an anti-Semitic newspaper
Sturmabteilung (SA), the Nazi militia
Ubikation, rooming space
Verruckt, mad, crazy
Volk, the people
Volk ohne Raum, people without enough living space
Volkszaehlung, head count of the people
Weseruebung, military exercises on the Weser River

About the Author

Gerda Schild Haas lives with her husband in Lewiston, Maine. She divides her time now between her work as cataloger at the Bates College Library, her civic responsibilities in state and local organizations and her commitment to the Holocaust. She lectures to audiences from high school to Elderhostel, from church groups to United Jewish Appeal meetings. Presently she is organizing a Holocaust Conference sponsored by the Maine Humanities Council and Bates College. But all activities temporarily slow down when father, stepmother, children and grandchildren come to visit. Then the house and garden are filled with life, love and laughter.

A Note on the Graphics

The Endpapers   The Hebrew letters on the endpapers are the Jewish names of those members of Gerda Haas' family and her husband's family who perished in the Holocaust: Her mother Breindl bas Gabriel; her sister Chava bas Yisroel; her husband's sister Breindl bas Yehuda Halevi; his sister Chava bas Yehuda Halevi. May their memories be a blessing.

The Star   The Jewish Star on the cover and within the text is a drawing of the star that Gerda Haas had to buy for 20 Pfennig at the Jewish Community Office in Berlin in September 1941 and had to sew onto her uniform or dress or jacket or coat. Since she had only one, the star is understandably frayed at the edges and points. How happy she was when she was finally told to tear it off in February 1945. She stuffed it into her pocket and forgot about it. Years later she found it again. It will go, together with all her other Holocaust items, to a Jewish museum.

The Phoenix on the Binding   Gerda Haas will always treasure the phoenix carved out of yellow metal that her friend Jirca gave her in Theresienstadt. Of course she didn't dare to wear it there, but once she was free, she wore it proudly and sadly. Although Jirca had died, and surely the artist who made it, to Gerda it still seems a symbol of hope, rebirth and joy, this mythical bird lifting its lovely neck from the depths of despair.

The Graphics Credits   The text of this book was set in Garamond on the Compugraphic Editwriter by the Sant Bani Press, Tilton, N.H. Printing and binding were done by the Halliday Lithograph Corporation, West Hanover, Massachusetts.

Manuscript and proof editing was handled by Stan Spiegel. Production coordination was directed by Mary Lou Bridge. Photograph enlargements were made by Joseph E. Kachinski. The jacket, binding, endpaper, text and map designs were created by Bonnie Spiegel.